S0-BAM-353

The Photographic History of The Civil War

In Ten Volumes

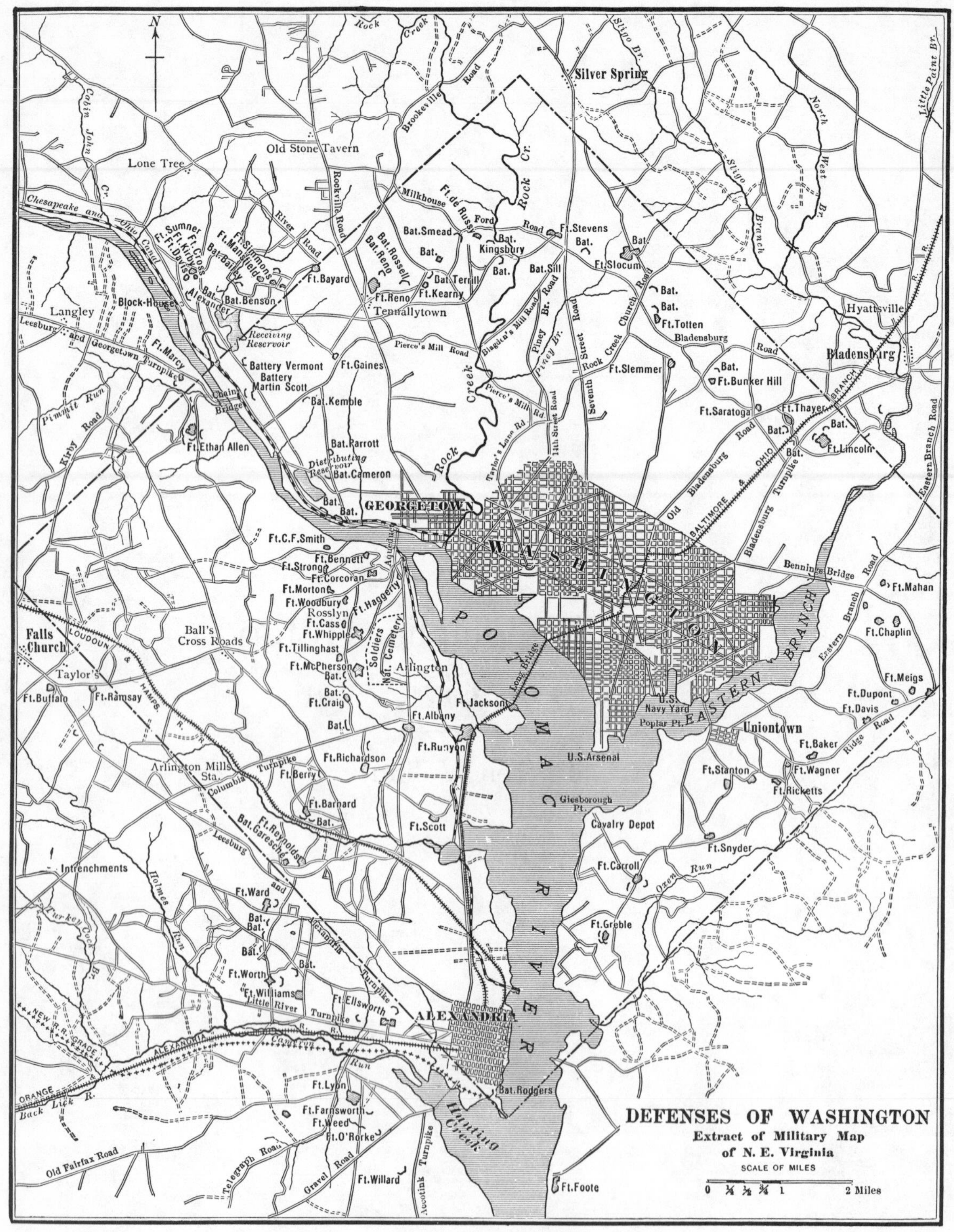

MAP SHOWING THE DEFENSES OF WASHINGTON

SPECIALLY COMPILED FOR THE PHOTOGRAPHIC HISTORY OF THE CIVIL WAR FROM THE OFFICIAL MAP OF THE ENGINEER BUREAU OF THE U. S. WAR DEPARTMENT, DRAWN 1865

FEDERAL GUNS IN THE GRAND REVIEW

BEFORE THE CAPITOL, MAY 24, 1865

ARTILLERY BRIGADE IN THE GRAND REVIEW

It was the artillery that defended Washington, as told in Chapter I of this volume. It was "heavy" artillery turned into infantry which sustained the greatest loss in battle—the First Maine and Eighth New York. On every hard-fought open field, it was the artillery that put heart into the infantry, supporting the charge or covering the retreat. No wonder a roar of applause went up on that sunny day in May, while the caissons clanked down Pennsylvania Avenue, and made the cannon rumble again in their bronze and iron throats.

The Photographic History
of The Civil War

Forts and Artillery

Francis Trevelyan Miller
Editor in Chief

Contributors

William H. Taft
President of the United States

Henry Wysham Lanier
Art Editor and Publisher

Eben Swift
Lieutenant-Colonel, U. S. A.

French E. Chadwick
Rear-Admiral, U. S. N.

George Haven Putnam
Major, U. S. V.

Marcus J. Wright
Brigadier-General, C. S. A.

Henry W. Elson
Professor of History, Ohio University

James Barnes
Author of "David G. Farragut"

CASTLE BOOKS ★ NEW YORK

This Edition Published by Arrangement
With A. S. Barnes & Co., Inc.

Manufactured in the United States of America

CONTENTS

PREFACE

IT was not a mere sneer that described Napoleon as "only an artillery officer." His method of massing great guns was almost unknown in America when the Civil War opened; the Confederates, to their cost, let two years go by before organizing so as to allow of quick artillery concentration; yet what else could have won Gettysburg for the Federals?

Proper defense against cannon was even less understood until the Civil War.

If Louis XIV's military engineer Vauban had come to life during any battle or siege that followed his death up to 1861, he could easily have directed the operations of the most advanced army engineers—whose fortifications, indeed, he would have found constructed on conventional lines according to his own text-books.

Thus the gunner in Blue or Gray, and his comrade the engineer, were forced not only to fight and dig but to evolve new theories and practices. No single work existed to inform the editors of this History systematically concerning that fighting and digging. No single work described Federals and Confederates alike, and readably told the story of the great events with the guns and behind the ramparts from '61 to '65. That gap it is hoped this volume will fill.

American resourcefulness here became epochal. For siege work great guns were devised and perfected which rendered useless, for all time, most of the immense brick and stone and mortar fortifications existing in the world. The introduction of rifled guns worked as great a revolution in warfare on land as that of the ironclad vessel on the sea.

The photographs in this volume follow the artillery in the field, both Federal and Confederate. They comprehensively illustrate the precaution taken by the Federal engineers to protect the Northern capital from capture. They supplement graphically the technical information in regard to the fabrication of guns and making of ammunition. A dramatic series of views follows the gradual reduction of the Confederate forts and batteries on Morris Island by the Federal besiegers, and the latter's attempts against Sumter.

The photographs in the latter part of the volume reflect the ingenuity of the American soldier in protecting himself on the battlefield; the bridging of broad rivers in the space of an hour by the Engineer Corps; the expert railroading under difficulties of the United States Military Railroad Construction Corps; the Confederate defenses along the James which baffled the Federal army, and preserved Richmond so long free though beleaguered.

I

WITH THE FEDERAL ARTILLERY

LIGHT ARTILLERY—TWO GUNS IN POSITION, READY TO FIRE

BATTERY A, FOURTH UNITED STATES ARTILLERY, FEBRUARY, 1864

Battery A, Fourth United States Artillery, was one of the celebrated horse batteries of the Army of the Potomac. These photographs, taken by Gardner in February, 1864, represented its four 12-pounder light brass Napoleons "in battery," with limbers and caissons to the rear, and the battery wagon, forge, ambulance, and wagons for transportation, embracing the entire equipage of a light battery in the field. At that time the battery was on the line of the Rappahannock. Three months later it accompanied Sheridan on his

THE BATTERY THAT RODE CLOSEST TO RICHMOND

famous Richmond raid, and on the night of May 12th its members heard men talking within the fortifications of Richmond, dogs barking in the city, and bought copies of the Richmond *Inquirer* from a small but enterprising Virginia newsboy who managed to slip within their lines with the morning papers. Below, beyond "A," another battery is seen in camp. The horses hitched in, and the open limber-chests indicate an approaching inspection. These formed part of Lieutenant-Colonel James Madison Robertson's brigade.

ON THE DAY OF BATTLE—SHELLING EARLY'S TROOPS IN FREDERICKSBURG

Here is no play at war. These guns were actually throwing their iron hail against Marye's Heights across the river on the very day that this photograph was taken by Captain A. J. Russell, the Government photographer. Early that morning the Union guns opened with a roar; at half past ten Sedgwick's gallant Sixth Corps charged up the hill where nearly 13,000 of their comrades had fallen the previous December. Before the assault the field artillery added its clamor to the heavy boom of the big guns, clearing the way for the intrepid Union columns which General Newton led up the once deadly hill to victory.

WORKING THE 32-POUNDERS ON MAY 3, 1863

With a charge of eight pounds of powder these sea-coast guns could throw a shot weighing 32.3 pounds 2,664 yards, or over a mile and a half, with a ten degree muzzle elevation. The town spread out before the frowning weapons was thus easily within range. The pieces are mounted on siege carriages. Two men are handling the heavy swab which must reach a distance nearly twice the length of a man. The man at the nearest breech is just sighting; the crew are at attention, ready to perform their tasks. In a companion photograph, taken at the same time (pages 126 and 127 of Volume II), they can be seen waiting to load the piece in the foreground.

THE FEDERAL ARTILLERY AND ARTILLERYMEN

By O. E. Hunt
Captain, United States Army

THE regular troops brought into Washington for its defense at the outbreak of the war included two batteries of field-artillery of exceptional drill and discipline. The presence of these guns and men helped materially to allay the feeling of apprehension, and General Scott, in command of the United States army at the time, was able to assure the inhabitants that he could hold Washington against several times the number that the Confederates could then bring against him, as he knew from experience that the troops which had been hastily enlisted for the Southern cause were still in a very unprepared state.

Most of the organizations participating in the first battle of the war were untried and undisciplined. A few regular companies and batteries made a leaven for the mass, and among those Federal organizations that most distinguished themselves were Ricketts' and Griffin's regular field-batteries.

About half-past two in the afternoon of July 21, 1861, these were ordered forward to the top of the Henry hill, where the battle of Bull Run was raging hottest. They went with a feeling that the regiments ordered to support them were unreliable. For a time there was a lull in the battle. But danger was close at hand. No sooner had Ricketts taken up his position than his men and horses began to fall under the well-directed fire of concealed Confederate sharpshooters. No foe was visible, but death sped from behind fences, bushes, hedges, and knolls. The battery fought with desperate

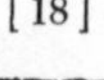

THE HENRY HOUSE—AFTER BULL RUN

THE ARTILLERY CENTER OF THE FIRST CIVIL WAR BATTLE

Thus stood the Henry house after the battle of Bull Run, on July 21, 1861. The building is no longer habitable—though the white plaster remaining shows that the destroying cannonade had not brought fire in its train. At first not in the direct line of fire, the little home suddenly became the center of the flood-tide of the first real conflict of the Civil War when at two-thirty General McDowell sent forward Ricketts' and Griffin's regular batteries. The former planted their guns within 1,500 yards of Captain (later Brigadier-General) John B. Imboden's Confederate batteries, which were stationed in a slight depression beyond. A terrific artillery duel at once ensued. Old Mrs. Henry, bedridden and abandoned by her relatives, lay alone in the house in an agony of terror till one of the first shots put an end to her life of suffering. The Thirty-third Virginia could restrain themselves no longer, and without orders advanced upon the Federal batteries. In the dust they were mistaken for a supporting Federal regiment until within point-blank range they fired a volley which annihilated both batteries. Thenceforth the contending forces surged over the prostrate bodies of cannoneers. Ricketts, severely wounded, was finally taken prisoner. At last Johnston's fresh troops arrived, the gray line surged forward, and the much-coveted guns were seized by the Confederates for the last time.

courage. Griffin's battery took its place alongside. There were eleven Union guns pouring shell into—what? Soon were uncovered no less than thirteen Confederate guns at short range. The Confederate batteries were well supported. The Federal guns were not.

The Confederate regiments, seeing the Union batteries exposed, were tempted to come out from their concealment. They pressed cautiously but stubbornly on Ricketts, whose battery, all this time, was wholly occupied with the Confederate artillery. Griffin, absorbed in the fire of his guns against the opposing artillery, was astounded to see a regiment advancing boldly on his right. He believed these troops to be Confederates, but was persuaded by other officers that they were his own supports. Instinctively, he ordered his men to load with canister and trained the guns on the advancing infantry. Persuaded not to fire, he hesitated a moment, and the two batteries were overwhelmed. The supporting regiment fired one volley and fled. The two disabled batteries now became the center of the contest of the two armies. In full view from many parts of the field, the contending forces surged back and forth between the guns, over the prostrate bodies of many of the cannoneers. Ricketts, severely wounded, was finally taken by the Confederates and retained a prisoner. Two more Federal batteries, one a regular organization, crossed the valley to take part in the fight, but were compelled to withdraw.

Finally, with the appearance of Johnston's fresh troops, including more field-artillery, the tide was turned for the last time, and the much coveted guns remained in the hands of the Confederates. Four pieces of Arnold's battery, four of Carlisle's battery, and five of the Rhode Island battery, practically all that were taken off the field, were lost at the clogged bridge over Cub Run. The entire loss to the Federals in artillery was twenty-five guns, a severe blow when ordnance was so precious.

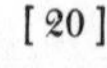

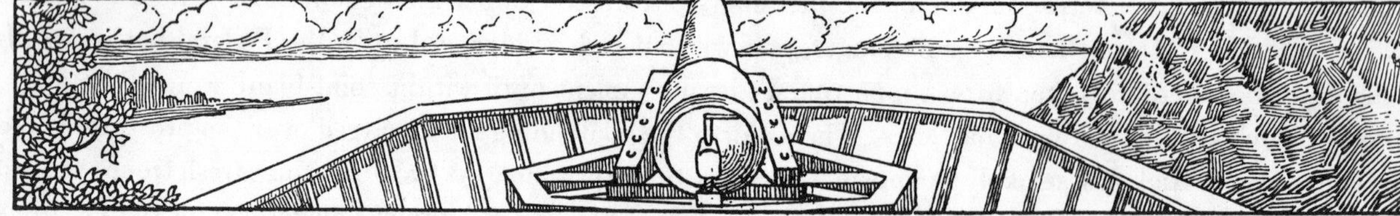

GENERAL GRIFFIN, WHO LED THE FIRST LIGHT BATTERY INTO WASHINGTON

Major-General Charles Griffin stands in the center of his staff officers of the Fifth Army Corps, of which he attained command on April 2, 1865. He was the man who led the first light artillery into Washington, the famous Battery D of the Fifth United States Artillery, known as the "West Point Light Battery." When war was threatening, Colonel Charles Delafield, then Superintendent of the Military Academy at West Point, directed Lieutenant Charles Griffin, then of the Second Artillery and instructor in the Tactical Department, to form a light battery of four pieces, with six horses to the piece, and enough men to make the command seventy strong. On February 15, 1861, it left for Washington with its four 12-pounder Napoleons. Reorganized July 4th as Company D of the Fifth United States Artillery, its organizer promoted to its captaincy, its strength increased to 112 men, and equipped with four 10-pounder Parrotts and two 12-pounder gun-howitzers, it proceeded to Arlington and thence to the battlefield of Bull Run. The "West Point Light Battery" was the first to enter the City of Washington in 1861, with Captain Charles Griffin, and Lieutenants Henry C. Symonds and Alexander S. Webb, his subordinates. At Bull Run the battery was wrecked, nearly all its horses killed, and one third of its men either killed or wounded. At West Point there is a memorial tablet to this battery bearing the following names: Bull Run, Mechanicsville, Hanover, Gaines's Mill, Malvern Hill, Manassas, Antietam, Fredericksburg, Rappahannock, Wilderness, Spotsylvania, North Anna, Cold Harbor, Weldon, Appomattox. General Griffin commanded the artillery at Malvern Hill, and as leader of the Fifth Corps he received the surrender of the arms of the Army of Northern Virginia at Appomattox. The Maltese Cross on the flag was the badge of his corps.

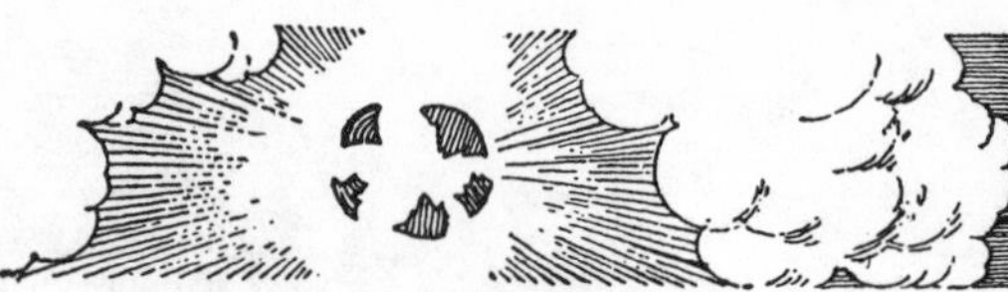

McClellan was called to Washington and placed in command, and immediately, by his great energy, tact, and professional skill, restored confidence. On his assuming command of the Military Division of the Potomac, the field-artillery of the division consisted of no more than parts of nine batteries, or thirty pieces of various and, in some instances, unusual and unserviceable calibers. Calculations were made for an expansion of this force, based on an estimated strength of the new Army of the Potomac, about to be formed, of one hundred thousand infantry.

Considerations involving the peculiar character and extent of the force to be employed, the probable field and character of the operations, and the limits imposed by the as yet undeveloped resources of the nation, led to the adoption, by General McClellan, of certain recommendations that were made to him by General W. F. Barry, his chief of artillery. The most important of these were: to have, if possible, three guns for each thousand men; one-third of the guns to be rifled and either Parrott or Ordnance Department guns; batteries to be of not less than four nor more than six guns, and then followed a number of important recommendations concerning the tactical organization of the arm.

A variety of unexpected circumstances compelled some slight modifications in these propositions, but in the main they formed the basis of the organization of the artillery of the Army of the Potomac.

The supply of ordnance matériel before the Civil War was in large measure obtained from private arsenals and foundries. This sudden expansion in the artillery arm of the country overtaxed these sources of supply, and the Ordnance Department promptly met the requisitions of the chief of artillery of the Army of the Potomac by enlarging, as far as possible, their own arsenals and armories. The use of contract work was in some instances the cause of the introduction of faulty materiel; and the loss of field-guns on several

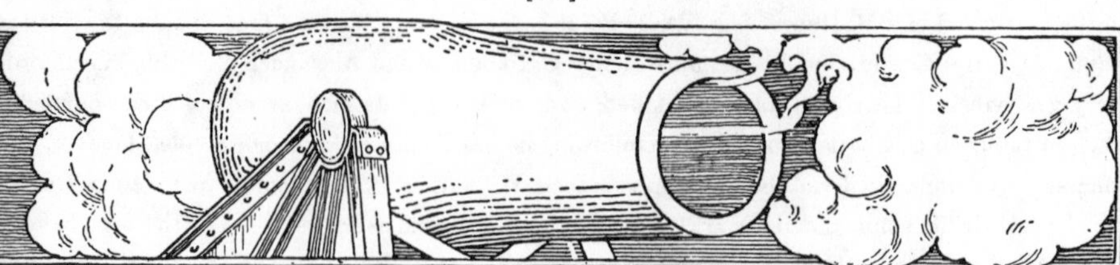

THE ONLY UNION BATTERY THAT FIRED ON YORKTOWN

This photograph of May, 1862, shows Federal Battery No. 1 in front of Yorktown. On May 3, 1862, all of McClellan's encircling guns, with the exception of two batteries, were waiting to open fire, and those two would have been ready in six hours more—when the Confederates evacuated the works defending the city. Fire was actually opened, however, only from this one. It was armed with two 200-pounder and five 100-pounder Parrott rifled guns. The garrison was one company of the famous First Connecticut Artillery, under Captain Burke. It was a great disappointment to the Federal artillerymen, who had worked for a month placing the batteries in position, that there was no chance to test their power and efficiency. McClellan has been criticised for dilatory tactics at Yorktown, but many old soldiers declare that the army under his command inflicted as much damage and suffered far less than the victorious army directed by Grant.

WATCHING THE APPROACH OF A SHELL, YORKTOWN, MAY, 1862

This photograph of Battery No. 4, planted for the bombardment of Yorktown, shows a sentinel on the watch, ready to give warning of the approach of a shell and thus enable every man to seek shelter. Beside him is the bombproof in which the troops remained under cover when the bombardment was continuous. At Yorktown, the Confederates had an 8-inch mortar with which they did rather indifferent shooting, but the moral effect on the Federal soldiers of the screeching shells was great.

The caliber of these mortars was thirteen inches, and on account of their tremendous weight, 17,000 pounds, it required great labor to place them in position. The projectiles, which were principally used for sea-coast operations, varied in weight, according to character. Their maximum weight was about 770 pounds, and these were fired with a maximum of about seventy-five pounds of powder. The bore of this mortar is 35.1 inches in length. This was a case of war's labor lost, as the Confederates left on May 3d, and McClellan's elaborate siege batteries never had a chance.

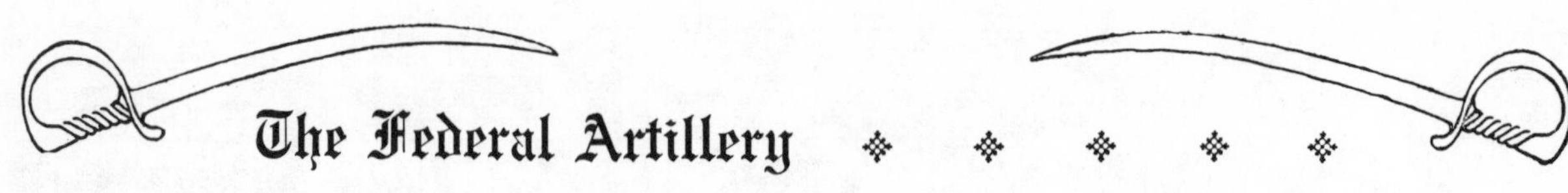

battlefields was laid to the breaking of gun-carriages. The Ordnance Department, however, was able to supply the deficiencies as soon as its own plants were running, and artillery officers thereupon expressed their complete satisfaction.

The field-guns were of two kinds—the 3-inch wrought-iron (10-pounder) rifle and the smooth-bore Napoleon 12-pounder. The first was made by wrapping boiler-plate around an iron bar to form a rough cylinder, welding it together, and then boring it out and shaping it up. The second was generally made of bronze, cast solid, then bored and prepared. For short ranges in rough country, the Napoleon gun was preferred to the rifle, as it carried heavier charges and the use of canister in it was more effective.

The siege-guns, in which mobility was less important, were of cast iron. Owing to the length of bore and the relatively small diameter, these guns were also usually cast solid. One of these pieces, the Parrott, was strengthened by a wrought-iron cylinder shrunk over the breech.

Sea-coast guns were generally of cast iron, and the best types were cast hollow and cooled by the Rodman process of playing a stream of water on the interior of the tube while the exterior was kept hot, thus regulating the crystallization of the iron and increasing its durability. To some of the sea-coast guns the Parrott principle of construction was applied.

The imperfectly equipped batteries which were left to the Army of the Potomac after the First Bull Run consisted, as has been noted, of only thirty guns. These had six hundred and fifty men and four hundred horses.

When the army took the field, in March, 1862, the light artillery consisted of ninety-two batteries of five hundred and twenty guns, twelve thousand five hundred men, and eleven thousand horses, all fully equipped and in readiness for field-service. Of this force, thirty batteries were regular and sixty-two volunteer. During the short period of seven months, all the immense amount of necessary matériel had been issued and

FIFTY-NINE AND A HALF TONS OF ORDNANCE EMPLACED IN VAIN

These mortars of Battery No. 4 were ready to let loose a stream of fire upon Yorktown on the night of May 3d. But that very night the Confederate host secretly withdrew. The great weight of the projectiles these guns could throw was sufficient to crash through the deck of a battleship. For that reason such mortars were generally used for sea-coast fortifications. The projectiles weighed up to 770 pounds. At times, the big mortars were used for siege purposes, although their great weight—17,000 pounds—made them difficult to emplace in temporary works. For thirty days the Union artillerymen had toiled beneath the Virginia sun putting the seven gigantic weapons, seen on the left-hand page, into place. Their aggregate weight was 119,000 pounds, or fifty-nine and a half tons. By garrisoning Yorktown and forcing the Federals to place such huge batteries into position—labor like moles at these elaborate, costly, and tedious siege approaches—General Magruder delayed the Union army for a month, and gained precious time for General Lee to strengthen the defenses of the threatened Confederate capital, while Jackson in the Valley held off three more Federal armies by his brilliant maneuvering, and ultimately turned upon them and defeated two.

the batteries organized, except that about one-fourth of the volunteer batteries had brought a few guns and carriages with them from their respective States. These were of such an odd assortment of calibers that there was no uniformity with the more modern and serviceable ordnance with which most of the batteries were being armed, and they had to be replaced with more suitable matériel. Less than one-tenth of the State batteries came fully equipped for service.

When the Army of the Potomac embarked for Fort Monroe and the Peninsula, early in April, 1862, fifty-two batteries of two hundred and ninety-nine guns went with that force, and the remainder that had been organized were scattered to other places, General McDowell and General Banks taking the greater portion. When Franklin's division of McDowell's corps joined McClellan on the Peninsula, it took with it four batteries of twenty-two guns; and McCall's division of McDowell's corps, joining a few days before the battle of Mechanicsville, also kept its artillery, consisting of the same number of batteries and guns as Franklin's. This made a grand total of sixty field-batteries of three hundred and forty-three guns with the Federal forces.

The instruction of a great many of these batteries was necessarily defective at first, but the volunteers evinced such zeal and intelligence, and availed themselves so industriously of the services of regular officers, that they made rapid progress and attained a high degree of efficiency.

The Confederates having taken a position at Yorktown and erected strong works, a regular siege of the place was ordered. Reconnaissances were made by the artillery and engineer officers to locate the works. A siege-train of one hundred and one pieces was sent down from Washington, and field-batteries of 12-pounders were also used as guns of position. The First Connecticut Heavy and the Fifth New York Heavy Artillery were in charge of the siege-train, and had for its operation a total of twenty-two hundred men.

MAJOR ASA M. COOK

The three photographs on this page give bits of daily camp-life with the light artillery. In the top photograph Major Asa M. Cook, of the Eighth Massachusetts Light Battery, who also had temporary command of the First, sits his horse before his tent. In the center the artillerymen of the First Massachusetts Light Battery are dining in camp at their ease. Below appear the simple accommodations that sufficed for Lieutenant Josiah Jorker, of the same battery. The First Massachusetts was mustered in August 27, 1861, and saw its full share of service. It fought through the Peninsula campaign, assisted in checking Pope's rout at Bull Run, August 30, 1862, and covered the retreat to Fairfax Court House, September 1st. It served at Antietam, Fredericksburg, and Gettysburg; at the Wilderness and in the "Bloody Angle" at Spotsylvania the following year. It fought at Cold Harbor, and went to Petersburg, but returned to Washington with the veteran Sixth Army Corps to defend the city from Early's attack. It then accompanied Sheridan on his Shenandoah Valley campaign and fought at the battle of Opequon. It was mustered out, October 19, 1864, at the expiration of its term. The Eighth Battery of Massachusetts Light Artillery was organized for six months' service June 24, 1862. It fought at the second battle of Bull Run, at South Mountain, and Antietam. The regiment was mustered out November 29, 1862.

DINNER TIME
FIRST MASSACHUSETTS LIGHT BATTERY IN CAMP

LIEUTENANT JOSIAH JORKER, WITH THE FIRST MASSACHUSETTS ARTILLERYMEN

The Federal Artillery ❖ ❖

Fourteen batteries of seventy-five guns and forty mortars were established across the Peninsula, the work of constructing emplacements beginning on April 17th and ending on May 3d. During the night of May 3d, the Confederates evacuated Yorktown, and the Federal troops took possession at daylight on the 4th.

The peculiarities of the soil and terrain in the vicinity of the opposing works made the labor of installing the siege-artillery very great. The heavier guns would often sink to the axles in the quicksand, and the rains added to the uncomfortable work. The efforts of the strongest and most willing of the horses with the heavy matériel frequently did not avail to extricate the guns from the mud, and it became necessary to haul them by hand, the cannoneers working knee-deep in mud and water. The First Connecticut Heavy Artillery and the Fifth New York Heavy Artillery excelled in extraordinary perseverance, alacrity, and cheerfulness.

The effect of the delay to the Army of the Potomac was to enable the Confederates to gain strength daily in preparation for the coming campaign. All the batteries of the Union line, with the exception of two, were fully ready to open fire when the Confederates evacuated their positions, and these two batteries would have been ready in six hours more. Circumstances were such, however, that fire was actually opened from only one battery, which was armed with two 200-pounder and five 100-pounder Parrott rifled guns.

The ease with which these heavy guns were worked and the accuracy of their fire on the Confederate works, as afterward ascertained, were such as to lead to the belief that the Confederates would have suffered greatly if they had remained in the works after the bombardment was opened. The desired result, however, had been achieved. The Union army had been delayed a month, and precious time had been gained for General Lee to strengthen the defenses of Richmond while Johnston held off his formidable antagonist.

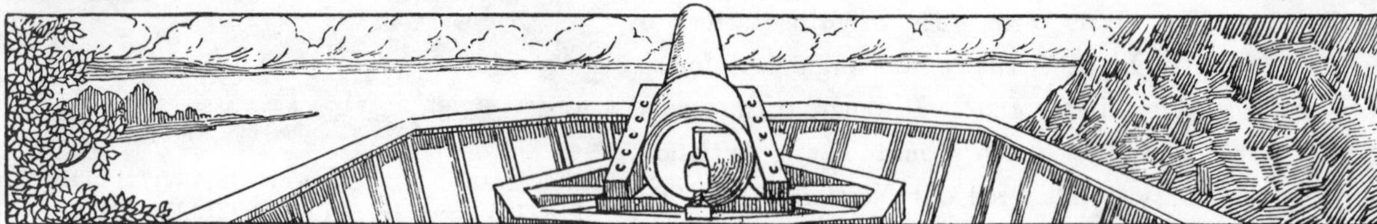

COWAN AND HIS MEN, MAY, 1862, JUST AFTER THE FIRST FIGHT

These four officers of the First New York Independent Battery seated in front of their tent, in camp on the left bank of the Chickahominy River, look like veterans, yet a year of warfare had not yet elapsed; and their first taste of powder at Lee's Mills had just occurred. First on the left is Andrew Cowan (later brevet-lieutenant-colonel), then lieutenant commanding the battery (he had been promoted to captain at Lee's Mills, but had not yet received his captain's commission). Next is First-Lieutenant William P. Wright (who was disabled for life by wounds received in the battle of Gettysburg), Lieutenant William H. Johnson (wounded at Gettysburg and mortally wounded at Winchester), and Lieutenant Theodore Atkins, sunstruck during the fierce cannonade at Gettysburg, July 3, 1863, and incapacitated for further service in the army. Private Henry Hiser, in charge of the officers' mess at the time, is leaning against the tent-pole. The first Independent Battery of Light Artillery from New York was organized at Auburn and mustered in November 23, 1861. It was on duty in the defenses of Washington until March, 1862, when it moved to the Peninsula by way of Fortress Monroe. Its first action was at Lee's Mills, April 5, 1861; it took part in the siege of Yorktown, and fought at Lee's Mills again on April 16th. It served throughout the Peninsula campaign, and in all the big battles of the Army of the Potomac throughout the war. It helped to repulse Early's attack on Washington, and fought with Sheridan in the Shenandoah. The battery lost during its service two officers and sixteen enlisted men killed and mortally wounded and thirty-eight enlisted men by disease.

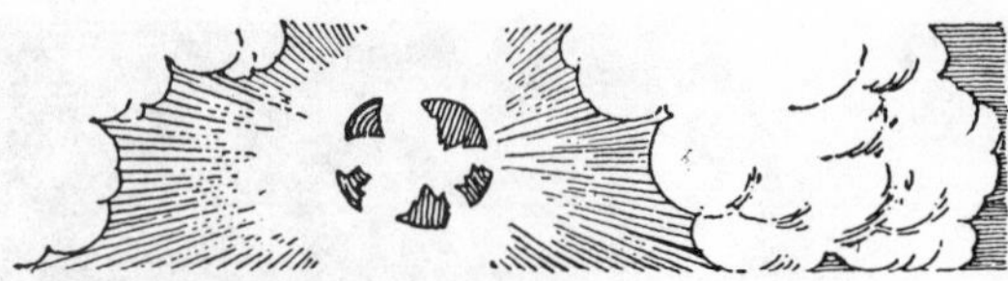

To the patient and hard-working Federal artillerymen, it was a source of keen professional disappointment that, after a month's exacting toil in placing siege-ordnance of the heaviest type, the foe did not give them a chance to test its power and efficiency.

It was found by the Federals that the Confederate works about Yorktown were strong. The chief engineer of the Army of the Potomac reported that the outline of the works immediately surrounding the town was almost the same as that of the British fortifications of Cornwallis in the Revolution, but that the works had been thoroughly adapted to modern warfare. Emplacements had been finished for guns of heavy type, of which about ninety-four could have been placed in position. The Federals captured fifty-three guns in good order.

From Yorktown to the front of Richmond, and on the march to the James, the gallant efforts of the artillery seconded the work of the other arms through the battles of Williamsburg, Hanover Court House, Fair Oaks, Mechanicsville, including Gaines' Mill, Savage's Station, Glendale, and Malvern Hill. As General W. F. Barry has stated, "These services were as creditable to the artillery of the United States as they were honorable to the gallant officers and enlisted men who, struggling through difficulties, overcoming obstacles, and bearing themselves nobly on the field of battle, stood faithfully to their guns, performing their various duties with a steadiness, a devotion, and a gallantry worthy of the highest commendation."

At Malvern Hill the artillery saved the army. The position was most favorable for the use of guns. The reserve artillery, under Colonel H. J. Hunt, was posted on the heights in rear of the infantry lines. Sixty pieces, comprising principally batteries of 20-pounders and 32-pounders, had a converging fire from General Porter's line, and all along the crest of the hill batteries appeared in commanding positions. The First Connecticut Heavy Artillery again distinguished itself for the

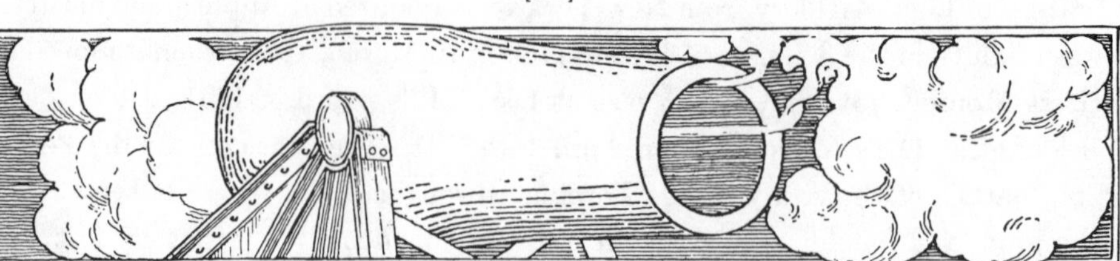

COWAN'S BATTERY ABOUT TO ADVANCE ON MAY 4, 1862

THE NEXT DAY IT LOST ITS FIRST MEN KILLED IN ACTION, AT THE BATTLE OF WILLIAMSBURG

Lieutenant Andrew Cowan, commanding, and First-Lieutenant William F. Wright, sit their horses on the farther side of the Warwick River, awaiting the order to advance. After the evacuation of Yorktown by the Confederates on the previous night, Lee's Mills became the Federal left and the Confederate right. The Confederate earthworks are visible in front of the battery. This spot had already been the scene of a bloody engagement. The First Vermont Brigade of General W. F. Smith's division, Fourth Corps, had charged along the top of the dam and below it on April 16th and had gained the foremost earthwork, called the "Water Battery." But General Smith received orders not to bring on a general engagement. The Vermonters were withdrawn, suffering heavily from the Confederate fire. Their dead were recovered, under a flag of truce, a few days later. The "slashing" in the foreground of this photograph was in front of earthworks erected by Smith's division after the withdrawal of the Vermonters. The earthworks themselves were about two hundred yards to the rear of this "slashing," and were occupied by the First New York Battery in the center, and strong bodies of infantry to its left and right. The battery is seen halted where a road ran, leading to the Williamsburg road. Loaded shells had been planted inside the Confederate works, so that the feet of the horses or the wheels of the guns passing over them would cause them to explode. The battle of Williamsburg or "Fort Magruder" was fought on May 5th. In that battle the battery lost its first men killed in action.

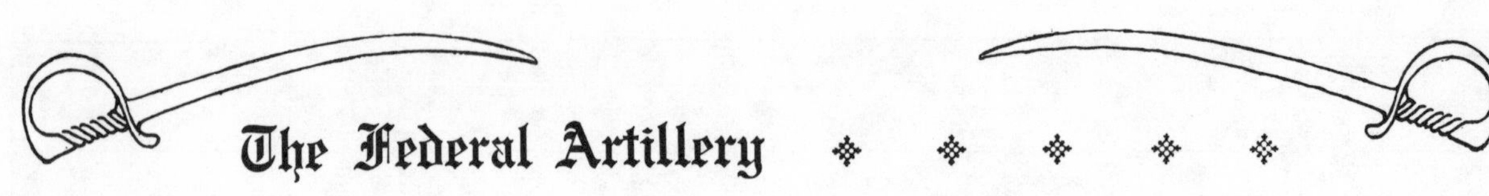

tremendous and skilful labors of placing its heavy guns on the crest.

During the entire morning of July 1st there was constant artillery fire. As often as bodies of the Confederates appeared within close range, the canister sent among them from the batteries on the crest was sufficient to drive them back to cover. General Magruder was sent by Lee against the Union lines in a supreme effort to break them, but his men never approached near enough to threaten the security of the Federal batteries. Some of the guns that were in exposed positions were limbered up and withdrawn to more secure positions, and there again opened fire on Magruder's advance. Part of the front line of the Confederates reached a position where the men could neither advance nor retire, but had to hug the inequalities of the ground to avoid the rain of canister.

Repeated efforts were made by the Confederates to pierce the Union line and get among the batteries that were creating such havoc, but the tenacity of the infantry line, bravely assisted by the guns massed behind it and sending destruction over it into the ranks of the foe, made it an impossible feat. The Confederates were repulsed, and the Federal army at last obtained rest from that fearful campaign. The artillery had saved it in the last great fight.

The Union Army of Virginia, under General John Pope, was organized on the day that the battle of Mechanicsville was fought, June 26, 1862. When the Peninsula campaign was over, and it was decided to withdraw McClellan, the main Federal army in front of Washington became that of General Pope, whose artillery as at first organized consisted of thirty-three batteries.

Pope's first duty was to prevent the concentration of all the Confederate armies on McClellan as the latter was withdrawing. Pope accordingly advanced on Culpeper Court House. Just after his leading troops passed that point, and before they reached the Rapidan, on the line of the Orange

"FLYING ARTILLERY" IN THE ATTEMPT ON RICHMOND

THE CANNONEERS WHO KEPT UP WITH THE CAVALRY—IN THIS SWIFTEST BRANCH OF THE SERVICE EACH MAN RIDES HORSEBACK

Here are drawn up Harry Benson's Battery A, of the Second United States Artillery, and Horatio Gates Gibson's Batteries C and G, combined of the Third United States Artillery, near Fair Oaks, Virginia. They arrived there just too late to take part in the battle of June, 1862. By "horse artillery," or "flying artillery" as it is sometimes called, is meant an organization equipped usually with 10-pounder rifled guns, with all hands mounted. In ordinary light artillery the cannoneers either ride on the gun-carriage or go afoot. In "flying artillery" each cannoneer has a horse. This form is by far the most mobile of all, and is best suited to accompany cavalry on account of its ability to travel rapidly. With the exception of the method of mounting the cannoneers, there was not any difference between the classes of field batteries except as they were divided between "light" and "heavy." In the photograph above no one is riding on the gun-carriages, but all have separate mounts. Battery A of the Second United States Artillery was in Washington in January, 1861, and took part in the expedition for the relief of Fort Pickens, Florida. It went to the Peninsula, fought at Mechanicsville May 23–24, 1862, and took part in the Seven Days' battles before Richmond June 25th to July 1st. Batteries C and G of the Third United States Artillery were at San Francisco, California, till October 1861, when they came East, and also went to the Peninsula and served at Yorktown and in the Seven Days.

and Alexandria Railroad, they encountered the foe. This brought on the battle of Cedar Mountain, the first engagement of the campaign, August 9th. Contact of the advance troops occurred in the morning, and, beginning at noon, the artillery duel lasted until about three o'clock in the afternoon. Then the infantry engagement began, and resulted in the Federal troops being pushed back. The Confederates followed the retiring troops until Federal reenforcements arrived. "Unaware of this," says J. C. Ropes, "Jackson undertook, in his anxiety to reach Culpeper before morning, to shell the Federal troops out of their position, but succeeded in arousing so many sleeping batteries that he shortly discontinued his cannonade, having suffered some loss. The battle of Cedar Mountain was over." The Union troops lost one gun, mired in the mud while withdrawing.

Pope retired across the Rappahannock and Lee concentrated his entire army against him. At the Rappahannock, the commanding positions of the Union artillery on the left bank enabled it to get a superiority of fire over the Confederate guns, which proved very distressing to Lee and baffled his first attempts to cross.

From the Rappahannock to Gainesville, the artillery had little opportunity to go into action. The marching and countermarching by both armies, each under the impression that the other was retreating, finally brought them together on the field of Gainesville, on August 28th. In this sanguinary fight the losses were great, the artillery sustaining its full proportion.

Pope's problem was now to prevent the union of Longstreet and Jackson. At Groveton, near the old Bull Run battle-ground, another bloody encounter took place, and the character of the fighting can best be understood when it is related that the men of General Hatch's division, after fighting for three-quarters of an hour in close range of the foe, retired in good order, leaving one gun in the hands of the Southerners.

A BATTERY THAT FOUGHT IN MANY CAMPAIGNS—"KNAP'S"

The upper photograph is of Independent Battery E of Pennsylvania Light Artillery, known as Knap's Battery, after its captain, Joseph M. Knap. Here the battery is within a strong fortification, guarded by a "slashing" of trees with branches pointing outward, visible beyond the walls. At Antietam, where the battery distinguished itself, there were no entrenchments to protect it from the fire of the Confederates; yet, practically unsupported, it broke up two charges in the thick of the action. Then McClellan's long-range guns materially assisted the Union advance, but later in the day the demand for artillery was so great that when General Hancock asked for more to assist his attenuated line, he could not get them until he finally borrowed one battery from Franklin. After the battle ended (September 17, 1862) and the Confederates withdrew to the south side of the Potomac, General Porter resolved to capture some of the Confederate guns commanding the fords. One of the five pieces taken in this exploit on the night of September 19th was a gun which had been captured by the Confederates at the First Bull Run, from Griffin's Battery, D of the Fifth United States Artillery. There is another photograph of Knap's battery in Volume II, page 61. It was organized at Point of Rocks, Maryland, from a company formed for the Sixty-third Pennsylvania and surplus men of the Twenty-eighth Pennsylvania Infantry in September, 1861. Its service included Pope's campaign in Northern Virginia, beside the Maryland campaign which culminated at Antietam. Its next important campaign was that of Chancellorsville, and then came the Gettysburg campaign. The scene of its activities was then transferred to the West, where it fought at Chattanooga, Lookout Mountain and Missionary Ridge. It was with Sherman in the Atlanta campaign, marched with him to the sea, and returned to Washington with the Army of Georgia in time for the Grand Review.

HEADQUARTERS FIRST BRIGADE HORSE ARTILLERY, BRANDY STATION, SEPTEMRER, 1863

Here are some followers of Brigadier-General James Madison Robertson, who won promotion as chief of horse artillery on many fields, from the Peninsula to the Virginia campaigns of 1864. The horse artillery was attached to the cavalry force.

The Confederates afterward said of this incident that the gun continued to fire until they were so close as to have their faces burnt by the discharges. Higher praise than this surely could not have been given the troops of either side.

Then followed the Second Battle of Manassas, a defeat for the Union army, but a hard-fought battle. The artillery continued to fire long after the musketry engagement had ceased, and after darkness had set in. The Federal army retired. General Pope claims not to have lost a gun, but Lee's report states that thirty pieces of artillery were captured during the series of battles. With the battle at Chantilly the campaign closed, and the Federal armies were again concentrated around Washington.

Early in September, Pope was relieved, and the Army of Virginia passed out of existence. Lee crossed into Maryland; McClellan moved up the Potomac with the reorganized Army of the Potomac, and the encounter came at Antietam, but in the mean time Harper's Ferry had again been taken by the Confederates, and seventy-three pieces of artillery and thousands of small arms were added to their store.

On the high ground in the center of his position at Antietam, McClellan placed several batteries of long-range guns. From this position almost the whole of the field of battle could be seen, and, further to the left, where the batteries of the Fifth Corps were placed, a still more complete view could be obtained. The conformation of the ground was such that nearly the entire Confederate line was reached by fire from these central Federal batteries. The Union advance was assisted materially by their fire, but several of them were effectively shelled by the Confederates, who, however, on their counter-attacks, in turn suffered severely from the fire of the Federal guns.

At 10 A.M., September 17th, two of Sumner's batteries were being closely assailed by Confederate sharpshooters, and Hancock formed a line of guns and infantry to relieve them. Cowan's battery of 3-inch guns, Frank's 12-pounders, and

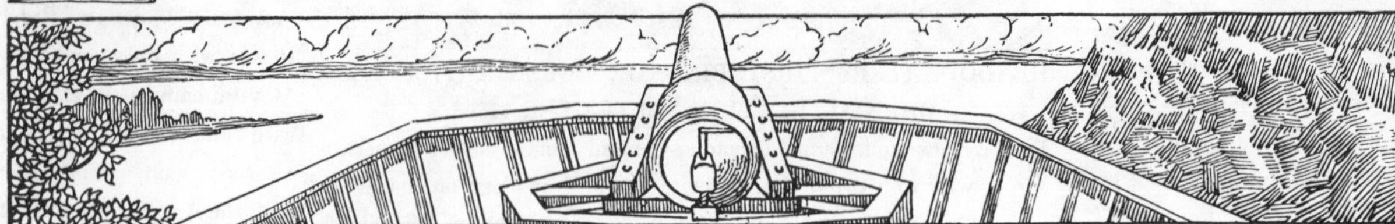

FROM PRIVATE TO BRIGADIER-GENERAL—ROBERTSON, A CHIEF OF ARTILLERY WHO HELPED THE FEDERALS TO WIN GETTYSBURG

Twenty-three years before the war Brigadier-General James Madison Robertson (first on the left above) was a private in battery F of the Second United States Artillery. Between 1838 and 1848 he became corporal, then artificer, and finally quartermaster-sergeant. On June 28th of that year he was made second-lieutenant, and four years later first-lieutenant. It was not until May 14, 1861, that he attained his captaincy. Then came war, and with it rapid advancement. His quarter of a century of preparation stood him in good stead. In the next four years he was promoted as many times for gallant, brave, and distinguished services on the field, attaining finally the rank of brigadier-general. While Pleasonton's cavalry at Gettysburg was preventing Stuart from joining in Pickett's charge, Robertson led the horse artillery which seconded the efforts of Pleasonton's leaders, Gregg and Buford and Kilpatrick, whose exploits were not second to those of the infantry. For gallant and meritorious service in this campaign Robertson was promoted to lieutenant-colonel. He had been promoted to major for his gallantry at the battle of Gaines' Mill on the Peninsula. He was made colonel May 31, 1864, for gallant and meritorious service in the battle of Cold Harbor, and brigadier-general for distinguished service while chief of horse artillery attached to the Army of the Potomac during the campaign from May to August, 1864, including the battles of the Wilderness, Cold Harbor, Hawes' Shop, and Trevilian Station. He died, a soldier "full of years and honors," January 24, 1891.

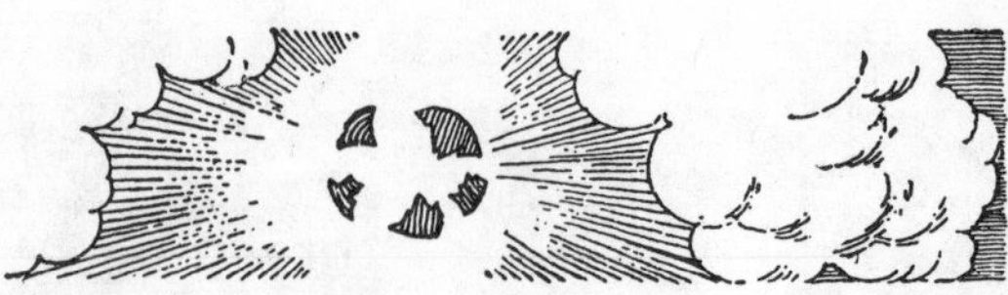

Cothran's rifled guns, with their supporting infantry, a brigade, drove away the threatening skirmishers and silenced the Confederate batteries.

The demand for artillery was so great that when General Hancock asked for more guns to assist his attenuated line, the request could not be complied with. However, he borrowed, for a time, from Franklin, one battery, and when its ammunition had been expended, another was loaned him to replace it.

The battle ended September 17th. On the night of the 18th the Confederates withdrew, and by the 19th they had established batteries on the south side of the Potomac to cover their crossing. Porter determined to clear the fords and capture some of the guns. The attempt was made after dark of that day, and resulted in the taking of five guns and some of their equipment. One of these had been taken by the Confederates at the First Bull Run, and belonged to Battery D (Griffin's), Fifth United States Artillery.

We now follow the fortunes of the army to Fredericksburg. Sumner, with fifteen brigades of infantry and thirteen batteries, arrived on the banks of the Rappahannock before a large Confederate force was able to concentrate on the opposite shore, but no attempt was made to cross until just before the battle of December 13, 1862. General Hunt, on the day of the fight, had one hundred and forty-seven guns on the crest above the left bank of the river, in position to command the crossing, and the ground beyond. Besides these, twenty-three batteries, of one hundred and sixteen guns, crossed the river at the lower bridges, and nineteen batteries, of one hundred and four guns, crossed with Sumner's command. The Federal guns were principally 3-inch rifles, 20-pounder Parrotts, and 4½-inch siege-guns. They engaged the Confederates at close range, and the duel was terrific. The reserve line, on the crest of the left bank, aided with all its power, but the result was disastrous to the Federal arms.

We cannot follow the fortunes of the heroes through all

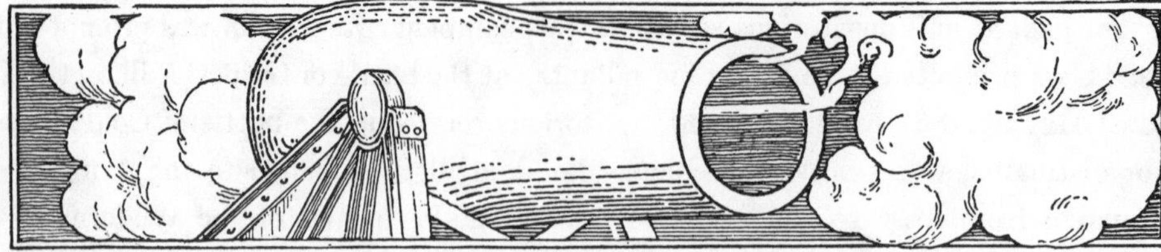

LIGHT ARTILLERY "IN RESERVE"—WAITING ORDERS

It is no parade-ground upon which this splendid battery is drawn up, as the untrodaen daisies plainly show. Thus the waving fields of Gettysburg smiled on those July days of 1863—until the hoofs and wheels had trampled all green things to the earth, where they lay crushed beneath the prostrate forms of many a brave soldier of the North and South fighting for what each thought the right. This battery is standing in reserve. At any moment the notes of the bugle may ring out which will send it dashing forward across field and ditch to deal out death and face it from the bullets of the foe. The battery was evidently serving with infantry, as the cannoneers have no mounts. They are standing beside the gun-carriages, upon which they will leap when the battery moves forward. It was no easy matter for them to retain their seats as the heavy wheels cut through the grass and flowers and rebounded from hummocks and tilted sharply over stones. At any moment a horse might fall crippled, and it was their duty to rush forward and cut the traces, and jump aboard again as the gun drove around, or, if necessary, over the wounded animal. The latter was harder for an artilleryman who loved his horses than facing the screaming shells and whistling bullets at the front.

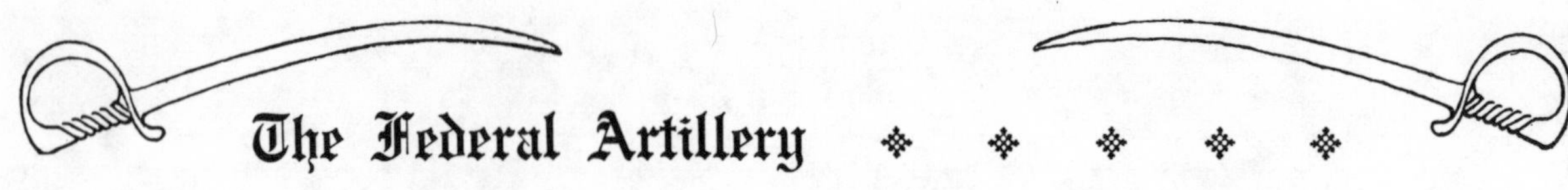

the vicissitudes of the following campaigns. On the Gettysburg field the artillery again contested with the Confederates in probably the most stubborn fighting of the war. General Meade had three hundred guns. The Federal advance was at first gradually forced back to Cemetery Hill, where General Doubleday rallied his troops, and his artillery did excellent service in checking the foe. He relates that the first long line that came on from the west was swept away by the Federal guns, which fired with very destructive effect. On the second day, the angle at the peach orchard furnished opportunities for nearly every phase of an artillery combat. " The power of the arm in concentration was well illustrated, the splendid devotion with which its destructive force was met and struggled against fixed our attention, and the skilful tactics by which its strength was husbanded for the decisive moment are especially to be praised."

Two Pennsylvania batteries on Cemetery Hill which had been captured by the Confederates were recovered in a gallant manner. The cannoneers, so summarily ousted, rallied and retook their guns by a vigorous attack with pistols, handspikes, rammers, stones, and even fence rails—the " Dutchmen " showing that they were in no way inferior to their " Yankee " comrades, who had been taunting them ever since Chancellorsville. After an hour's desperate fighting the Confederates were driven out with heavy loss.

The Federal artillery from Little Round Top to Cemetery Hill blazed " like a volcano " on the third day of the fight. Two hours after the firing opened, the chief of artillery, with the approval of General Meade, caused his guns to cease firing in order to replenish their ammunition supply. This deceived the Confederates, and Pickett's famous charge was made. No sooner was the advance begun than the Federal artillery belched forth all along the line, firing only at the approaching infantry. The brave assailants advanced even to the muzzles of the guns, the mass gradually diminishing as it

A VETERAN BATTERY FROM ILLINOIS, NEAR MARIETTA IN THE ATLANTA CAMPAIGN

Battery B of the First Illinois Light Artillery followed Sherman in the Atlanta campaign. It took part in the demonstrations against Resaca, Georgia, May 8 to 15, 1864, and in the battle of Resaca on the 14th and 15th. It was in the battles about Dallas from May 25th to June 5th, and took part in the operations about Marietta and against Kenesaw Mountain in June and July. During the latter period this photograph was taken. The battery did not go into this campaign without previous experience. It had already fought as one of the eight batteries at Fort Henry and Fort Donelson, heard the roar of the battle of Shiloh, and participated in the sieges of Corinth and Vicksburg. The artillery in the West was not a whit less necessary to the armies than that in the East. Pope's brilliant feat of arms in the capture of Island No. 10 added to the growing respect in which the artillery was held by the other arms of the service. The effective fire of the massed batteries at Murfreesboro turned the tide of battle. At Chickamauga the Union artillery inflicted fearful losses upon the Confederates. At Atlanta again they counted their dead by the hundreds, and at Franklin and Nashville the guns maintained the best traditions of the Western armies. They played no small part in winning battles.

approached. Their comrades watched them breathlessly until they disappeared in the cloud of smoke. Only a few disorganized stragglers were finally swept back. The deadly canister had broken the spirit of that great Army of Northern Virginia.

In the West, the value of the artillery was no less than in the East. It will be impossible to notice the minor affairs in which field-batteries took an active and a decisive part. In Missouri particularly was this the case. General Lyon, before his untimely death, used this effective weapon to its full capacity, as did Pope, Fremont, Grant, and the other Union leaders who participated in shaping up the campaign against the Confederacy in Missouri and Kentucky.

Early in 1861 the Confederates took possession of a line from Columbus to Bowling Green, Kentucky. Forts Henry and Donelson were in the center, and formed the keystone of the arch. Grant saw their value, and directed himself to their capture. He obtained permission from Halleck and McClellan to reconnoiter up the Tennessee and Cumberland rivers, and sent General C. F. Smith with two brigades from Paducah.

On the strength of Smith's report, Grant made strong representation to Halleck, his immediate superior, that the move was advisable. After some delay, the orders were issued, and Grant moved up the Tennessee with seventeen thousand men. The immediate assault on Fort Henry was threatened by General McClernand, with two brigades, each having two batteries. The work was a solidly constructed bastion fort with twelve guns on the river face, and five bearing inland. It was evacuated without attack from the land forces, as the gunboat bombardment was sufficient to drive out the defenders, but not without considerable damage to the fleet.

Fort Donelson, on the Cumberland, was the next objective. On the 8th of February, 1862, Grant telegraphed to Halleck that he proposed to take Fort Donelson with infantry and cavalry alone, but he moved out from Fort Henry with fifteen thousand men and eight field-batteries. Some of the guns were

A WISCONSIN LIGHT BATTERY AT BATON ROUGE, LOUISIANA

The First Wisconsin Independent Battery of Light Artillery saw most of its service in Tennessee, Mississippi, and Louisiana. Its first active work was in the Cumberland Gap campaign, from April to June, 1862. It accompanied Sherman's Yazoo River expedition in December, 1862, and went on the expedition to Arkansas Post in January, 1863. At the siege of Vicksburg it participated in two assaults, May 19th and 22d, and after the fall of Vicksburg, July 4th, it went to the siege of Jackson, Mississippi. The battery was then refitted with 30-pounder Parrotts, and ordered to the Department of the Gulf. It left New Orleans April 22, 1864, to go on the Red River campaign. This was taken by the Confederate photographer, A. D. Lytle.

Battery C of the First Illinois Light Artillery served throughout the Western campaigns and accompanied Sherman on his march to the sea. It took part in the siege of Savannah, December 10 to 21, 1864, and served throughout the campaign of the Carolinas, January to April, 1865. After being present at the surrender of Johnston and his army, it marched to Washington via Richmond, and took part in the grand review. It was mustered out on June 14, 1865.

OFFICERS OF A LIGHT BATTERY THAT MARCHED TO THE SEA

20- and 24-pounders, rifles, and howitzers. Grant's fifteen thousand men found themselves confronted by about twenty thousand entrenched. McClernand pressed to the right, up the river. His artillery was very active. Sometimes acting singly, and then in concert, the batteries temporarily silenced several of those of the Confederates and shelled some of the camps. Outside the main work, about fourteen hundred yards to the west, the Confederates had, after the surrender of Fort Henry, constructed a line of infantry entrenchments, which circled thence to the south and struck the river two and one-quarter miles from the fort. The guns of eight field-batteries were placed on this line.

On the 15th, McClernand's right was assailed and pressed back, and a part of the garrison escaped, but Grant received the unconditional surrender of about fourteen thousand men and sixty-five guns. His own artillery had not increased beyond the eight batteries with which he marched from Fort Henry. These were not fixed in position and protected by earthworks, but were moved from place to place as necessity dictated.

The brilliant feat of arms of Pope and his command in the capture of Island No. 10 added to the growing respect in which the artillery was held by the other combatant arms.

About seven in the morning on April 6, 1862, the Confederate artillery opened fire on the Union camps at Shiloh. Thereupon ensued one of the most sanguinary conflicts of the whole war. Although the Federal artillery was under the direct orders of the division commanders, the fighting was so fragmentary that no concerted attempt was made to use the batteries until, on the retirement of Hurlbut to the vicinity of Pittsburg Landing, some batteries of heavy guns were placed in position to cover the possible retirement of the troops from the front. About forty guns were finally assembled, and their work had an important part in saving the army, for this group of batteries was a large factor in repulsing the attempt of the

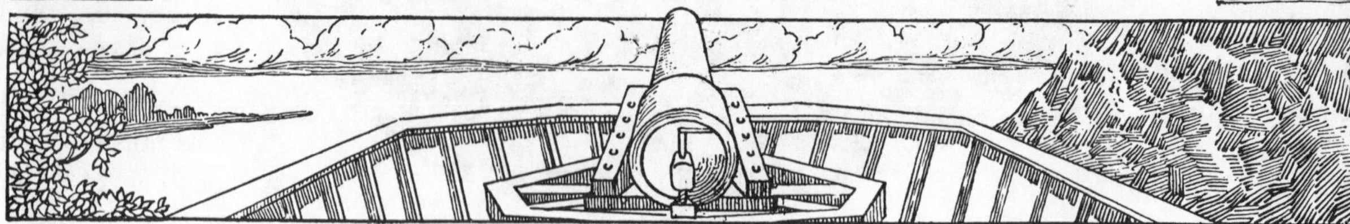

HEAVY ARTILLERY THAT MADE MARVELLOUS INFANTRY—DRILLING BEFORE THE WILDERNESS

Save for the drills in the forts about Washington, the big heavy artillery regiments with a complement of 1,800 men had an easy time at first. But in 1864, when General Grant took command of the armies in the field, the heavy artillery regiments in the vicinity of Washington were brigaded, provisionally, for service at the front. On May 19th, at the battle of Spotsylvania, the veterans cracked no end of jokes at the expense of the new troops. "How are you, heavies?" they would cry. "Is this work heavy enough for you? You're doing well, my sons. If you keep on like this a couple of years, you'll learn all the tricks of the trade." They had no more such comments to make after they had seen the "heavies" in action. They bore themselves nobly. Many of the severest casualties during the war were sustained by the heavy artillerists in the Wilderness campaign and at Petersburg.

A LIGHT BATTERY THAT FOUGHT BEFORE PETERSBURG—THE 17TH NEW YORK

The Seventeenth Independent Battery of New York Light Artillery, known as the "Orleans Battery," was organized at Lockport, New York, and mustered in August 26, 1862. It remained in the artillery camp of instruction and in the defenses of Washington until July, 1864, when it was ordered to Petersburg. It took part in the pursuit of Lee, and was present at Appomattox.

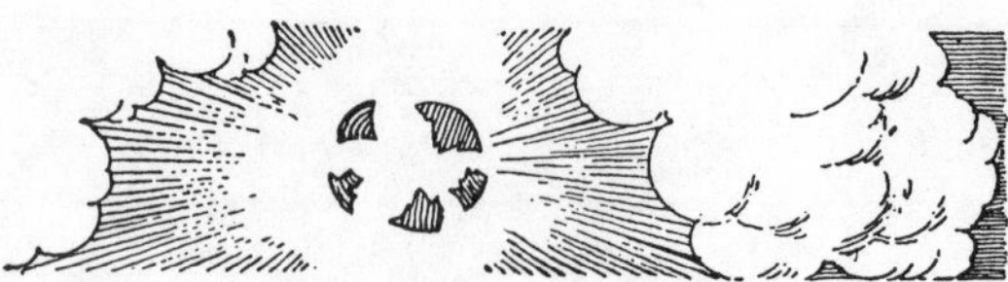

Confederates to seize the Landing and cut off Buell's army from crossing to Grant's assistance.

At the battle of Murfreesboro, or Stone's River, the artillery was especially well handled by the Federals, although they lost twenty-eight guns. On the second day, the Confederates made a determined assault to dislodge the Federals from the east bank of the river. The infantry assault was a success, but immediately the massed batteries on the west bank opened fire and drove Breckinridge's men back with great loss. Federal troops were then sent across the river to reenforce the position and the day was saved for the Union cause. The effective fire of the artillery had turned the tide of battle.

In assailing Vicksburg, Grant made four serious attempts to get on the flanks of the Confederate position before he evolved his final audacious plan of moving below the city and attacking from the southeast. In all the early trials his artillery, in isolated cases, was valuable, but the character of the operations in the closed country made it impossible to mass the guns for good effect. The naval assistance afforded most of the heavy gun-practice that was necessary or desirable against the Confederates.

On the last attempt, however, when the troops had left the river and were moving against Pemberton, Grant's guns assumed their full importance. His army consisted of the Thirteenth Army Corps, Major-General McClernand; the Fifteenth Army Corps, Major-General Sherman, and the Seventeenth Army Corps, Major-General McPherson, with an aggregate of sixty-one thousand men and one hundred and fifty-eight guns. The superb assistance rendered to the infantry by the ably handled guns made it possible for Grant to defeat his antagonist in a series of hard-fought battles, gradually move around him, and press him back into Vicksburg. Once there, the result could not be doubtful if the Federal army could hold off the Confederate reenforcements. This it was able to do. The progress of the siege we shall not here consider, except to

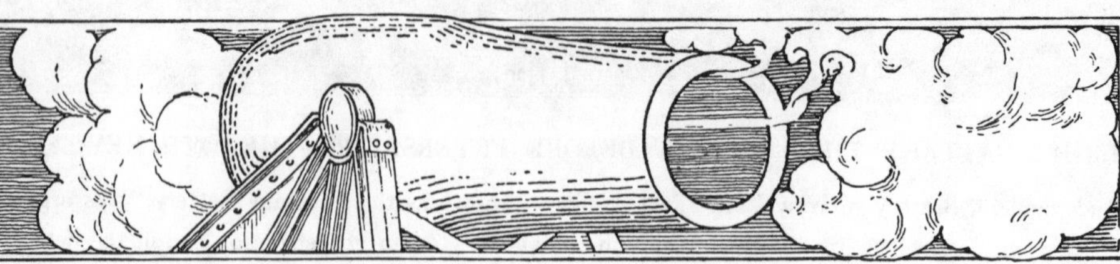

THIS BATTERY STOOD FIFTH IN ITS NUMBER OF CASUALTIES

The First Independent Battery of New York Light Artillery, under command of Captain Andrew Cowan, lost two officers and sixteen enlisted men killed and mortally wounded out of its complement of 150 men. Only four other batteries suffered a greater loss. "Cooper's" Battery B, First Pennsylvania Artillery, lost twenty-one men; "Sands'" Eleventh Ohio Battery lost twenty men (nineteen of them in one engagement in a charge on the battery at Iuka); "Philips'" Fifth Massachusetts Battery lost nineteen men; and "Weeden's" Battery C, First Rhode Island Artillery, lost nineteen men. This photograph shows Cowan's Battery in position within the captured Confederate works on the Petersburg line. The officers and men lived and slept in a work captured from the Confederates, and the horses were picketed back of the emplacements and in the gun-pits as seen underneath.

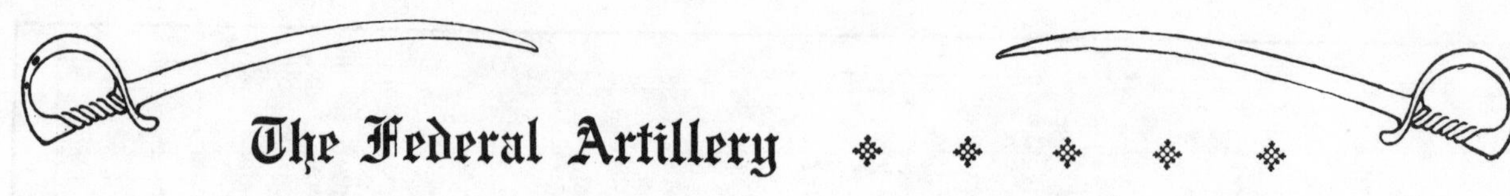

say that for scientific artillery work on the part of the besiegers it was not surpassed elsewhere in the conduct of the war. Twelve miles of trenches were constructed and armed with two hundred and eight light field-guns and twelve heavy siege-guns. The total loss in guns for the Confederacy during the series of operations was two hundred and sixty, of which one hundred and seventy-two were lost in the city of Vicksburg, and eighty-eight during the preceding campaign. Sixty-seven of these were siege-guns and the rest lighter field-pieces.

From Tullahoma to Chickamauga, Rosecrans skilfully maneuvered his army, to encounter a check that caused a temporary halt in the Union progress. During the first day's fierce fighting at Chickamauga, there were several interchanges of batteries—captures and recaptures. At half-past two in the afternoon of September 19, 1863, the Confederates made a determined assault on the Federal right. Hood's corps met with fearful loss from heavy artillery fire, six batteries opening with canister as the columns approached. On they came relentlessly, but the stubborn courage of the Federal troops, now reenforced, finally drove them back. As darkness was approaching, General Thomas, on the Union left, while re-forming his lines, was fiercely attacked, and the assault was so determined that some confusion resulted, but the artillery again came to the rescue, and, after dark, the Confederates were repulsed, and the first day's conflict ended as a drawn battle.

On the morning of the second day, the attack was made on the Federal left by Polk, but Thomas had entrenched his men and batteries, and the tremendous efforts to dislodge him were repulsed by a storm of musketry and canister, and the attacks failed. After the Federal right was pushed off the field and the conflict raged around Thomas on Horseshoe Ridge, the artillery of Thomas' command created havoc in the ranks of the assaulting columns. As the final attacks were made the ammunition was exhausted, and, in their turn, the infantry saved the artillery by receiving the foe with cold steel. That night

THE "ABOUT-FACED" REDOUBT THREE DAYS AFTER ITS CAPTURE BY THE FEDERALS

A photograph of June 21, 1864—three days after Cowan's Battery captured this work and turned it against its Confederate builders. When the Eighteenth Army Corps had made its advance on Petersburg, followed by the gallant charges of the Fifteenth, and the fighting of the two following days, all the captured redoubts were occupied and strengthened. Of course, they were made to face the other way. The sand-bag reënforcements were removed and placed on the eastern side, new embrasures and traverses were constructed, and face to face the armies sat down to watch one another, and to begin the huge earthworks and fortifications that became the wonder of the military world. All night long for many months the air was filled with fiery messengers of death. The course of the bomb-shells could be plainly followed by the lighted fuses which described an arc against the sky. The redoubt pictured here is one captured, "about faced," and occupied on June 18th by Cowan's First New York Independent Battery, in the Artillery Brigade of the Sixth Corps. Thus the Union lines advanced, trench by trench, until Lee's army finally withdrew and left them the works so long and valiantly defended. The view looks northwest to the Appomattox.

BRIGADIER-GENERAL C. H. TOMPKINS

GENERAL TOMPKINS

Starting as captain of a Rhode Island Battery May 2, 1861, Charles Henry Tompkins became a major August 1, 1861, colonel September 13, 1861, and brevet brigadier-general of volunteers August 1, 1864, for gallant and meritorious service, in the campaign before Richmond, and in the Shenandoah Valley.

the Federal army retired to Chattanooga. The Confederate victory had been dearly bought.

Sherman started his campaign with fifty-three batteries of two hundred and fifty-four guns. For most of the time the weather was almost as great an antagonist as the Confederates. Crossing swollen streams without bridges, dragging heavy guns through mud and mire, and most of the time stripped of all surplus baggage and equipage, the artillery soldier had few pleasures, no luxuries, and much very hard work.

On the 17th of July, the Confederate Government removed Johnston, and detailed Hood to command his army. The news was received with satisfaction by the Federal troops, for now they were certain of getting a fight to their hearts' content. And so it developed. The battle of Peach Tree Creek, in front of Atlanta, gave a splendid opportunity for the employment of the energies of the batteries that had been dragged so far through the mud by the patient men and animals of Sherman's artillery. " Few battlefields of the war had been so thickly strewn with dead and wounded as they lay that evening around Collier's Mill."

Atlanta captured, Sherman rested his army and then started for the sea, sending Thomas back into Tennessee to cope with Hood. At Franklin and Nashville, the guns maintained the best traditions of the Western forces, and victory was finally achieved against one of the best armies ever assembled by the Confederacy.

The consolidated morning report of the Army of the Potomac for April 30, 1864, showed with that army forty-nine batteries of two hundred and seventy-four field guns, of which one hundred and twenty were 12-pounder Napoleons, one hundred and forty-eight 10-pounder and 3-inch rifles, and six 20-pounder Parrott rifles. In addition to these guns, there were eight 24-pounder Coehorn mortars. Two hundred and seventy rounds of ammunition were carried for each gun. The

"DICTATOR"—THE TRAVELING MORTAR IN FRONT OF PETERSBURG, 1864

This is the 13-inch mortar, a 200-pound exploding shell from which threw a Confederate field-piece and its carriage above its parapet, at a range of nearly two miles. The 17,000 pounds of this mortar made it difficult to move, so it was mounted on an ordinary railroad-car strengthened by additional beams, and plated on top with iron. This engine of destruction was run down on the Petersburg & City Point Railroad to a point near the Union lines, where a curve in the track made it easy to change the direction of the fire. The recoil from a charge of fourteen pounds of powder shifted the mortar less than two feet on the car, which moved a dozen feet on the track. Even the full charge of twenty pounds of powder could be used without damage to the axles of the car. This mortar, whose shell would crush and explode any ordinary field-magazine, terrorized the Confederate gunners, and succeeded in silencing their enfilading batteries on Chesterfield Heights. The activities of this great war machine were directed by Colonel H. L. Abbot, of the First Connecticut Heavy Artillery. Other photographs of it, with officers and men, are shown on pages 186 and 187, Volume III.

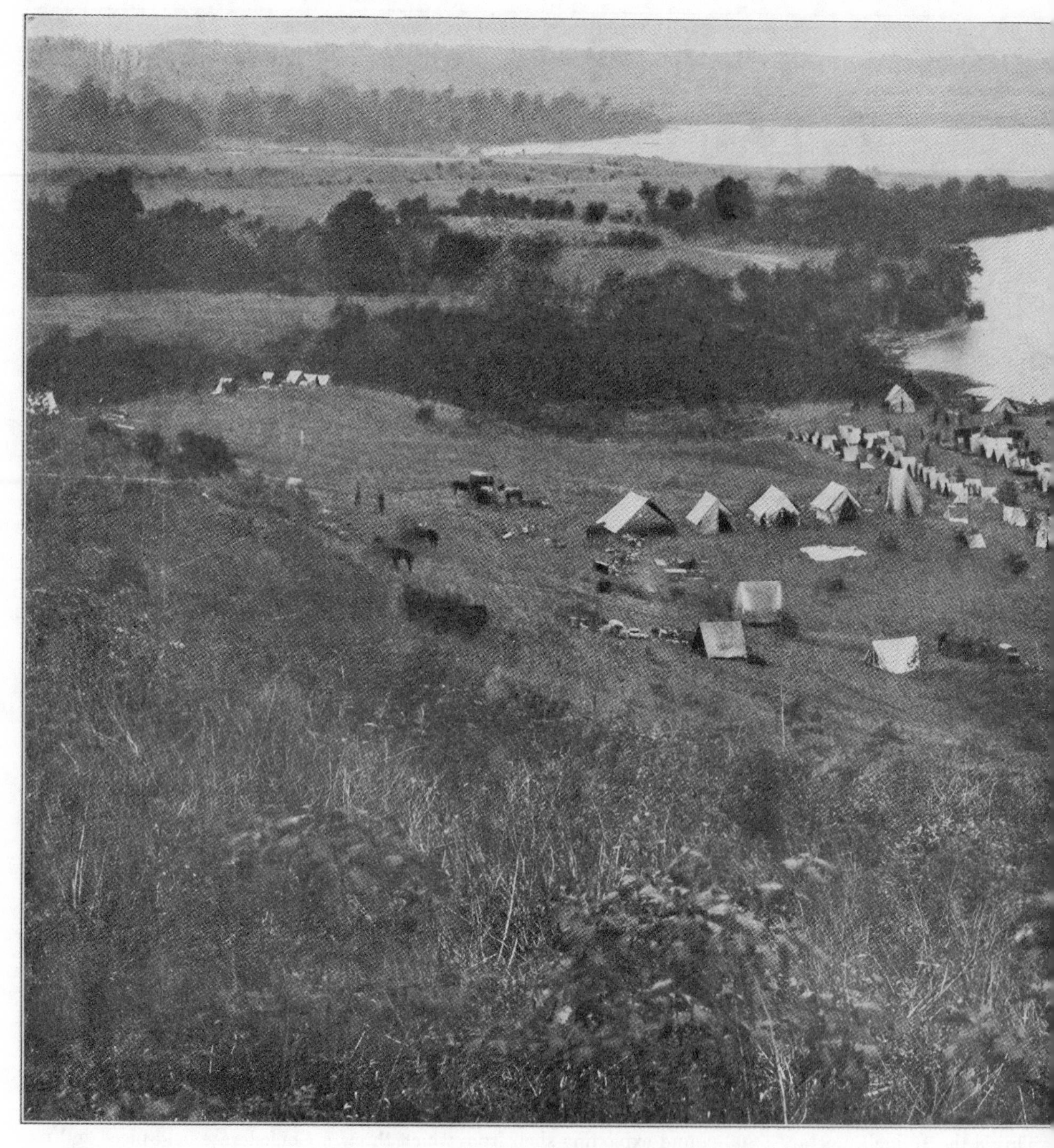

CAMP OF HEAVY ARTILLERY ON THE WAY TO PETERSBURG

On May 16, 1864, the date of this sweeping photograph, the movement against Petersburg had begun. The heavy guns which these two regiments were about to serve before Petersburg were sent by steamer and rail, so no ordnance is visible in this peaceful-looking camp on the banks of the beautiful river. The First Massachusetts Heavy Artillery had been ordered from the defenses of Washington to join the Army of the Potomac at Belle Plain, Virginia. It was to form part of the second brigade, third division, Second Army Corps, of the

THE FIRST MASSACHUSETTS AND SECOND NEW YORK AT BELLE PLAIN, 1864

Army of the Potomac, from May, 1864, to May, 1865. A month after landing at Belle Plain it was at the siege of Petersburg. At Belle Plain it was met by the Second New York Heavy Artillery, also from the defenses of Washington, which formed part of the first brigade, first division, Second Army Corps of the Army of the Potomac, from that time till June, 1865. The latter regiment also proceeded to Petersburg but by a more circuitous route. May 18th to 21st it served at Spotsylvania; June 1st to 12th, it was at Cold Harbor.

succession of battles and flank marches through the Wilderness to the James, up to Petersburg, thence to Appomattox, had taxed the energies and showed the devotion of the men with the guns in the hardest campaign of the war, finally causing the surrender of a remnant of the proud Army of Northern Virginia.

While at Petersburg, an interesting experiment was tried which resulted successfully. A large 13-inch Coehorn mortar was mounted on an ordinary railroad platform car, run down to a point within range of the Confederate works, and halted on a curve so that by a slight movement of the car the direction of the piece could be changed. The mortar, fired with fourteen pounds of powder, recoiled less than two feet on the car, which, in turn, was moved only ten or twelve feet on the track. The firing excited much apprehension in the Confederate works, and was effective in preventing their batteries from enfilading the right of the Union lines.

Major E. S. May, of the British army, has this to say of the Federal artillery in the Civil War:

"We have not by any means exhausted that rich repository of brilliant deeds, and many bright examples are reluctantly omitted. Enough, however, has been said to show that this arm can scarcely be with justice reproached for lack of enterprise during the great struggle. . . . As regards the conduct of officers and men in action, efficient service of guns, and judicious handling on the part of its more prominent leaders, the artillery showed itself in no degree unworthy of the great traditions handed down to it from the previous era, and may point with satisfaction to what it accomplished."

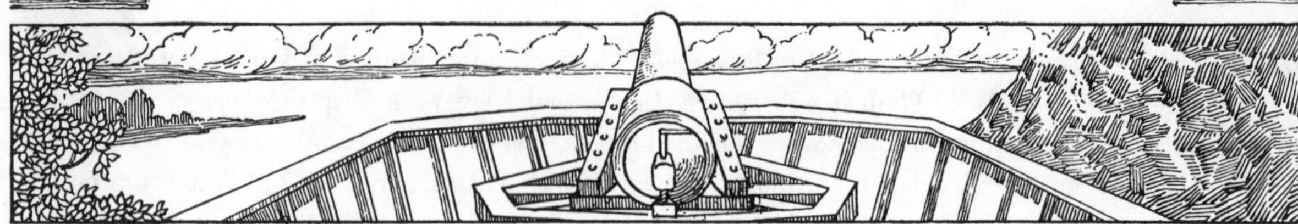

II

CONFEDERATE GUNS AND GUNNERS

THE LARGEST CONFEDERATE GUN AT YORKTOWN—A 64-POUNDER BURST IN THE EFFORT TO REACH FEDERAL BATTERY NO. 1 IN McCLELLAN'S WORKS BEFORE THE BELEAGUERED CONFEDERATE CITY

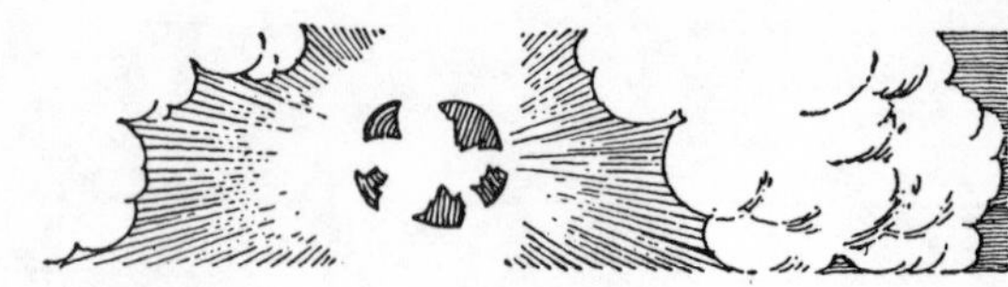

THE CONFEDERATE ARTILLERY—ITS ORGANIZATION AND DEVELOPMENT

By David Gregg McIntosh

Colonel of Artillery, Confederate States Army

THE organization of the Confederate field-artillery during the Civil War was never as symmetrical as that of the cavalry and infantry, and its evolution was slow. This was due in part to the lack of uniformity in the equipment of single batteries, and the inequality in the number of men in a company, running all the way in a 4-gun battery from forty-five to one hundred, and also to the tardiness with which the batteries were organized into battalions with proper staff-officers.

The disposition of the Government was to accept all bodies which volunteered for a particular branch of the service, and this did not tend to due proportions between the different branches. Outside of a limited number of smooth-bore guns in possession of certain volunteer associations, the Government had no equipment of field-artillery to start with. What was found in the arsenals in the Southern States which fell into the hands of the Confederate Government, consisted of old iron guns mounted on Gribeauval carriages, manufactured about 1812, but there was not a single serviceable field-battery in any arsenal.

The few guns belonging to the different States were short of harness, saddles, and other equipment. Not a gun or gun-carriage, and, except during the Mexican War, not a round of ammunition had been prepared in any of the Confederate States for fifty years. When hostilities began, the only foundry for casting cannon was at the Tredegar works in Richmond, and with the exception of a battery of Blakely guns, imported by the State of South Carolina, and a single battery

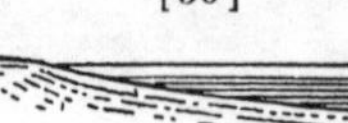
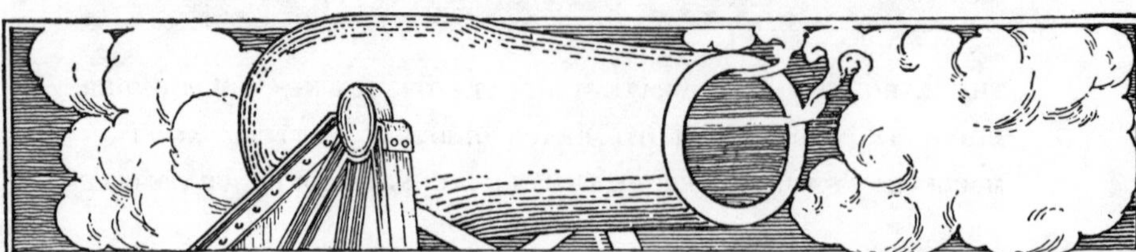

INSIDE A CONFEDERATE "WATER BATTERY," PENSACOLA HARBOR, IN 1861

THIS AND THE FOLLOWING THREE PHOTOGRAPHS WERE TAKEN WITHIN THE CONFEDERATE LINES IN 1861

This vivid view of great events in the making reveals the green Confederate volunteers without uniforms and still inexperienced. They show more enthusiasm than efficiency as they awkwardly handle the guns. It was not long before these quickly recruited gunners had become expert enough to give a good account of themselves. On November 22 and 23, 1861, they sustained and replied to a bombardment by the United States vessels *Niagara* and *Richmond* and by Fort Pickens and the neighboring Union batteries. Although Fort McRee was so badly injured that General Bragg entertained the idea of abandoning it, the plan of the Union commanders to "take and destroy it" was not executed. Time and again when the Federal blockading fleet threatened various points along the Confederate coast, requisitions were sent for these guns, but they were always needed in this fort. At the outset of the Civil War not a gun or gun-carriage, and, excepting during the Mexican War, not a round of ammunition had been prepared in the States of the Confederacy for fifty years. They were forced to improvise all of the vast paraphernalia necessary for war.

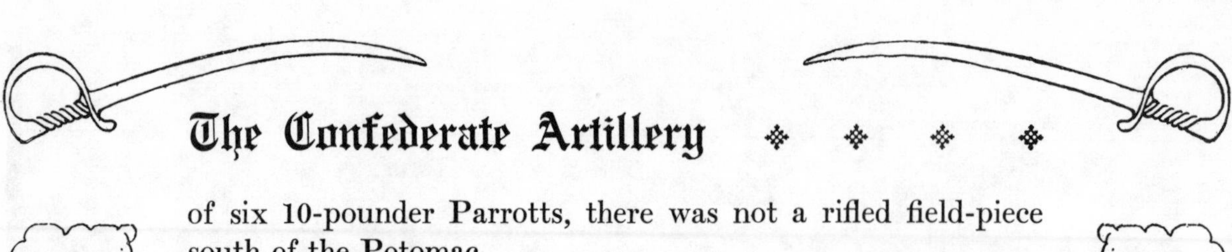

of six 10-pounder Parrotts, there was not a rifled field-piece south of the Potomac.

The first step to supply this want was to ream out a number of old 4-pounder iron guns belonging to the State of Virginia to get a good bore, and then rifle them after the manner of the Parrott. Besides these, that State purchased a few Parrott guns, used by Colonel Magruder at Big Bethel, in June, 1861.

Of the volunteer associations, the Washington Artillery, of New Orleans, organized in 1838, and having seen service as Company A in Persifal Smith's regiment in the Mexican War, was best known. In 1861, the organization consisted of five batteries, four of which served in Virginia, and one in the Army of Tennessee. On May 3, 1861, the battalion, through Judah P. Benjamin, offered its services to the Confederate Government, and was mustered in on the 26th of that month. The battalion made its mark at Bull Run on July 18th, but its most conspicuous service was at Fredericksburg, in December, 1862, when from Marye's Heights it played an important part in repulsing repeated assaults of the Union troops. Its strength was afterward much reduced, and in Virginia the batteries consisted of three guns each.

Next in importance was the Richmond Howitzers, organized at the time of the John Brown raid by George W. Randolph, afterward Confederate Secretary of War. In 1861, it was recruited up to three companies and formed into a battalion, though in the field the first company was never associated with the other two. It has been said that the flower of the educated youth in the South gravitated toward the artillery, and it is claimed that over one hundred men were commissioned from this corps, of every rank from that of second lieutenant to Secretary of War. One of its features was the Howitzer Glee Club, led by Crouch, the author of "Kathleen Mavourneen"; another was the Howitzer Law Club, in which moot-courts were held. Many of its members were from the

THE CONFEDERATE GUNNERS IN 1861

It is clear that these Confederate gunners at Pensacola are untried and undisciplined, but it is also evident that they are enthusiastic. They are manning the guns which are to open later on Fort Pickens, the first fort on the Confederate coast seized by the Federals, and held by them throughout the war. This was due to the enterprise of Lieutenant Adam J. Slemmer, ably seconded by Lieutenant J. H. Gilman. Lieutenant Slemmer's report says of Lieutenant Gilman: "During the whole affair we have stood side by side, and if any credit is due for the course pursued, he is entitled to it equally with myself." The demand was refused, and Fort Pickens never passed into the hands of the Confederates. The battery seen in this photograph was at Warrington, nearly opposite Fort Pickens. It commanded the entrance to the harbor. General Pendleton, who was a graduate of West Point in the class of 1830, was chief of artillery in Lee's army of Northern Virginia. He entered the war as captain in the artillery corps July 19, 1861, and became colonel and chief of artillery July 21, 1861. The mortar in this photograph is an old style piece dating from before the Mexican war. The new Confederate soldiers had at times to content themselves with very old guns.

BRIGADIER–GENERAL W. N. PENDLETON

University of Virginia, where out of six hundred and four students in 1861 over one-half entered the Confederate service.

Besides these organizations, was the Washington Artillery, of Charleston, South Carolina, organized in 1784; the Marion Artillery, of the same place; Delaware Kemper's Artillery, of Alexandria, and a number of other organizations.

The great bulk of the artillery, however, was composed of companies which volunteered for that branch of the service, and were compelled to accept such equipment as the Government could furnish. This embraced a great variety. There was the small 6-pounder gun, at first largely predominating, and afterward the 12-pounder known as Napoleon, and also the 12-pound and 24-pound howitzer, all of bronze. The rifled guns were somewhat nondescript. Those turned out by the Ordnance Department were generally of 3-inch caliber with five or seven grooves adapted to the same ammunition, though not uniform in length or shape, and varying in weight. Many of these were withdrawn and replaced by guns of the Parrott type, or the 3-inch U. S. pattern.

It was extremely rare at any period of the war to find a battery with uniform equipment. There was at no time in the Army of Northern Virginia more than six or eight batteries of Napoleon guns, and a less number of 3-inch rifles. It seems to have been thought desirable to have a section of rifles and a section of smoothbores. But it was not unusual to find in the same section rifles of different caliber, or a Napoleon with a 6-pounder, or perhaps a howitzer; and in a battery of four guns, there was not infrequently at least three different calibers which required different ammunition. This made the supply of ammunition more difficult and impaired the effectiveness of the battery. Experience taught the value of concentrated fire, and that four Napoleons or four rifles were more effective than the fire of a mixed battery.

The Napoleon and the 3-inch rifle, U. S. pattern, were the favorite guns; the former, because it was equally adapted to the

BRIGADIER-GENERAL E. P. ALEXANDER, WHO COMMANDED LONGSTREET'S ARTILLERY AT GETTYSBURG

E. P. Alexander was the Confederate officer who commanded Longstreet's eighty guns in the great artillery battle which preceded Pickett's charge at Gettysburg. He entered the Engineer Corps of the Confederate army April 2, 1861, and served on the staff of General G. T. Beauregard as engineer and chief of signal service till August of that year. As chief of ordnance of the Army of Northern Virginia, he distinguished himself on the bloody field of Antietam. He directed the eighty pieces on Longstreet's front at Gettysburg, which prepared the way for Pickett's charge until they had shot away practically all their ammunition. He was acting chief of artillery in Longstreet's corps from September 25, 1863, till February 26, 1864, and was appointed chief of artillery of the corps with which he remained till Appomattox, serving in the Wilderness, at Spotsylvania, and the siege of Petersburg. On February 26, 1864, he had been appointed brigadier-general of Artillery. Within two weeks after Lee's surrender he was at the Brandreth House in New York city attempting to arrange for a commission in the Brazilian army. Later, he became general manager and president of various Southern railroads, Government director of the Union Pacific Railroad Company from 1885 to 1887, and in 1901 engineer arbitrator in charge of the mooted boundary survey between Costa Rica and Nicaragua.

use of shell, spherical case, or canister, and was most effective at close quarters; the latter, because it was light and easily handled, and its range and accuracy remarkable. At the siege of Petersburg, in the summer of 1864, a battery of 20-pound Parrotts from a Confederate work shelled passing trains behind the Union lines, which excited the ire of some 3-inch rifle batteries. The Confederate work was heavily built and well provided with embrasures for the guns, but these were torn away day by day and replaced at night. The range was finally so accurate that if a Confederate cap on a stick was raised over the edge of the parapet, it would immediately be cut down by a shot. The Confederate 30-pound Parrotts did not prove a success. Two of them mounted on Lee's Hill, at the battle of Fredericksburg, burst, one at the thirty-ninth, the other at the fifty-seventh discharge.

Besides the home-made guns, which were all muzzle-loaders, a number of guns of various make, Whitworth, Armstrong, James, Blakely, and Hotchkiss, were brought in through the blockade. Two Whitworths were sent to the Army of Northern Virginia. They had a great reputation for range and accuracy of fire, but beyond the shelling of distant columns and trains, proved a disappointment. The length and weight of the guns were above the average, making them difficult to transport, and the care and length of time consumed in loading and handling impaired their efficiency for quick work.

Transportation, after all, was one of the most difficult problems with the Confederate artillery. Four horses to a piece, and the same to a caisson, was the utmost allowance, excepting, perhaps, the 20-pounder Parrott gun. In consequence, the cannoneers were required to walk, and General Jackson issued more than one order on the subject. When A. P. Hill's artillery was hurrying from Harper's Ferry to Antietam to General Lee's assistance, the first battery to arrive on the field was worked by less than half the complement of men, officers, commissioned and non-commissioned, lending a hand.

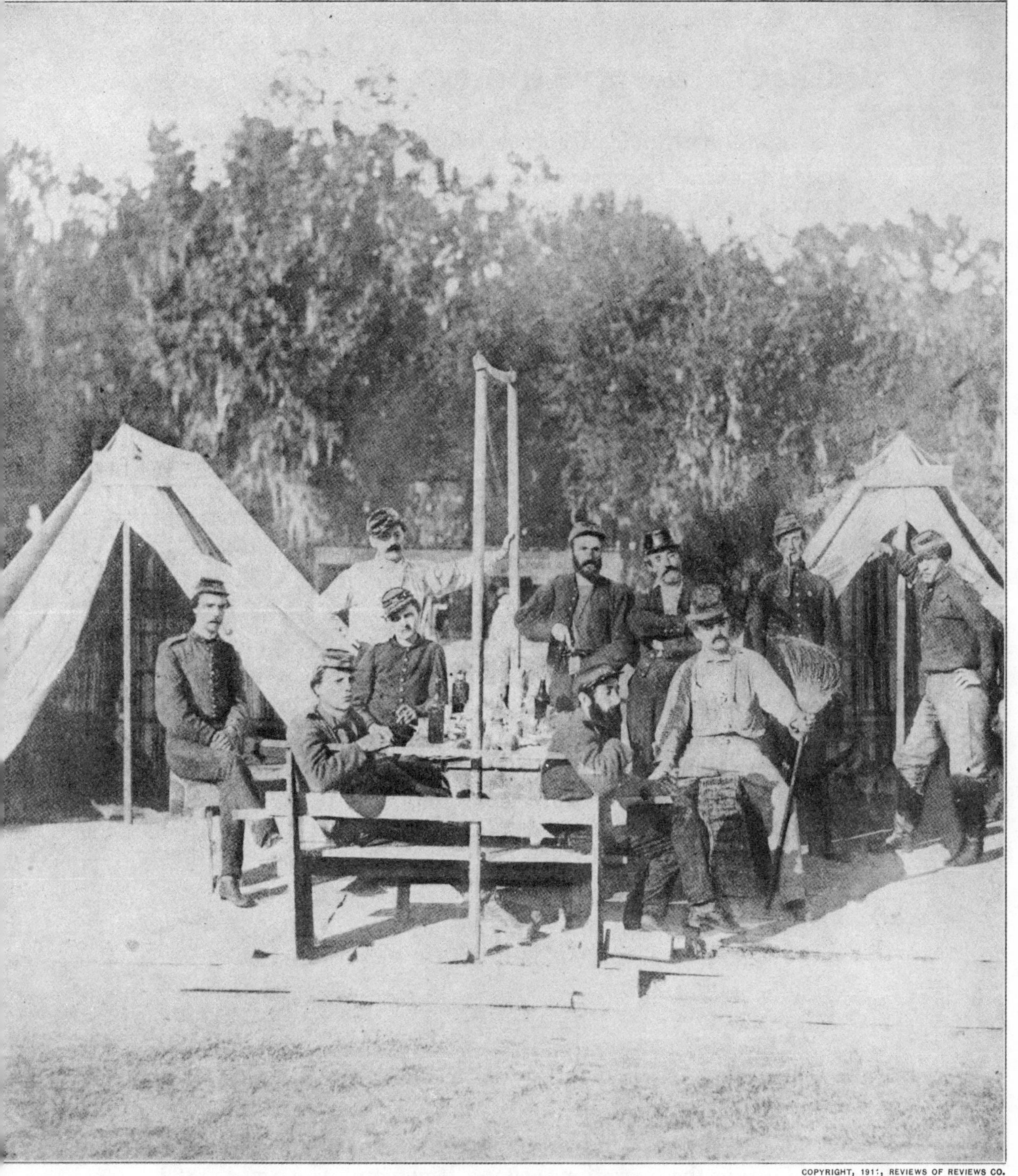

CONFEDERATE ARTILLERISTS

These Confederate artillerists, members of the famous Washington Artillery of New Orleans, had but few field-pieces with which to ace their foes when this photograph was taken, early in '62. Some ordnance stores had been secured when the Confederate Government eized coastwise guns and forts. But a visit to the artillery camps later in the war would have revealed the fact that most of the three-nch rifles, the Napoleons, and the Parrott guns had been originally "Uncle Sam's" property, later captured in battle; and an inspection f the cavalry would have shown, after the first year, that the Southern troopers were armed with United States sabers taken from he same bountiful source. During the first year, before the blockade became stringent, Whitworth guns were brought in from abroad But that supply was soon stopped, and the Southerners had to look largely to their opponents for weapons. The Tredegar Iron Works n Richmond was almost the only factory for cannon, especially for pieces of heavy caliber. It is estimated by ordnance officers hat two-thirds of the artillery in the South was captured from the Federals, especially the 3-inch rifles and the 10-pound Parrotts.

The forces under General Johnston in May, 1861, while at Harper's Ferry were supplied with the 6-pounder gun and 12-pounder howitzer. When Johnston joined Beauregard at Manassas in July, he brought four brigades with four batteries and two in reserve. Beauregard had eight brigades with thirty-four guns, which, under orders of July 20th, he distributed for the action as follows: Six pieces to Ewell, eight to Jones, eight to Longstreet, and twelve to Cocke. The Washington Artillery at this time had four 12-pound howitzers, four 6-pounders, and three rifles, distributed among the different batteries. Twenty-eight pieces captured in the battle added to the supply.

General Henry A. Wise, in West Virginia, reports about the same time having "ten small pieces, six of iron, three of brass, and one piece, private property," with nine officers and one hundred and seventy-seven men.

In April, 1862, the artillery in Johnston's army had grown to thirty-four batteries, McLaws' Division of four brigades having nine batteries, Toombs' Division of three brigades having two battalions, Longstreet's Division of five brigades having five batteries, with Pendleton's Artillery, thirty-six pieces, and the Washington Artillery in reserve.

In July, 1862, the batteries were distributed as follows:

Longstreet's	Division:	6	brigades,	8	batteries
A. P. Hill's	"	6	"	9	"
Jones'	"	2	"	3	"
D. H. Hill's	"	6	"	7	"
Anderson's	"	3	"	6	"
McLaws'	"	4	"	4	"

This gave thirty-seven batteries to twenty-seven brigades, with Pendleton's First Virginia Artillery of ten companies, Cutt's Georgia Artillery of five companies, and three battalions of eleven companies in reserve.

During the operations around Richmond in August, 1862, the artillery of the army was distributed as follows:

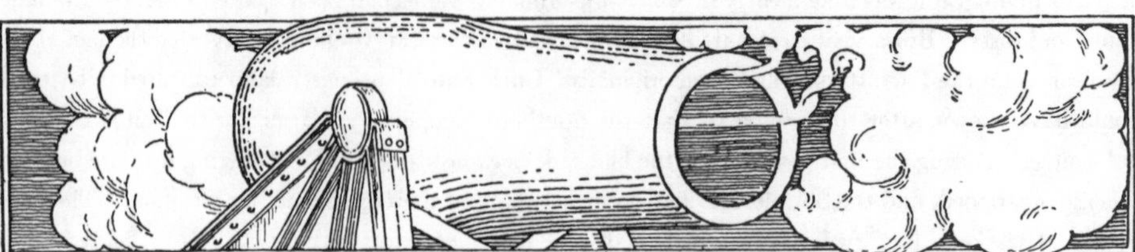

A DISTINGUISHED CONFEDERATE BATTERY FROM TENNESSEE—"RUTLEDGE'S"

his photograph shows the officers of Rutledge's Battery, Company A, First Tennessee Light Artillery. It as taken at Watkin's Park, Nashville, in the latter part of May, 1861, just after the battery was mustered . The cannon for this battery were cast at Brennon's Foundry, at Nashville, and consisted of four 6-ounder smooth-bore guns, and two 12-pounder howitzers. During the first year of the war the battery took art in several engagements and two notable battles—Mill Springs, or Fishing Creek, and Shiloh. The ficers here shown from left to right, starting with the upper row are: Frank Johnson, George W. Trabui, ck B. Long, James C. Wheeler, E. T. Falconet, A. M. Rutledge, Joe E. Harris, George E. Purvis, J. P. umphrey, J. Griffith, and M. S. Cockrill. Three of the officers in this picture—Falconet, Rutledge, and ockrill—were promoted. Captain Rutledge was promoted to be major of artillery and assigned to duty on e staff of General Leonidas Polk. First-Lieutenant Falconet became a captain in the cavalry service, and cond-Lieutenant Cockrill was appointed first-lieutenant and assigned to duty in the ordnance department. ence, and because of heavy losses, the battery was merged, at the expiration of the year for which it had listed, with McClurg's Battery, and its history after that time is the history of that battery.

Jackson's	Corps:	4 divisions,	14 brigades,	17 batteries
Magruder's	"	2 "	6 "	13 "
Longstreet's	"	3 "	15 "	22 "

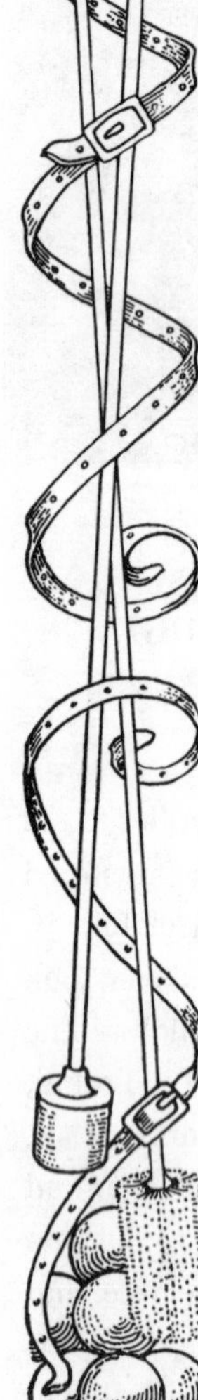

Pendleton with five battalions, twenty batteries, was held in reserve, and five more unattached, making a total of seventy-seven batteries.

In the Seven Days' Battles around Richmond, General Lee must have found his artillery something of an encumbrance. The artillery numbered about three hundred guns, nearly four guns to every thousand men, of which ninety-eight were in the general reserve. It has been said of the artillery during that time by a critic not unfriendly to the cause, that "it left only the faintest trace of its existence." Its use, generally, was fragmentary and detached, and nowhere did it achieve results comparable to the concentrated fire of the Union batteries at Malvern Hill. It was not until Second Manassas, when S. D. Lee brought eighteen guns to bear on the heavy masses attacking Jackson's right and succeeded in breaking them up in a short half-hour, that the value of concentrated artillery fire was learned. At Fredericksburg, fourteen guns were massed on Jackson's right at Hamilton's Crossing, and were used with brilliant results.

General Lee must have been impressed with the fact that his artillery was unwieldy, for in the expedition into Maryland, in the following fall, many batteries were left behind. In the right wing were one hundred and twelve pieces: forty-five rifles, thirteen Napoleons, and fifty-four short-range. In the left wing one hundred and twenty-three pieces: fifty-two rifles, eighteen Napoleons, fifty-three short-range; and in the reserve fifty-two guns.

On October 14, 1862, fourteen of these batteries were disbanded under general orders, and the men and guns distributed to other commands, and four batteries consolidated into two.

In the winter of 1862–63, the practice of assigning batteries to infantry brigades ceased, and the artillery was organ-

A CONFEDERATE ARTILLERY WRECK AT ANTIETAM

A TRAGEDY OF THE TREMENDOUS CANNONADE—WHY LEE DID NOT RENEW THE BATTLE

The battery-horses lie dead beside the shattered caissons and the litter of corn-cobs where, only a few hours before, they had munched at their last meal. The heavy loss to Lee's artillery in horses, caissons, and guns affected his decision not to renew the battle. From researches of Henderson, the British military historian, it appears that on the morning of September 18, 1862, after the roar of Antietam had died away, General Lee sent for Colonel Stephen D. Lee, and told him to report to General Jackson. They rode together to the top of a hill on which lay wrecked caissons, broken wheels, human corpses, and dead horses. Their view overlooked the Federal right. "Can you take fifty pieces of artillery and crush that force?" asked General Jackson. Colonel Lee gazed earnestly at the serried Union lines, bristling with guns unlimbered and ready for action, but could not bring himself to say no. "Yes, General; where will I get the fifty guns?" "How many have you?" asked General Jackson. "About twelve out of the thirty I carried into the action yesterday." "I can furnish you some, and General Lee says he can furnish you some." "Shall I go for the guns?" "No, not yet," replied General Jackson. "Colonel Lee, can you crush the Federal right with fifty guns?" Although Colonel Lee evaded the question again and again, General Jackson pressed it home. Reluctantly the brave artillery officer admitted: "General, it cannot be done with fifty guns and the troops you have near here." "Let us ride back, Colonel." Colonel Lee reported the conversation to General Lee, and during the night the Army of Northern Virginia, with all its trains and artillery, recrossed the Potomac at Boteler's Ford.

ized into a number of battalions, usually of four batteries, with one or two field-officers with the rank of major or lieutenant-colonel to each. These battalions were supplied with an ordnance officer and a quartermaster. An adjutant was usually detailed from one of the batteries. The battalion commanders reported to the chiefs of artillery of the army corps, and on the march or in battle acted with, and received orders from, the general of the division with which they happened to be.

In the Chancellorsville campaign, Longstreet with two divisions was absent. With the remaining divisions of that corps, there were two battalions of artillery and ten batteries in reserve. With the Second Corps there were four battalions and ten batteries in reserve, with a further general reserve of six batteries, making a total of fifty-one batteries.

On June 4th, prior to the Gettysburg campaign, the army having been divided into three corps, an officer of the rank of colonel was assigned to the command of the artillery of each corps, the battalion organization continuing as before.

Of these, five battalions, with twenty-two batteries, were assigned to the First Corps; five battalions, with twenty batteries, were assigned to the Second Corps; five battalions, with twenty batteries, were assigned to the Third Corps.

The equipment was as follows:

31 rifles,	42 Napoleons,	10 howitzers	=	83 in the 1st Corps
38 "	32 "	12 "	=	82 in the 2d Corps
41 "	26 "	15 "	=	82 in the 3d Corps
	Total			247

The particular equipment in the battalions of the Third Corps was as follows:

Cutts:	10 rifles,	3 Napoleons,	4 howitzers	=	17
Garnett:	11 "	4 "	2 "	=	17
McIntosh:	10 "	6 "		=	16
Pegram:	8 "	9 "	2 "	=	19
Cutshaw:	2 "	5 "	7 "	=	14

AFTER THE BATTLE OF CHATTANOOGA—CAPTURED CONFEDERATE GUNS

The Confederate artillery was never equal in number or weight to that of the Union armies. In the West these ancient 12-pounder howitzers were mounted on rough wooden carriages, those above, for instance. These guns are aligned in front of General Thomas' headquarters. They were taken late in November, 1863, at the battle of Chattanooga, and the photograph was made early in 1864. Behind the guns can be seen the pole to one of the caissons. When the Confederate armies captured a gun they almost invariably whirled it around, detailed artillerymen to man it, and set it promptly to work, but by this time the Union armies were so well equipped that captured guns might be parked. Many pieces had changed hands several times, and had barked defiance at both armies. The equipment of the Confederate batteries was seldom uniform. Among four guns there might be found three different calibers, requiring different ammunition. The batteries' efficiency was still further impaired during the fight by the inability of the chief of artillery to select positions for his guns, which were often placed so far apart that he was unable to assemble them for concentrated fire. This was due to the custom of apportioning the field-artillery to infantry divisions, and placing them under orders of the brigadier-general, who could not give them proper attention. The plan was not changed until the early part of 1863. In the face of all these difficulties the Confederate artillery made a glorious record.

There were in Richmond, at this time, three battalions of light artillery and five batteries unattached, besides two divisions with two battalions each of heavy artillery.

The battalion organization continued to the close of the war, the exigencies of the service producing minor changes, and shifting of commands at various times. As many as six or eight batteries were sometimes assigned to a battalion commander.

At the battle of Cold Harbor, the opposite lines at one point approached quite near, and it was discovered that the Union troops were laying a mine, the approach to which was along an open trench. The battalion commander took advantage of a ravine in his rear, and sinking the trail of a smoothbore gun so that it could be used as a mortar, threw shells with a slight charge of powder and time-fuses aimed to fall and explode in the trench. When the Union forces withdrew and the ground was examined, a number of shells were found in the trench unexploded, showing accuracy of fire, but failure of the fuse.

The organization as described was adopted generally in the Southern and Western armies. In the Department of North Carolina, General Holmes had, in 1861, three brigades to which six batteries were assigned. In the Army of Kentucky, six batteries were assigned to six brigades, with two in reserve.

In 1862, in Bragg's Army of the Mississippi, Polk's Corps contained one division of four brigades, and a battery assigned to each brigade. In Hardee's Corps the batteries were assigned to brigades or divisions, indiscriminately. In Van Dorn's Army of West Tennessee, a battery was assigned to each brigade of infantry. In Kirby Smith's Army of Tennessee, there were two divisions, four brigades to each, and a battery attached to each brigade.

CAPTAIN JOHN DONNELL SMITH

This photograph well reflects the bearing of a representative artillery officer in the Army of Northern Virginia. At the time—May, 1863—he was in Richmond, following the battle of Chancellorsville. He was then First-Lieutenant of Jordan's Battery, Alexander's Battalion of Artillery, First Corps, Army of Northern Virginia. Battery A of Huger's (formerly Alexander's) battalion of Artillery, Longstreet's Corps, Army of Northern Virginia, of which John Donnell Smith later became captain, was then in camp near Bowling Green, Caroline County, Virginia. Captain Smith helped to serve the guns at Gettysburg. On June 4, 1863, prior to the Gettysburg campaign, the army having been divided into three corps, five battalions with twenty-two batteries were assigned to the first, five battalions with twenty batteries were assigned to the second, and five battalions with twenty batteries to the third. The total number of Confederate guns at Gettysburg, including rifles, Napoleons, and howitzers was two hundred and forty-eight. These opposed 320 Union guns, all in action.

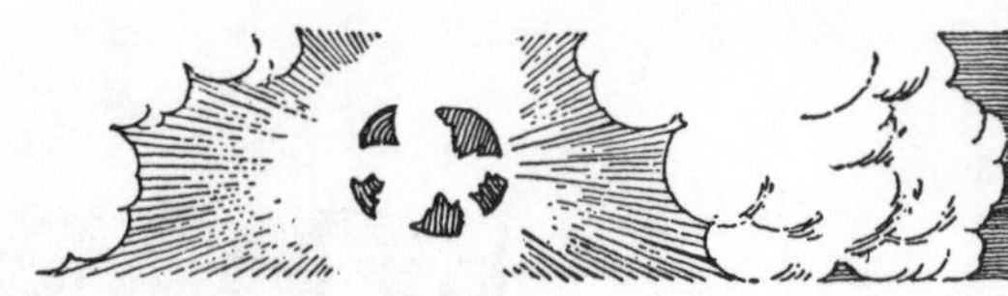
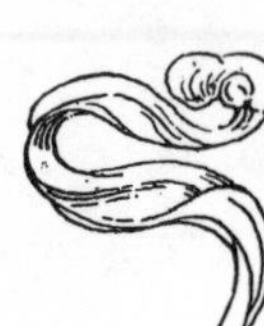

MEMORIES OF GETTYSBURG

By F. M. Colston *

ALEXANDER'S battalion of artillery, which I joined in the spring of 1863, had gained renown under Colonel, afterward Lieutenant-General, Stephen D. Lee, especially at Second Manassas and Sharpsburg. This renown was increased under the command of Colonel E. Porter Alexander, afterward brigadier-general and chief of artillery of Longstreet's corps. He had graduated No. 3 at West Point, in 1857, and entered the Engineer Corps of the United States Army. He was more consulted by General Lee than any other artillery officer in the Confederate service. In later life he became president of several railroads, Government director of the Union Pacific Railroad, and engineer arbitrator of the boundary survey between Costa Rica and Nicaragua.

The battalion was composed of six batteries—two more than customary—four Virginia, one South Carolina and one Louisiana. Together with the more noted Washington Artillery of New Orleans, with four batteries, it composed the reserve artillery of Longstreet's corps, Army of Northern Virginia. They were called the "reserve" because they were not specially attached to any division, but kept for use whenever and wherever wanted. Hence the battalion explanation that "we were called 'reserve' because never in reserve."

After taking part in the battle of Chancellorsville, our battalion was moved down to Milford, Caroline County, to refit. On June 3d commenced the forward march that ended at Gettysburg. When we went into action there, July 2d, just south of the peach orchard, the batteries actually charged, action front, with a front of over four hundred yards—the finest sight imaginable on a battlefield. One of the batteries, which was short-handed, had borrowed five men from the adjacent Mississippi regiment. In the fight two were killed and

* Lieutenant and Ordnance Officer in Alexander's Battalion of Artillery, Longstreet's corps.

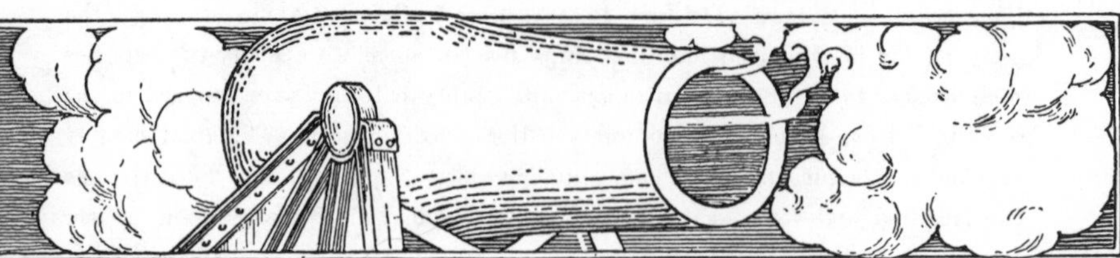

LIEUTENANT-COLONEL FRANK HUGER

CONFEDERATE ARTILLERY OFFICERS

After General Alexander became acting chief of artillery, Huger succeeded to the command of his battalion. The fine faces of these officers recall the trying times through which they passed. For the last two years especially, the Confederate field-artillery fought against the odds of lack of horses. Behind them stood no such supply depot as Giesboro outside of Washington, which furnished the Federal armies thousands of fresh horses, and cared for sick ones. A Confederate artillery piece seldom boasted more than four horses after 1862. When some of these were killed, the gun was handled by the horse or horses left and the men of the battery. However, Huger's battalion went through the campaigns of Chancellorsville, Gettysburg, East Tennessee, the Wilderness, Spotsylvania Court House—fought with the Army of Northern Virginia through the siege of Petersburg—and "never had to run." The men boasted they occupied their ground after every fight, and buried their own dead.

PROBLEMS OF LEE'S ARTILLERY

W. T. Poague was captain of the Rockbridge Artillery in the Stonewall brigade before he became lieutenant-colonel of artillery, Third Corps. This was in the Army of Northern Virginia. The efficiency of its artillery was crippled until the winter of 1862–63 by the system of attaching the batteries to various brigades and divisions, and not handling it as a separate corps so that its batteries could be massed. The chief of artillery was not even allowed to choose the positions for his guns. But during that winter the artillery was organized into a number of battalions, and the battalion commanders reported to the chiefs of artillery of the army corps, and on the march or in battle acted with and received orders from the general of the division with which they happened to be. After the batteries could be massed they were much more effective as they abundantly proved on the battlefield of Gettysburg and in the later Virginia campaigns.

LIEUTENANT-COLONEL W. T. POAGUE

one wounded, so that we could return only two—which the regiment seemed to think a small return of borrowed property! We then took a position in front of the Emmittsburg road and a little north of the peach orchard. We lay all night there, opposite the center of the Federal line, the cemetery being a little to our left front, and the Round Tops on our right.

At one o'clock the next day the great artillery duel, the heaviest in the history of war to that time and probably not exceeded since, was opened by the previously arranged signal-gun of the Washington Artillery. It was promptly answered by the Federals—and the din of war was on.

The roar of our guns was terrific. The explosion of the Federal shells, with a different sound, added to the tumult. In the midst of it our officers and men engaged were busy with their work, pausing only to give a cheer at the sight of an exploding caisson of the Federals. The work went on mechanically. Few orders were given and those had to be shouted. As soon as Pickett's division passed through our guns on their way to the charge a respite was gained, the dead were removed, the wounded cared for, and the survivors breathed more freely.

The question is often asked, "How does a man feel in such an action?" Comparatively few men are physical and moral cowards. Even when the courage is wanting, the example and opinion of comrades often acts in place of it. Brave men cheerfully acknowledge their appreciation of the danger. The most trying time is "waiting to go in." The silence before the coming battle is oppressive. Many mental and physical exhibitions will be noticed, and if the battle is on, the sight of the wounded men streaming back is disheartening.

But when once engaged, the sense of duty and the absorption of occupation will greatly overcome every other sensation. Every man has his duty to do, and if he does it he will have little time to think of anything else. No place can be considered safe. In this action, a man was standing behind a tree near our battalion, safe from direct fire. But a passing shell exploded just as it passed; the fragments struck him and tossed his dead body out. The sight reassured those who were in the open.

I

DEFENDING THE NATIONAL CAPITAL

BLOCKHOUSE AT THE CHAIN BRIDGE, ABOVE GEORGETOWN

THIS APPROACH WAS DEFENDED BY FORTS ETHAN ALLEN AND MARCY ON THE VIRGINIA SIDE, AND BY BATTERIES MARTIN SCOTT, VERMONT, AND KEMBLE ON THE MARYLAND SIDE OF THE POTOMAC

IN A WASHINGTON FORT

Erect on the parapet is the tall, soldierly figure of Colonel Michael Corcoran of the Sixty-ninth New York, who was subsequently captured and chosen by lot to meet the same fate as Walter W. Smith, prizemaster of the Southern schooner *Enchantress*, taken prisoner, July 22, 1861, and tried for piracy. Neither was executed. The men pictured in their shirt-sleeves, and the heavy shadows cast by the glaring sun, indicate that the time is summer. The soldier with the empty sleeve has evidently suffered a minor injury, and is carrying his arm inside his coat. Several of the officers peer over the parapet, watching for the approach of danger. The first forts located in the defenses south of the Potomac were Fort Runyon, at the land end of the approach of Long Bridge, and Fort Corcoran, covering the approach to the aqueduct. On the night of May 23, 1861, three columns of Federal soldiers crossed the Potomac, one by the aqueduct, one by Long Bridge, and one by water to Alexandria. The smooth-bore guns in the armament of Fort Corcoran were two 8-inch howitzers *en barbette*. The rifled guns consisted of three 3-inch Parrotts *en embrasure*. The term "*en barbette*" refers to the placing of a gun so that the muzzle projected over a wall. "*En embrasure*" indicates a cannon in an opening in the fortification with no protection in front of it. The gun around which the officers above are grouped is an 8-inch sea-coast howitzer. These guns were of iron, and were used principally to flank the ditches of permanent works. They fired especially grape-shot for this purpose. The howitzer is a cannon employed to throw large projectiles with comparatively small charges of powder. It is shorter and lighter than most guns of the same caliber. The chief advantage was in the fact that it could produce at short ranges a greater effect, due to its ability to throw hollow projectiles with bursting charges and case shot. The weight of this gun was about 3,000 pounds, and the usual charge was about four pounds of powder. It is mounted on a wooden carriage. Before it lies a pile of grape-shot.

COLONEL MICHAEL CORCORAN

AND HIS OFFICERS OF THE 69TH NEW YORK, IN FORT CORCORAN, 1861

The First Connecticut Heavy Artillery was organized from the Fourth Connecticut Infantry in January, 1862, and remained on duty in Fort Richardson till April. The regiment acquired a high reputation by serving continuously throughout the four years of warfare actively in the field as heavy artillery. Very few of the other "heavy" regiments in the army saw any service aside from garrison duty, except while acting as infantry. The First Connecticut Heavy Artillery served in the two big sieges of the Army of the Potomac, Yorktown, April and May, 1862, and Petersburg, June, 1864 to April, 1865. Fort Richardson lay on the Virginia line of the Washington defenses about halfway between Fort Corcoran and Fort Ellsworth, in front of Alexandria. Its smooth-bore armament consisted of three 24-pounders on siege carriages *en barbette*, two 24-pounders on barbette carriages *en embrasure*, one 24-pounder field howitzer *en embrasure* and one 24-pounder field howitzer *en barbette*. Its four rifled guns consisted of one 100-pounder Parrott *en barbette*, two 30-pounder Parrott *en embrasure* and one 30-pounder Parrott *en barbette*. It also contained two mortars, one 10-inch siege mortar and one 24-pounder Coehorn.

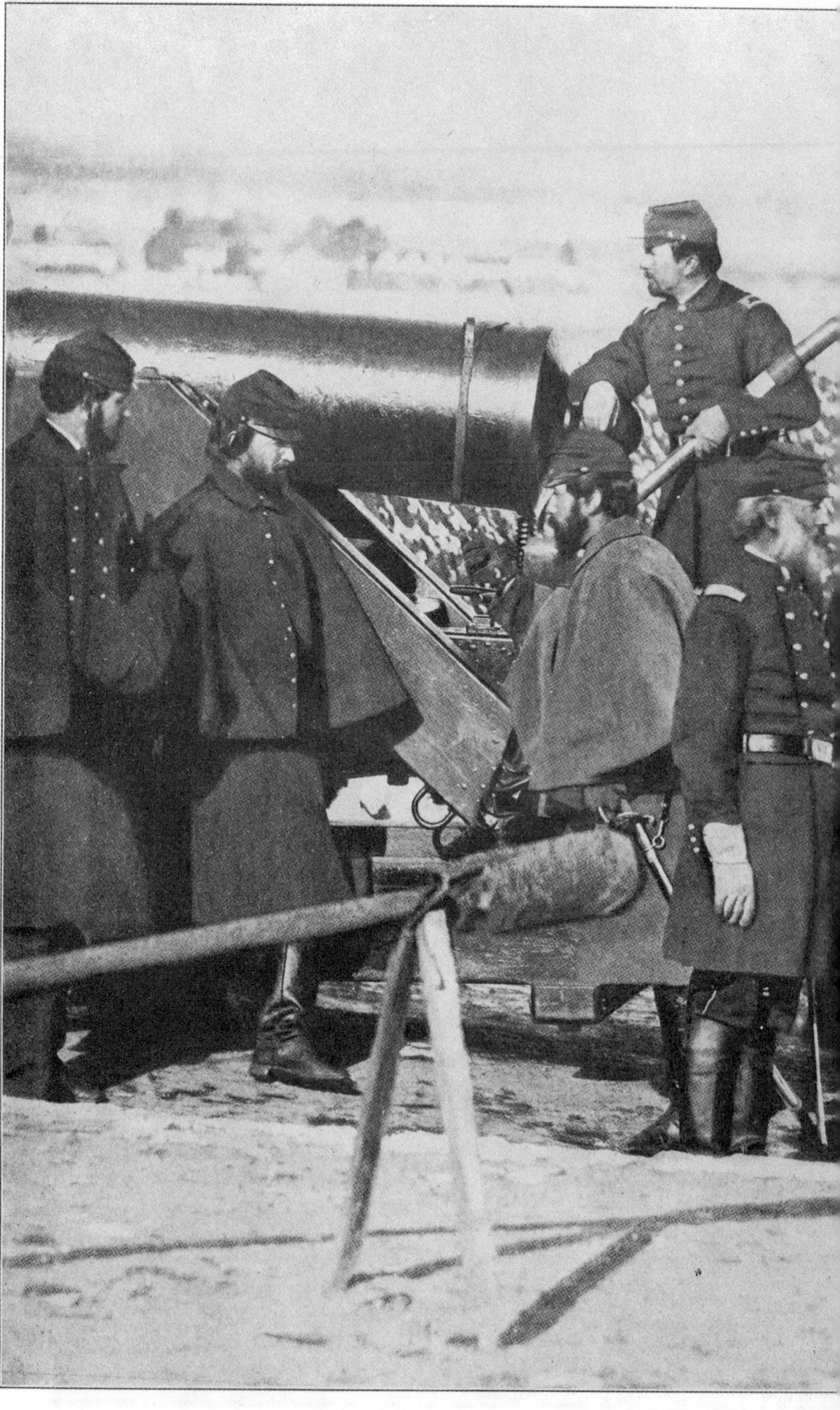

OFFICERS OF THE FIRST CONNECTICUT HEAVY ARTILLERY IN FORT RICHARDSON

A WINTER SCENE IN THE DEFENSES OF WASHINGTON

DEFENDING THE NATIONAL CAPITAL

By O. E. Hunt
Captain, United States Army

THE following conversation took place early in 1861 between General Winfield Scott and Colonel Charles P. Stone, inspector-general of the District of Columbia:

General Scott: "Gosport navy-yard has been burned."

Colonel Stone: "Yes, General."

General Scott: "Harper's Ferry bridge has been burned."

"Yes, General."

General Scott: "The bridge at Point of Rocks was burned some days since."

"Yes, General."

General Scott: "The bridges over Gunpowder Creek, beyond Baltimore, have been burned."

"Yes, General."

General Scott: "They are closing their coils around us, sir."

"Yes, General."

General Scott: "Now, how long can we hold out here?"

"Ten days, General, and within that time the North will come down to us."

General Scott: "How will they come? The route through Baltimore is cut off."

"They will come by all routes. They will come between the capes of Virginia, up through Chesapeake Bay, and by the Potomac. They will come, if necessary, from Pennsylvania, through Maryland, directly to us, and they will come through Baltimore and Annapolis."

INSIDE
FORT TOTTEN—THREE
SHIFTING SCENES IN A BIG-GUN DRILL

Constant drill at the guns went on in the defenses of Washington throughout the war. At its close in April, 1865, there were 68 enclosed forts and batteries, whose aggregate perimeter was thirteen miles, 807 guns and 98 mortars mounted, and emplacements for 1,120 guns, ninety-three unarmed batteries for field-guns, 35,711 yards of rifle-trenches, and three blockhouses encircling the Northern capital. The entire extent of front of the lines was thirty-seven miles; and thirty-two miles of military roads, besides those previously existing in the District of Columbia, formed the means of interior communication. In all these forts constant preparation was made for a possible onslaught of the Confederates, and many of the troops were trained which later went to take part in the siege of Petersburg where the heavy artillery fought bravely as infantry

Later, General Scott asked, "Where are your centers?" and received the reply: "There are three, General. First, the Capitol, where have been stored some two thousand barrels of flour, and where Major McDowell remains every night with from two to three hundred of my volunteers. Second, the City Hall hill, a commanding point, with broad avenues and wide streets connecting it with most important points, having in its vicinity the Patent Office and the General Post Office, in each of which I place a force every night. In the General Post Office we have stored a large quantity of flour. Third, the Executive Square, including the President's house, the War, Navy, State, and Treasury departments, in each of which, and in Winder's building, I place a force every night after dusk.

"The citadel of this center is the Treasury building. The basement has been barricaded very strongly by Captain Franklin of the Engineers, who remains there at night and takes charge of the force. The front of the Treasury building is well flanked by the State Department building, and fifty riflemen are nightly on duty there. The building opposite is also occupied at night. The outposts at Benning's Bridge and the pickets in that direction will, in case of attack in force, retire, fighting, to the Capitol. Those on the northeast and north will, if pressed, retire by Seventh Street to City Hall hill, while those on the northwest and west will, in case of attack, fall back and finally take refuge in the Treasury building, where they will be joined by the detachments guarding the river front when the attack shall have become so marked and serious that only the centers can be held. In the Treasury building are stored two thousand barrels of flour, and perhaps the best water in the city is to be found there. The city is so admirably laid out in broad avenues and wide streets centering on the three points chosen, that concentration for defense on any one of the three is made easy.

"The field-battery can move rapidly toward any outpost where heavy firing shall indicate that the attack there is serious,

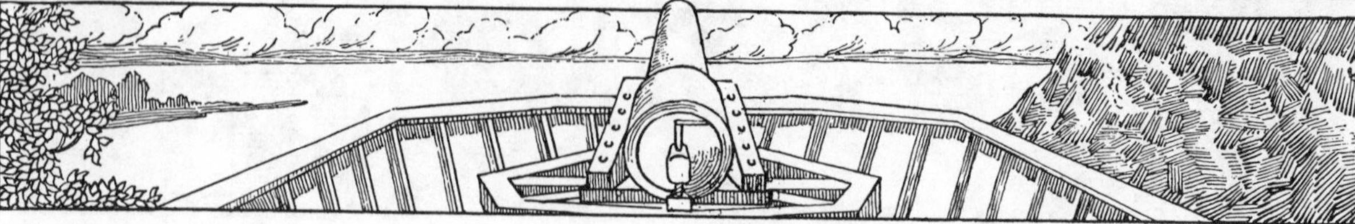

THE SEVENTEENTH NEW YORK ARTILLERY DRILLING BEFORE THE CAPITAL

In the background rises the dome of the Capitol which this regiment remained to defend until it was ordered to Petersburg, in 1864. It appears in parade formation. The battery commander leads it, mounted. The battery consists of six pieces, divided into three platoons of two guns each. In front of each platoon is the platoon commander, mounted. Each piece, with its limber and caisson, forms a section; the chief of section is mounted, to the right and a little to the rear of each piece. The cannoneers are mounted on the limbers and caissons in the rear. To the left waves the notched guidon used by both the cavalry and light artillery.

A LIGHT BATTERY AT FORT WHIPPLE, DEFENSES OF WASHINGTON

This photograph shows the flat nature of the open country about Washington. There were no natural fortifications around the city. Artificial works were necessary throughout. Fort Whipple lay to the south of Fort Corcoran, one of the three earliest forts constructed. It was built later, during one of the recurrent panics at the rumor that the Confederates were about to descend upon Washington. This battery of six guns, the one on the right hand, pointing directly out of the picture, looks quite formidable. One can imagine the burst of fire from the underbrush which surrounds it, should it open upon the foe. At present it is simply drilling.

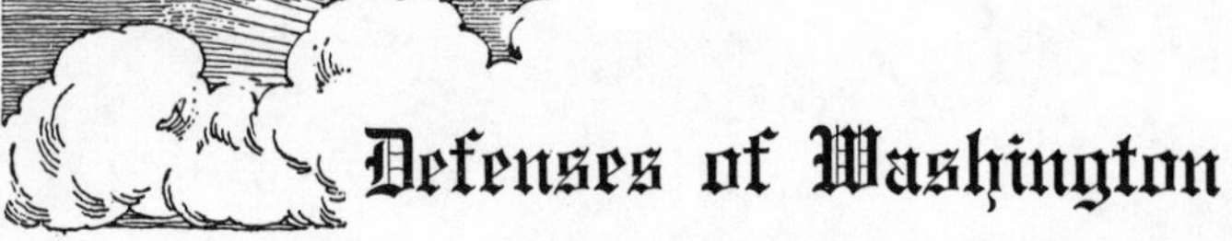

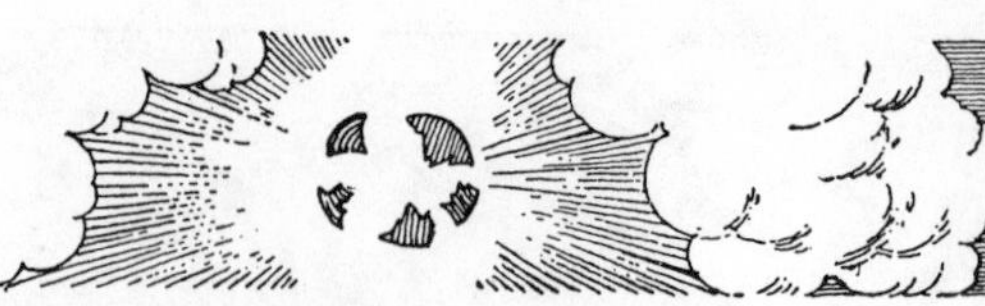

and with the aid of this battery the retreat from that point can be made slowly enough to give time for concentration on that line of the outlying companies in positions not threatened. In case a sharp resistance outside the city may fail to prevent the advance of the enemy, we can occupy the centers until the North shall have had time to come to our relief. All our information tends to show that the force of the enemy which can immediately act against the capital does not exceed five thousand organized men, and before that number can be largely increased our relief will come. These District of Columbia volunteers would be fighting in defense of their homes and would fight well."

After considering the plan outlined General Scott thus replied to Colonel Stone:

"Your plan is good. Your pickets will have to fight well, and must not try to fall back more than fifteen paces at a time and to fire at least once at each halt. This requires good men and good, devoted officers. These soldiers of the District will probably fight as well in defense of their homes as the enemy in attacking them. But you have too many centers. You cannot hold three. You will need all your force concentrated to hold one position against an energetic force equal, or superior in numbers, to all you have. The first center to be abandoned must be the Capitol. It is a fire-proof building. There is little in it that is combustible excepting the libraries of Congress and the Supreme Court, and I do not believe that any Americans will burn public libraries and archives of courts of justice. The second center to be abandoned will be the City Hall hill. Finally, if necessary, all else must be abandoned to occupy, strongly and effectively, the Executive Square, with the idea of firmly holding only the Treasury building, and, perhaps, the State Department building, properly connected. The seals of the several departments of the Government must be deposited in the vaults of the Treasury. They must not be captured and used to deceive

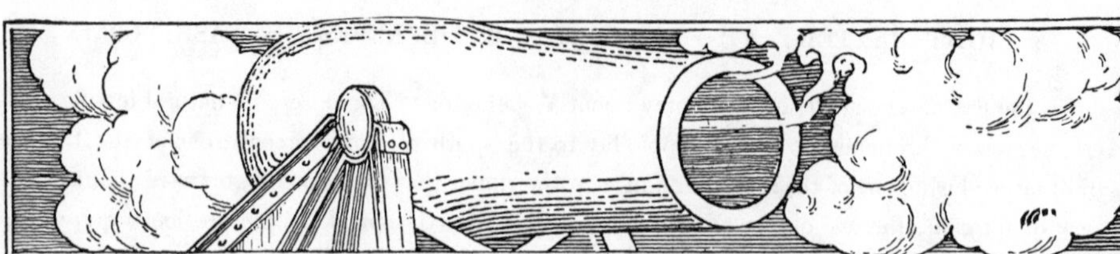

A TRIP AROUND THE DEFENSES OF WASHINGTON—FORT LYON

This photograph is the first of a series illustrating the thirty-seven miles of forts and batteries which surrounded Washington. After Fort Lyon, in this series, one of the farthest forts to the southwest, comes Battery Rodgers, south of Alexandria; then the entrance to Long Bridge; Forts Corcoran and Woodbury, defending the Aqueduct Bridge; Fort Marcy, the farthest north across the Potomac from Washington; Fort Sumner, the farthest north on the other side of the Potomac; Fort Stevens, farther east; Fort Totten, east of Fort Stevens; Fort Lincoln, still farther south; and finally Fort C. F. Smith, to show the type of construction of the later forts. Thus the reader completely encircles Washington, and beholds varied types of sixty-eight forts and batteries. These mounted 807 guns and ninety-eight mortars, with emplacements for 1,120 guns more. There were also 35,711 yards of rifle-trenches and three blockhouses. Fort Lyon, above pictured, lay across Hunting Creek from Alexandria. The Parrott guns were rifled cannon of cast-iron, strengthened at the breech by shrinking a band of wrought-iron over the section which contained the powder charge. The body of the larger Parrott guns was cast hollow and cooled by the Rodman process—a stream of water or air flowing through the interior. About 1,700 of these guns were purchased by the Federal Ordnance Department during the war and used in the defense of Washington and in the great sieges.

and create uncertainty among public servants distant from the capital."

Then he added: " Should it come to the defense of the Treasury building as a citadel, then the President and all the members of his cabinet must take up their quarters with us in that building. They must not be permitted to desert the capital!"

This conversation, quoted from a Washington historian of the war-time period (Doctor Marcus Benjamin), shows, in brief, the inadequate preparations for the defense of the capital of one of the greatest nations on the face of the globe! On April 19, 1861, troops began to arrive from the North, and the extreme apprehension was for a time quieted, until the battle of Bull Run, on July 21st, threw the country, and especially the population of Washington, into a state of the most intense excitement.

Except for certain river defenses, twelve miles below the city, Washington was entirely undefended at the outbreak of the war. From a hasty glance at the topography, we find that there are no natural fortifications around the city, and that artificial works were necessary throughout. The problem of defense was made greater, also, by the fact that the city was spread out over so much ground. At the time of the Civil War the effective range of the heaviest artillery was between three and four miles, and the engineers recognized the great difficulty of erecting adequate defenses. We find also that public opinion fluctuated and affected the action of Congress in regard to these defenses, to the frequent consternation of the officers charged with their maintenance.

Obviously the first direction from which danger was apprehended was that of the Virginia side. The heights commanding the river were a constant menace to Washington until they could be occupied in force by the Federals. Since no attempts theretofore had been made to fortify the city, it does not appear that sufficient information upon which even

BATTERY RODGERS

ITS 15-INCH GUN

Battery Rodgers, about half a mile from the southern outskirts of Alexandria, overlooked the Potomac and the mouth of Hunting Creek. Its site was a bluff rising about twenty-eight feet above high water. It was armed with five 200-pounder Parrott guns and a 15-inch Rodman smooth-bore, emplaced in pairs. The parapet was twenty-five feet thick. The 15-inch Rodman gun visible above the bomb-proofs, can be studied below closer at hand. This monster of its time became possible through the discoveries made by Captain Rodman, of the United States Ordnance Department. It is mounted on a center-pintle carriage—that is, the tracks carrying the carriage are completely circular, and the pivot on which it revolves is under the center of the carriage. The timber revetment of the interior slope of the parapet affords greater protection to the garrison; the men can stand close to the wall, and are less apt to be struck by high-angle fire. In the foreground are the entrances to the bomb-proofs, guarded by two sentries who accommodatingly faced the camera.

ALL QUIET ALONG THE POTOMAC, MAY 18, 1864

AN INTIMATE VIEW OF THE GREAT RODMAN GUN SHOWN ON THE PAGE PRECEDING

The 15-inch Rodman gun in Battery Rodgers, near Alexandria, with a gun-detachment around it. The scene was quiet the day this photograph was taken. The gunners little thought that within a few weeks the city would be in a turmoil of excitement from Early's attack on the northern defenses of Washington. This battery was erected to guard the south side of Washington from an attack by the Confederate fleet. The distance to mid-channel was 600 yards, and no vessel of a draft of twenty feet could pass at a greater distance than half a mile. The battery also enfiladed the channel for the full range of its guns. The main face of the work was 135 feet long, and it had flanks of sixty and eighty feet. The wharf at Alexandria is visible to the left, with a steamer loading supplies and a lighter close by. The size of the gun can be judged from the little photograph, on the opposite page, of a soldier who has crawled, feet first, into the muzzle.

a tentative line of works could be planned was at hand, and engineer officers examined the ground as well as they could at the termination of Long Bridge, on the Virginia shore, and also at the Virginia side of the aqueduct. Confederate pickets were observed from the first outbreak of hostilities, and while these parties were apparently unarmed, the officers making reconnaissances to determine the location of works, had necessarily to be prudent in their movements, and accurate observations were impossible.

The first forts located were Fort Runyon, at the land end of the approach to Long Bridge, about a half a mile from the Virginia end of the bridge proper, and Fort Corcoran, covering the approach to the aqueduct. These footholds were secured by a crossing in force on the night of the 23d of May, 1861, of three columns, one by the aqueduct, one by Long Bridge, and one by water to Alexandria. The nearness of Alexandria, and the fact that it commanded the river, made its occupation a matter of prime importance from the outset. Fort Ellsworth, on Shuter's Hill, one half-mile west of the town, was located and fortified by the column crossing by water. During the eight weeks following the crossing, and up to the time of General McDowell's advance on Manassas, officers and troops were hard at work on the entrenchments, thus established at three points, to the total neglect of the protection of the city on the eastern and northern sides. These first three works constructed were larger than most of those which followed—the perimeter of Fort Runyon, indeed, exceeding that of any subsequent work.

Of course, these three points were intended to be only footholds for further development of the works, and were, themselves, badly located for isolated defense. Fort Runyon was overlooked by the heights of Arlington, as was Fort Corcoran, though the latter was better situated than the former. Fort Ellsworth was but a weak field-fortification.

The main efforts of the officers were to strengthen the

COPYRIGHT 1911, REVIEW OF REVIEWS CO.

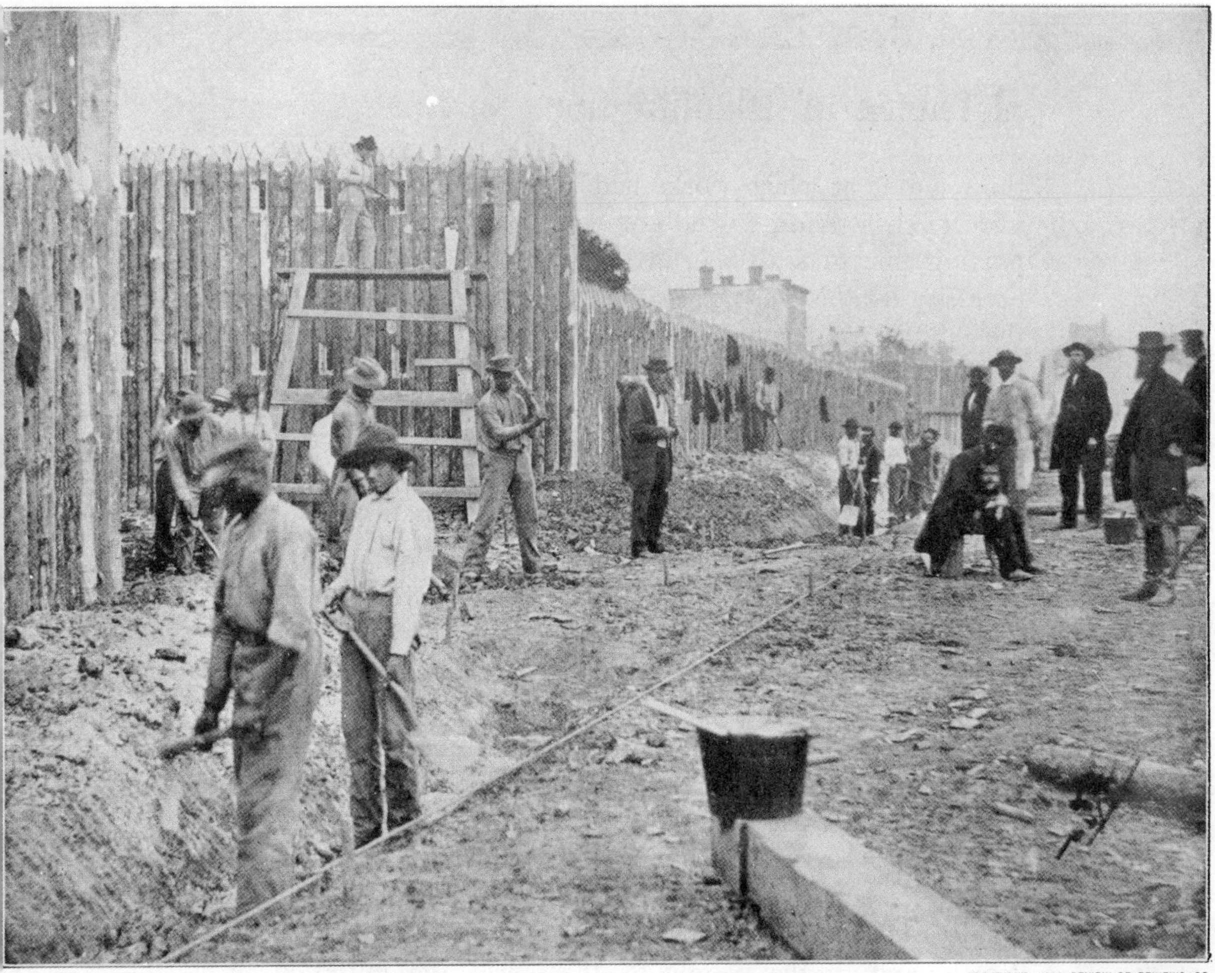

COMPLETING THE BARRICADE AT ALEXANDRIA

When Brigadier-General Herman Haupt was put in charge of all the railroads centering in Washington in 1861 his first care was to safeguard them as far as possible from the destructive Confederate raiders. He built a stockade around the machine shops and yard of the Orange & Alexandria Railroad, with blockhouses at the points most vulnerable to raiders. The citizens of Alexandria, terrified by their exposed position across the Potomac close to the battlefield of Bull Run, entrenched themselves as best they could, before the great forts about them were completed. The lower view is looking up Duke Street from Pioneer Mill. The heavy stockade, inside the city, suggests how acute were the apprehensions of its inhabitants. The barrier is solid enough to stop a cavalry charge, with the big gates closed. A couple of field pieces, however, could batter it down in short order. Later in the war, such stockades as this would have been built with twenty-five feet of earth banked up in front of them. After the hurried preparations shown in the photograph, the tide of war rolled away into southern Virginia. The stockade for a while remained as a memento of a passing fear.

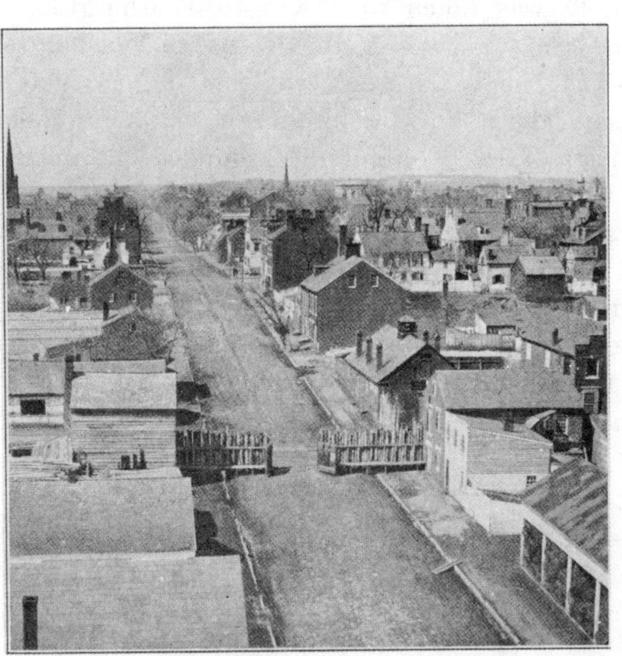

A STOCKADE IN THE STREET

three points at which works had been begun, and no attempts were made looking to the erection of a continuous or a supporting line to stop the advance of the Confederates. The necessity for this was not realized. But the first disaster awoke the military and civil authorities of Washington to the grim fact that the war was not a thing of probably a few weeks' duration, and in the face of a victorious foe there was the great menace of the capture of the Nation's capital with all the dire consequences. It was not the extent of the fortifications that impeded the Confederate army after Manassas, but the fact that there *were* fortifications, and that the Confederates were as badly defeated as the Federals. General Johnston says:

"We were almost as much disorganized by our victory as the Federals by their defeat," and it was conceded by everybody that disorganization and the moral deterrent effect of "fortifications" were mainly responsible for the Confederates not pressing their victory to the logical conclusion of occupying the capital.

The stream of fugitives crowding across Long Bridge and Aqueduct Bridge after the disaster of Bull Run, July 21st, announced to the people of Washington, to the people of the North, and to the people of the world the initiation of a mighty struggle. The echo rang southward, where the cry immediately was taken up, "On to Washington." In the North the echo was, "On to the defense of Washington." Despair in the North was replaced by a dogged determination to prosecute the war to the bitter end, and a few weeks' delay on the part of the Confederates sounded the doom of their chances to take the capital, for every energy of the North was bent, first, to organizing for its defense, and, second, to taking the field in an offensive movement against the Confederates.

General Scott, who had fought in two wars against foreign foes, was bowed down with age, and the tremendous energy necessary to cope with so appalling a situation had left him; so he asked to be relieved by a younger man. All

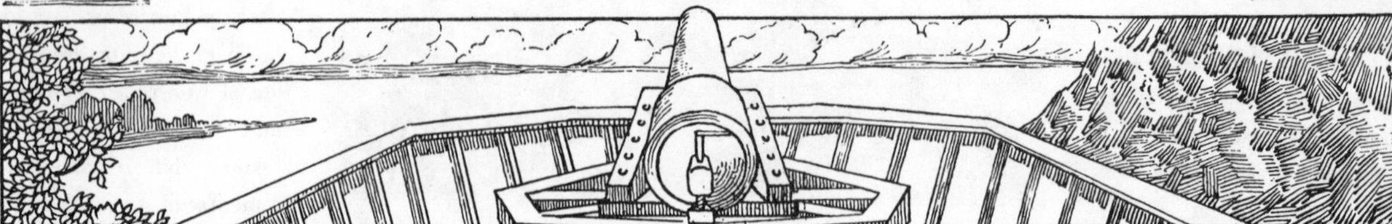

DEFENDERS OF LONG BRIDGE—A BATTERY DRILL

The little boy on the corner is not looking at the cannoneers. Real soldiers and 12-pounder Napoleon field-guns are no novelty to him by now. He is staring at something really new in the summer of '64—the camera. He finds the curious looking box vastly more interesting. The soldiers stationed at the Virginia end of Long Bridge were "caught" by the pioneer photographer at drill. They are in correct position ready for action. The duty of the soldiers with the long swabs on the right of the guns near the muzzle is to sponge them out, and to ram home the new charge. The men on the left near the muzzle place the charge in the gun. The men on the right, back of the wheel, cover the vents until the charge is rammed home. The men on the left, back of the wheel, have duties more complex. They prick the cartridge, insert a friction primer attached to a lanyard, step back, and at the order: "Fire!" explode the primer. Still further to the left of the guns stand the sergeants who are chiefs of pieces. The men behind the limbers cut the fuses for the length of time required and insert them in the shell. It is the duty of the men at their left to carry the charge from the limber and deliver it to the loaders who place it in the gun. Finally, the corporals directly behind the cannon are the gunners who sight the pieces. The remainder are to help prepare and bring up the ammunition from the limber, and to take the places of any disabled. All this is familiar to their companions lounging about the hotel. The time is evidently summer. The boy is barefoot, and the trees are in full bloom.

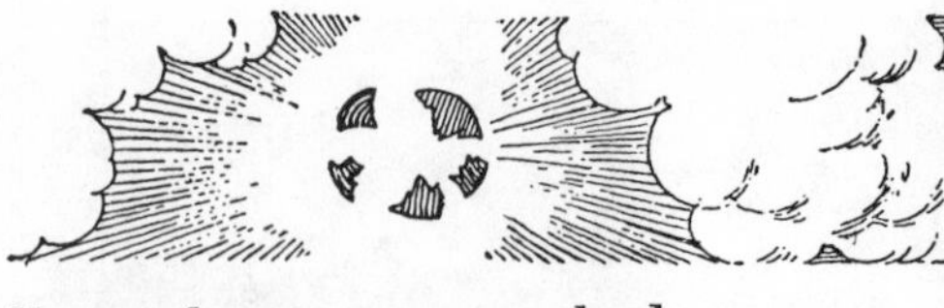

eyes were directed to General McClellan, whose successes had already made him a marked man, and under the direction of that able organizer a more secure feeling immediately appeared. He directed the immediate completion of the fortifications of the city, and also bent his energy to organizing the great Army of the Potomac.

Once the positions on the right bank of the Potomac were reasonably secure through the works just mentioned and such additional defenses as Fort Albany, Fort Scott, and various lines of connecting fortifications, attention was given to the Washington side of the river. In the summer and autumn the Potomac is fordable at points not far above Washington, and as the river became lower apprehension increased that the victorious foe, who still rested at Manassas, would avoid the works on the Virginia side, cross above Georgetown, and attack from the Maryland side of the city. To meet the emergency, works were hurriedly thrown up without that careful preliminary study of the topography which the occasion really demanded.

The securing of the roads was the first consideration. The main road which followed the general line of the crest between Rock Creek and the Potomac, branched at Tennallytown, about a mile south of the District line, and entering and leaving the town were other important roads. As this was on fairly high ground it was selected as a proper point for a work, and Fort Pennsylvania (afterward Fort Reno) was placed there. Thus was established one point of the line of works. Fort Stevens, commanding the Seventh Street Road, running north, and Fort Lincoln, commanding the Baltimore turnpike and the Baltimore and Ohio Railroad, together with Forts Totten and Slocum, between these latter roads and the Seventh Street Road, were all simultaneously started. All these works were on the crest of a somewhat irregular ridge overlooking the valley of Sligo Branch. This carried the general project from Tennallytown, within two miles of the Potomac, around to the north and east of the capital to Anacostia Branch.

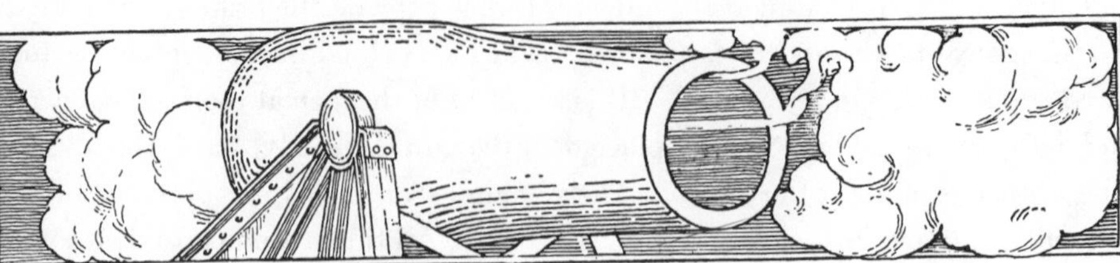

UNION ARCH OF THE WASHINGTON AQUEDUCT

GUARDING THE AQUEDUCT

FORTS AT AN UPPER POTOMAC APPROACH TO WASHINGTON

The forts on the south side of the Potomac, grouped immediately about the Aqueduct Bridge, were Forts Bennett, C. F. Smith, Strong, Morton, Woodbury, and Corcoran. The latter was a *tete-du-pont,* or defense of a bridge, covering the Virginia end of the Aqueduct Bridge. It was on a slight plateau above the river, but was itself commanded by higher ground around Arlington Heights. In the two center photographs cannoneers are loading big guns in Forts Corcoran and Woodbury. These are both cast-iron muzzle-loading 32-pounder guns, mounted on wooden carriages with front pintles. Technically, the upper part of the mount is the carriage, and the lower part, running on the traverse wheels, is the chassis. The front pintle allowed the gun to rotate through an arc of 180 degrees. An interesting aspect of the loading of

LOADING 32–POUNDERS IN CORCORAN AND WOODBURY

the big gun in Fort Corcoran is the officer holding his thumb over the vent. This was to prevent the influx of oxygen while the charge was being rammed home. After the gun was heated by several discharges, it was possible to fire it merely by removing the thumb from the vent. Woe to the man handling the rammer if the officer inadvertently removed his thumb before the charge was rammed home! The premature discharge following would blow him into atoms, that is, if he should be thoughtless enough to expose his body before the muzzle of the cannon. Many distressing accidents occur in this way, both in peace and war, where amateurs handle the guns. The well-trained artillerist stands aside from the muzzle when ramming home the charge. Fort Corcoran was constructed to defend this important bridge from assault on the Virginia side of the Potomac. Fort Strong was originally Fort De Kalb and with Forts Corcoran, Bennett and Woodbury constituted the defense of the bridge at the time the capital was threatened by the Confederates after Lee's defeat of General Pope's army in August, 1862.

DOWN THE POTOMAC FROM UNION ARCH

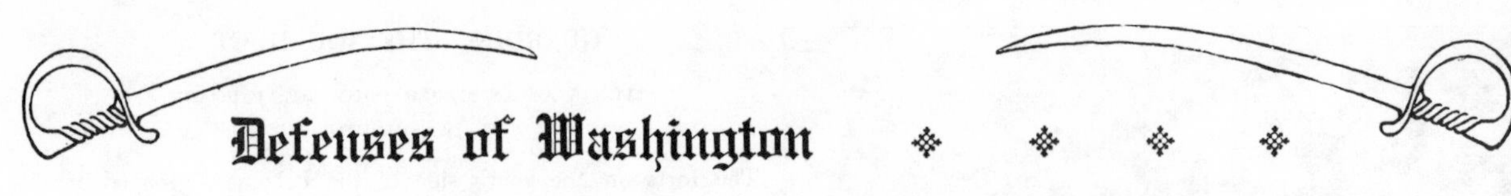

The line once established by the location of the larger forts, the process already employed on the Virginia side was used to fill in the gaps. Supporting works of usually less strength, were placed within rifle-range along the crest.

The problem of resting the left of the line on the Potomac, however, was more difficult. There were two matters of paramount importance, the consideration of which indicated a position for the line quite different from that indicated by the topography. It must be remembered that the Chain Bridge crossed the Potomac about three miles above Georgetown, and the receiving reservoir which supplied most of Washington and Georgetown with water was about three and one-half miles from the latter place. The value of the bridge and reservoir rendered their protection necessary. But the high ground, upon which naturally the line of forts should be placed, ran toward the Potomac on a line south of Powder-Mill Run, the stream supplying the reservoir, which approached the river at the point where the bridge crossed. It was obvious that works placed on these heights would not protect the reservoir, and that the bridge would be in the zone of fire of any force attacking the forts. Hence the line of works was broken, and three isolated works, afterward united into one, were placed on high ground to the north of the reservoir, and far enough above the bridge to prevent artillery fire from reaching it.

South of Anacostia Branch the problem at first appeared to be capable of solution by placing bridge-heads, or small forts covering the approaches to the bridges, on the south side. There were two bridges, one at the navy-yard, about two miles up the creek, and Benning's Bridge, some two and one-half miles above the first. In addition, it appeared that there should be at least one large fort overlooking and protecting the navy-yard and the arsenal, which latter was on the point at the confluence of the Anacostia and the Potomac, and which contained large quantities of war-supplies of all kinds. A more critical examination, however, showed the necessity of

A VIEW FROM FORT MARCY—COMPANY A, FOURTH NEW YORK HEAVY ARTILLERY

In front of the tent at the right of the picture sits William Arthur, brother of Chester A. Arthur, the future President. This view was taken from the fort down toward the camp. The Fourth New York Heavy Artillery was organized at New York, November, 1861, to February, 1862. It left for Washington on February 10th. Its first camp was five miles from Chain Bridge, and its second at Fort Marcy. These unusually clear photographs were treasured half a century by T. J. Lockwood, a member of the regiment.

LOOKING FROM THE CAMP TOWARD FORT MARCY

Marcy was the northernmost fort on the west side of the Potomac, lying above Chain Bridge. Its armament consisted of three 24-pounders *en barbette*, two 12-pounder howitzers, six 30-pounder Parrotts, three 20-pounder Parrotts and three 10-pounder Parrotts, all *en embrasure.* It also mounted one 10-inch siege mortar and two 24-pounder Coehorn mortars. It overlooked the Leesburg and Georgetown Turnpike.

fortifying the entire length of the crest between the Anacostia and Oxen Run, a distance of about six miles. This was done, and toward the end of the year 1861 these works were well toward completion. Likewise were the works along the entire perimeter of the defensive line encircling the capital, on both sides of the Potomac.

By the spring of 1862 there were, surrounding Washington, twenty-three forts on the Virginia side of the Potomac, fourteen forts and three batteries from the Potomac around by the north and east of the city to the Anacostia, and eleven forts south of the Anacostia, with the right of the line resting on the Potomac. Of these, Fort Runyon, already noted as covering Long Bridge on the Virginia side, was the largest, with a perimenter of one thousand five hundred yards, but the size of the remainder varied to a minimum of one hundred and fifty-four yards. Most of them were enclosed works, and some were lunettes, or partially closed works, with the unclosed side occupied by stockades. The armament was principally 24- and 32-pounders, some smooth-bore and some rifled, with a few lighter field-guns. Magazines were provided that had a capacity each of about one hundred rounds of ammunition, and some of the most important works had bomb-proof shelters, where about one-third of the garrison could sleep secure from artillery fire.

The curious fluctuation of public feeling toward the fortifications can be seen when we remember that, before the Manassas campaign, they were very lightly regarded; immediately after that campaign and the defeat of Bull Run, there was a fever heat of apprehension and demand for protection. When General McClellan's splendidly organized army took the field against the foe, there was a certainty that the war was about to be ended, and a corresponding decrease of regard for the defenses; and we shall see later how the ebb of the tide again caught the public and sent it scurrying behind the forts. When McClellan left Washington for the front, the act

IN FORMIDABLE FORT SUMNER
APRIL 5, 1864

ort Sumner, a semi-closed work, lay highest up the river of all the forts defending Washington. It was northwest of the receiving ·servoir, overlooking the Potomac, and commanded by the fire of its heavy guns the opposite shore in front of the works of the Virginia de. Its great armament made it a formidable fort. Of smooth-bore guns it had three 8-inch siege-howitzers and two 32-pounder a-coast guns *en embrasure,* and six 32-pounder and four 24-pounder sea-coast guns *en barbette.* Its rifled guns were two 100-pounder arrotts *en barbette,* four 4½-inch rifles *en embrasure,* two 4½-inch rifles *en barbette,* and six 6-pounder James rifles *en embrasure.* It so boasted three mortars, one 10-inch siege-mortar, and two 24-pounder Coehorns, and there were thirteen vacant platforms for eld and siege-guns. The terrain on which the work was placed was such as to enable it to shelter a large body of troops with natural ver. The first gun on the right in this photograph is a 32-pounder sea-coast gun in an embrasure; the second is a 4½-inch rifle an embrasure; the third is a 100-pounder Parrott *en barbette;* and the gun on the left is a 4½-inch rifle *en barbette.* The first and urth guns are on wooden sea-coast carriages; the second on a siege-carriage; and the Parrott rifle on a wrought-iron sea-coast carriage.

ONE OF THE HEAVY ARTILLERY REGIMENTS THAT WASHINGTON LACKED IN '64

he Third Pennsylvania heavy artillerists, as they drill in Fort Monroe, April, 1864, are the type of trained big gun fighters that Washgton needed by thousands when Early swept up to Fort Stevens, threatening to take it three months after this picture was taken.

of Congress making appropriations for the defenses of the capital read as follows:

"Be it enacted, etc., etc., that the sum of one hundred and fifty thousand dollars be, and the same is hereby, appropriated, out of any money in the Treasury not otherwise appropriated, for completing the defenses of Washington; *Provided,* That all arrearages of debts incurred for the objects of this act shall be first paid out of this sum: *And Provided Further,* That no part of the sum hereby appropriated shall be expended in any work hereafter to be commenced."

General J. G. Barnard, who, prior to the passage of the act above quoted, had been in engineering charge of the works, was, after the disasters of the first campaign under McClellan, placed also in command. He says that it was evident to all that the line north of the Potomac was not adequately defended at the time of the above act, and that after the disasters in Virginia the work was prosecuted with all vigor, new works being thrown up and the old ones strengthened, notwithstanding the act of Congress. Public opinion demanded these measures as imperative necessities, thus demonstrating the return of affection for forts and bombproofs. Even with the utmost endeavors of General Barnard, assisted by a large force of competent engineers, the defenses, in December, 1862, were far from satisfactory. Congress had not removed its prohibition against the commencement of new works, but here we witness one of the exhibitions of the masterful nature of the great war secretary, Stanton. He authorized General Barnard to continue the work of construction, and to begin such new works as were necessary. It was evident, however, that the expenditures would continue indefinitely, and ultimately would amount to a very large sum. In order to have a sufficient justification in the face of the Congressional prohibition, Secretary Stanton convened a board of officers whose judgment could be relied on for an unbiased decision. This board spent two months in examining

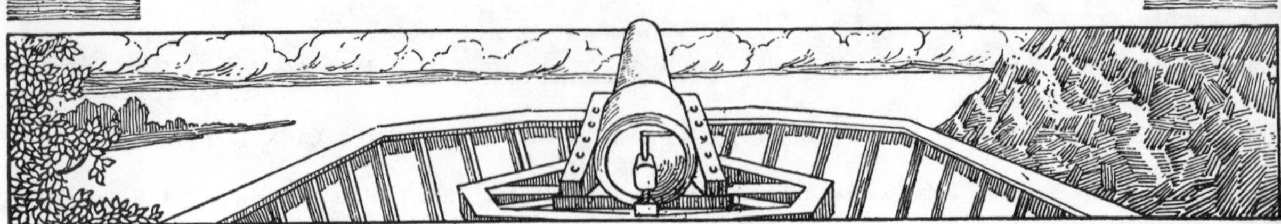

MEN OF THE THIRD MASSACHUSETTS HEAVY ARTILLERY IN FORT STEVENS

Fort Stevens, on the north line of the defenses of Washington, bore the brunt of the Confederate attack in the action of July 12, 1864, when Early threatened Washington. The smooth-bore guns in its armament were two 8-inch siege-howitzers *en embrasure,* six 24-pounder siege-guns *en embrasure,* two 24-pounder sea-coast guns *en barbette.* It was also armed with five 30-pounder Parrott rifled guns, one 10-inch siege-mortar and one 24-pounder Coehorn mortar. Three of the platforms for siege-guns remained vacant.

COMPANY K, THIRD MASSACHUSETTS HEAVY ARTILLERY, IN FORT STEVENS, 1865

Washington was no longer in danger when this photograph was taken, and the company is taking its ease with small arms stacked—three rifles held together by engaging the shanks of the bayonets. This is the usual way of disposing of rifles when the company is temporarily dismissed for any purpose. If the men are to leave the immediate vicinity of the stacks, a sentinel is detailed to guard the arms. The Third Massachusetts Heavy Artillery was organized for one year in August, 1864, and remained in the defenses of Washington throughout their service, except for Company I, which went to the siege of Petersburg and maintained the pontoon bridges.

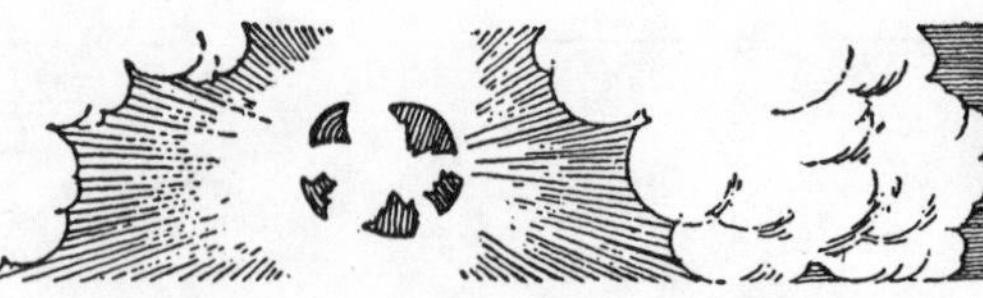

critically all the works, completed, under construction, and projected. The findings of the board were, in brief, as follows:

That there were (in December, 1862) surrounding Washington, fifty-three forts and twenty-two batteries; that the perimeter of the entire line of fortifications was thirty-seven miles; that the armament consisted of six hundred and forty-three guns and seventy-five mortars; that the total infantry garrison needed for a proper manning of the defenses was about twenty-five thousand; that the total artillery garrison necessary was about nine thousand, and that a force of three thousand cavalry was necessary to make reconnaissances in order to give warning of the approach of the foe. In accordance with the recommendations of the board, Congress raised the embargo on funds for further defense preparation, and, during 1863, several important new works were opened and completed, and the old ones kept in a high state of efficiency. One of the most notable new works was Battery Rodgers at Jones' Point, near Alexandria, for defense against the Confederate vessels. During 1864, one large fort, McPherson, was commenced on the Virginia side between Long Bridge and Aqueduct Bridge but not completed, and some smaller ones built. With these exceptions the time was devoted to keeping in good repair those already constructed. These included some water batteries that had been constructed in 1862 as a supplementary aid to the forts in repelling naval attacks.

The amount of work that was expended on the defenses of Washington during the war was indicated by the fact that, at the close of the war, in April, 1865, the fortifications consisted of sixty-eight enclosed forts and batteries, whose aggregate perimeter was thirteen miles, eight hundred and seven guns, and ninety-eight mounted mortars, and emplacements for one thousand one hundred and twenty guns, ninety-three unarmed batteries for field-guns, thirty-five thousand seven hundred and eleven yards of rifle-trenches, and three blockhouses. The

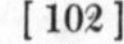

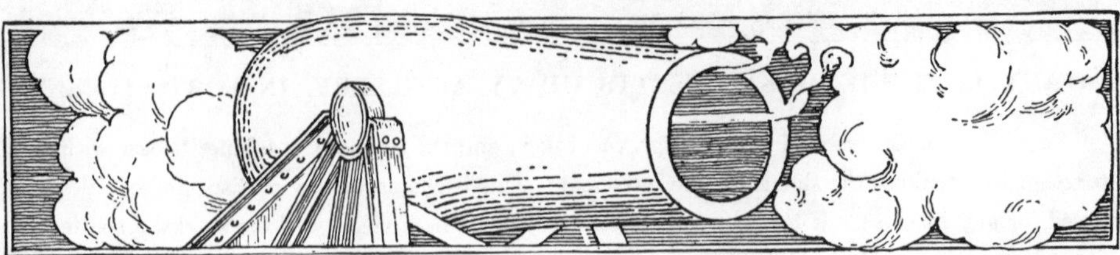

JAMES RIFLES BEHIND THE FORT TOTTEN RAMPARTS

The first gun, in the foreground, is a James rifle on a siege-carriage, the second a James rifle on a sea-coast carriage, the third a James rifle on a siege-carriage, and the fourth a Columbiad on a sea-coast carriage. Fort Totten had many magazines and bomb-proofs.

WITH THE COLUMBIADS AT FORT TOTTEN

The total armament of Fort Totten consisted of two 8-inch howitzers, eight 32-pounder sea-coast Columbiads, one 100-pounder Parrott rifle, three 30-pounder Parrott rifles, four 6-pounder James rifles, one 10-inch siege-mortar, and one 24-pounder coehorn mortar.

entire extent of front of the lines was thirty-seven miles. Thirty-two miles of military roads, besides those previously existing in the District of Columbia, formed the means of interior communication.

"Sensitiveness for the safety of Washington influenced every combination and every important movement of troops in the Virginia theater." General McClellan proposed, in January, 1862, to transfer the Army of the Potomac to the lower Chesapeake, for an advance on Richmond. A council of division commanders decided that McClellan's plan was good, but that the forts on the right bank of the Potomac for the defense of the capital must be garrisoned by a full quota, and that those on the Washington side be occupied in force—in brief, not less than forty thousand men ought to be left for the defense of Washington. McClellan sought to combine his own necessities with the exigencies which had arisen in connection with the protection of the capital, and included in the number of troops left for the defense those which he sent to the Shenandoah. The field-commanders always insisted that the best way to defend Washington was to attack Richmond. However, the Secretary of War decided that McClellan's inclusion of the Shenandoah troops in the defenders of the capital was not justifiable, and the recall of McDowell from the Army of the Potomac and all the subsequent controversies growing therefrom are matters of record.

Although General Pope's army operated between the Confederates and Washington, there was a great feeling of uneasiness on account of the inadequacy of the works, and the fact that the garrison had been reduced to add to Pope's field-army. But "nevertheless they deterred Lee from pushing further against Washington his offensive movements . . . and thereby saved the Nation from much greater calamities than actually befell us in this most disastrous year." The garrisons were "commanded, generally, by artillery officers of the army, and by them instructed in the service of sea-coast-, siege-, and

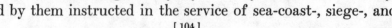

Eighteen forts, four batteries of heavy artillery, and twenty-three of light artillery were located between Fort Sumner, on the Potomac above Georgetown, and Fort Lincoln, near Bladensburg, commanding the Baltimore and Ohio Railroad and the upper Anacostia. Fort Lincoln was profusely but not heavily armed. It had two 8-inch siege-howitzers, six 32-pounder sea-coast guns, one 24-pounder siege-gun, three 24-pounder sea-coast guns, four 12-pounder field-guns, and eight 6-pounder field-guns *en barbette,* with two 24-pounder field-howitzers *en embrasure.* This concludes the list of the smooth-bores, but there were also a 100-pounder Parrott and four 20-pounder Parrotts. Fort Lincoln was a bastioned fort of four faces. One of the 20-pounder Parrotts is just visible over the top of the storehouse, and the 100-pounder is in full view in the far corner of the fort. This was one of the first points fortified on the Northern lines about Washington. The spade, seen leaning against the house to the left of the pile of boxes, was the great weapon of warfare. The lower photograph shows Company H of the Third Massachusetts Heavy Artillery manning the guns. Their muskets have been leaned against the parapet, and the pile of shells to the right makes the great guns glaring down the valley seem formidable indeed. The Third Massachusetts was organized from unattached companies of heavy artillery in August, 1864, for the defense of Washington.

THE INTERIOR OF FORT LINCOLN

COMPANY H, THIRD MASSACHUSETTS HEAVY ARTILLERY, IN FORT LINCOLN

field-guns of the forts," and "they soon became an unrivaled body of artillerymen. Their long connection with particular works inspired them with pride in their perfection and preservation, while the zeal and military knowledge of their commanders prompted and enabled them to render aid to the engineers in modifying and strengthening the forts and in developing the lines."

Such was the confidence felt by everyone in General Grant that when, in 1864, he withdrew practically the entire garrison of Washington for his field-army—a thing that McClellan had wanted to do and was prevented—there was little or no opposition raised. But this very action left Washington a tempting morsel for a daring raider, and the Confederate commander was not long in taking advantage of that fact. Lee was hard pressed, and he sought to create a diversion by sending Early to threaten, and, if possible, to capture Washington. This ruse of threatening the national capital had been successful before, and he hoped that Grant also might be influenced by it. Early left Lee's army under orders to attack and destroy General Hunter's army in the Shenandoah and then to threaten Washington. Several times during the raid, Lee communicated with Early, leaving the decision of returning or moving on to the judgment of Early, according to the circumstances in which he found himself. On the 10th of July he was within sixteen miles of Washington, in Maryland, and defeated a small detachment of Federal cavalry. Hasty preparations were made in the defenses to muster all the troops possible to repel the invader.

General Early attacked the works on the Seventh Street Road but was repulsed, and during the night of the 12–13th of July, 1864, he withdrew and retired toward Conrad's Ferry; on the Potomac. He stated later: "McCausland [one of his brigade commanders] reported the works on the Georgetown pike too strong for him to assault. We could not move to the right or left without its being discovered from a signal

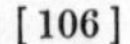

THE GARRISON OF FORT C. F. SMITH—COMPANY F, SECOND NEW YORK HEAVY ARTILLERY

COMPANY L, AT DRILL

In these photographs of 1865, the defenses of Washington have served their turn; it is more than a year since they were threatened for the last time by General Early and his men. But the panoply of war continues. Everything is polished and groomed. During four long years the guns in Fort C. F. Smith have been swabbed out daily and oiled, to be ready for a thunderous reception to the Confederates. The fort, one of the later constructions, lay to the northwest of Fort Corcoran. Its armament of smooth-bore guns consisted of one 8-inch seacoast howitzer *en barbette,* four 24-pounders on siege carriages *en embrasure,* and three 12-pounder howitzers *en embrasure.* Of rifled guns it boasted six 4½-inch Rodmans *en embrasure,* and two 10-pounder Parrotts *en embrasure.* It also mounted three 8-inch siege-mortars. There were six vacant platforms for further guns. The Second New York Heavy Artillery remained in the defenses of Washington till May, 1864, when it joined the Army of the Potomac. It lost 114 officers and men killed and mortally wounded, and 247 by disease.

station on the top of Soldiers' Home, which overlooked the country, and the enemy would have been enabled to move in his works to meet us. Under the circumstances, to have rushed my men blindly against the fortifications without understanding the state of things, would have been worse than folly. If we had any friends in Washington none of them came out with any information, and this satisfied me that the place was not undefended. . . . After interchanging views with my brigade commanders, being very reluctant to abandon the project of capturing Washington, I determined to make an assault on the enemy's works at daylight the next morning, unless some information should be received before that time showing its impracticability, and so informed those officers. During the night a despatch was received from General Bradley T. Johnson, from near Baltimore, informing me that he had received information, from a reliable source, that two corps had arrived from Grant's army, and that his whole army was probably in motion. This caused me to delay the attack until I could examine the works again, and, as soon as it was light enough to see, I rode to the front and found the parapets lined with troops. I had, therefore, reluctantly to give up all hopes of capturing Washington, after I had arrived in sight of the dome of the Capitol and given the Federal authorities a terrible fright."

This was the last time Washington was threatened; and the fortifications saved the city. The garrison unaided could not have done so.

[The defenses of Washington presented many problems in the nature of formal fortification and concentration of troops that did not apply to the capital of the Confederacy. Lee's army was the surest defense of Richmond whose fall necessarily followed the defeat of the Confederate forces. Nevertheless, a scheme of defense was early adopted and this will be found discussed in an interesting chapter, in the preparation, of which Captain Hunt has received the valuable assistance of Colonel T. M. R. Talcott, commanding the engineer troops of the Army of Northern Virginia.—The Editors.]

V

ATTACK AND DEFENSE AT CHARLESTON

THE MORNING AND EVENING GUN—SUMTER

THIS PIECE THAT TIMED THE GARRISON OF THE BELEAGUERED FORT LOOKS OUT ACROSS THE MARSHES OF CHARLESTON HARBOR—IN THESE GILLMORE'S MEN SET UP THEIR BATTERIES, WITH WHAT RESULTS THE FOLLOWING SERIES OF PICTURES SHOWS

GILLMORE STUDYING THE MAP OF CHARLESTON IN 1863, WHILE HE DREW HIS "RING OF FIRE" ROUND THE CITY

MAP EXPLAINING THE PHOTOGRAPHS ON THE PAGES THAT FOLLOW

Brigadier-General Quincy Adams Gillmore is the man who surrounded Charleston with a ring of fire. On the map which he is studying the words "East Coast, South Carolina" are plainly legible. A glance at the map to the right will reveal that coast, along which his guns were being pushed when this photograph was taken, in 1863. It will also reveal the progress illustrated by the succession of photographs following—the gradual reduction of Battery Wagner, at the north end of Morris Island before Charleston, by a series of parallels. On the facing page are scenes in Battery Reynolds on the first parallel and Battery Brown on the second. Then come Batteries Rosecrans and Meade on the second parallel, shown on successive pages. The "Swamp Angel" that threw shells five miles into the city of Charleston comes next, and then the sap-roller being pushed forward to the fifth and last parallel, with Battery Chatfield on Cumming's Point. On the next page is Battery Wagner. The

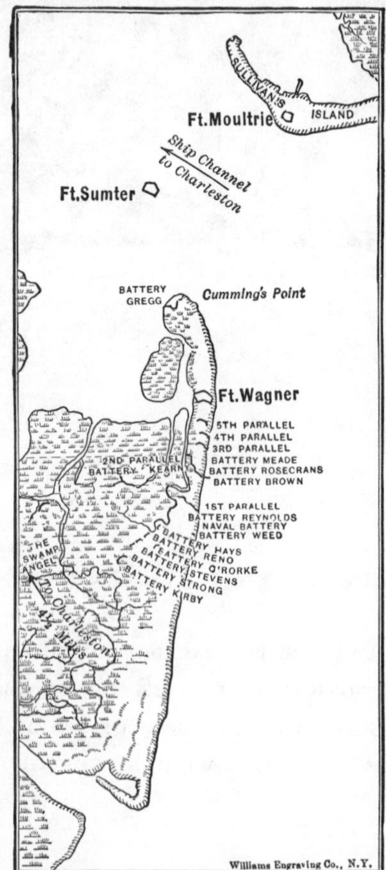

remaining scenes are inside Charleston. Th last page shows the effect of the bombardmen of Fort Sumter. Thus a sequent story is tol in actual photographs of the siege opera tions about Charleston. Quincy Adams Gil more was graduated first in his class at Wes Point. He served as an assistant enginee in the building of Fortress Monroe from 184 to 1852, and later became assistant instructo of practical military engineering at Wes Point. When the war broke out he ha abundant opportunity to put his learning t the test, and proved one of the ablest militar engineers in the Federal service. He acte as chief engineer of the Port Royal expedi tionary corps in 1861–62; was chief enginee at the siege of Fort Pulaski, Georgia, fron February to April, 1862, conducted the lan operations against Charleston, fought a Drewry's Bluff, and in the defense of Wash ington against Early. On March 13, 1865 he was brevetted successively brigadier general and major-general in the regula army, and on December 5, 1865, he resignec from the volunteer service He was the autho of many engineering books and treatises

THE PARROTT IN BATTERY STRONG

This 300-pounder rifle was directed against Fort Sumter and Battery Wagner. The length of bore of the gun before it burst was 136 inches. It weighed 26,000 pounds. It fired a projectile weighing 250 pounds, with a maximum charge of powder of 25 pounds. The gun was fractured at the twenty-seventh round by a shell bursting in the muzzle, blowing off about 20 inches of the barrel. After the bursting the gun was "chipped" back beyond the termination of the fracture and afterwards fired 371 rounds with as good results as before the injury. At the end of that time the muzzle began to crack again, rendering the gun entirely useless.

TWO PARROTTS IN BATTERY STEVENS

Battery Stevens lay just east of Battery Strong. It was begun July 27, 1863. Most of the work was done at night, for the fire from the adjacent Confederate forts rendered work in daylight dangerous. By August 17th, most of the guns were in position, and two days later the whole series of batteries "on the left," as they were designated, were pounding away at Fort Sumter.

GUNS IN BATTERY RENO TRAINED ON BATTERY WAGNER

Both the batteries on this page were "on the left," that is, across a creek from Morris Island proper. Battery Hays was begun July 15, 1863, in preparation for an attack on Battery Wagner set for July 18th. Within sixty hours from breaking ground, t platforms were made, the earthworks thrown up and revetted with sand-bags—as shown—magazines constructed and fifteen Parr guns in place, ready to open fire. At ten o'clock they began the bombardment of Wagner, in conjunction with the fleet, and kept up until dusk, when a determined but unsuccessful assault was made. Battery Reno was one of the "breaching batteries" against F Sumter. The work was begun July 27th, and on August 17th four 100-pounder Parrott rifle guns, one 8-inch and one 10-inch Parrott gu the largest guns then made, were in place. The ground was flat and marshy. No obstructions interfered with the bombardme

PARROTTS IN BATTERY HAYS TRAINED ON SUMTER

BATTERY REYNOLDS, ON THE FIRST PARALLEL AGAINST BATTERY WAGNER

The surprised Confederates discovered at dawn of July 24, 1863, the new line thrown forward from Battery Reynolds and the naval battery on the first Union parallel. Two direct assaults on Battery Wagner having been repulsed with great loss of life, the advance upon the work was made by a series of parallels. The batteries were ready in sixty hours from the time of breaking ground, most of the work being done in the night during heavy rains. The second parallel, six hundred yards in advance, was established July 23d, by a flying-sap along the narrow strip of shifting sand. The moon was so bright until midnight that no work could be done, but from twelve till dawn a parapet ten feet thick and one hundred seventy-five feet long was completed, six howitzers were placed, an entanglement was put up a hundred yards in advance, and a large bomb-proof magazine finished in the center of an old graveyard. Slowly but surely the Federal forces were working their way to the northern end of Morris Island.

SAILORS IN THE NAVAL BATTERY

BATTERY BROWN, ON THE SECOND PARALLEL

BURST GUN IN BATTERY ROSECRANS—LIFE IN THE "PARALLELS"

It was not the bursting of a gun in the works that caused the troops most concern, but the Confederate fire. Major Thomas B. Brooks describes dodging shells in the parallels on Morris Island in August, 1863: "The fire from Wagner, although inflicting much less real injury, up to this time, than the aggregate fire from the other batteries of the enemy, still gives far greater interruption to the working parties, on account of our nearness to the fort. 'Cover—Johnson or Sumter,' gives sufficient warning for those in the trenches to seek partial shelter, if the shell is seen to be coming toward them; but 'Cover, Wagner,' cannot be pronounced before the shell has exploded and done its work. At these cautionary words, I have often observed soldiers, particularly Negroes, fall flat on their faces, under the delusion that they were obtaining cover from mortar-shells exploding over them, when, in truth, their chances of being hit were much increased . . . On one occasion, a soldier was observed to place an empty powder-barrel over his head, to shield him from heavy shells."

THE 100-POUNDER PARROTTS IN BATTERY ROSECRANS

"'WARE SHARPSHOOTERS!'"—SERVING THE PARROTTS IN BATTERY MEADE

ıt ten o'clock on the night f July 28th, orders were ssued to construct Battery leade and Battery Rose-rans in the second parallel. 'he positions were laid out nd work begun on them efore midnight. Work pro-ressed rather slowly, how-ver, because the Confeder-te sharpshooters picked off very man who stuck his ead above the parapet. everal men were wounded t a distance of thirteen undred yards. Conse-uently all the work that re-uired any exposure was one at night. Another ause of delay was the lack f earth; when trenches were ug more than three feet eep the spring tides flooded hem. Besides, the work 'as frequently interrupted y finding dead bodies, ither in coffins or wrapped 1 blankets only. On an old map Morris Island was called "Coffin Land"; it had been used as a quarantine burying-ground for Charleston. In spite of such discouragements, the men standing in front of the headquarters at the bottom of the page continued their labors. By August 17th the five immense Parrott guns stood ready to fire against Sumter. Thus the Federal army advanced, parallel by parallel, toward Battery Wagner at the end of Morris Island, until the final "flying-sap" took them up to its very walls, and it was carried by assault. But the defenders had other strings to their bow, as Gillmore's amphibious diggers discovered. Though now occupying the stronghold that commanded the harbor from the south, the Federals got no farther.

HEADQUARTERS OF THE FIELD OFFICER OF THE SECOND PARALLEL

One of the most famous guns in the Civil War was the "Swamp-Angel." The marsh here surely deserved the name. The two engineers who explored it to select a site for the battery carried a fourteen foot plank. When the mud became too soft to sustain their weight, they sat on the plank and pushed it forward between their legs. The mud was twenty feet deep, and men on such a plank could start waves rippling across the oozy surface by jumping up and down. It is said that one of the officers detailed for the construction of the platforms called for "twenty men, eighteen feet long!" In spite of these difficulties piles were driven in the marsh at a point that commanded the city of Charleston and a platform at length laid upon it. On August 17, 1863, an 8-inch, 200-pounder Parrott rifle was skidded across the marsh and mounted behind the sand-bag parapet. On the night of August 21st, after warning had been sent to the Confederate commander, General Beauregard, the gun was fired so that the missiles should fall in the heart of Charleston. Sixteen shells filled with Greek fire were sent that night. On August 23d, at the thirty-sixth discharge, the breech of the gun was blown out and the barrel thereby thrown upon the sand-bag parapet as the photograph shows. From the outside it looked to be in position for firing, and became the target for Confederate gunners. Two weeks later two 10-inch mortars were mounted in place of the Parrott. It was later mounted in Trenton.

THE "SWAMP-ANGEL"—ONE OF THE FAMOUS GUNS OF '63

AFTER THE 36TH SHOT—THE "SWAMP-ANGEL" BURST

SAP-ROLLER AT THE HEAD OF THE FLYING-SAP

This remarkable picture was taken while the flying-sap was being pushed forward to the fifth (and last) parallel. The action of September 6th is thus reported by Major T. B. Brooks: "The general commanding ordered General Terry to take and hold the ridge, and place the resources of the command at his disposal for that purpose. It was accomplished at 6:30 P.M. by a brilliant charge of the Twenty-fourth Massachusetts Volunteers, Colonel Francis A. Osborn commanding, supported by the Third New Hampshire Volunteers, Captain Randlett commanding. Sixty-seven prisoners were captured. They were afraid to retire on account of their own torpedoes, as they informed us, and had too little time, even if there had been no torpedoes. No works, excepting rude rifle-pits in the excellent natural cover afforded by the ridge, were found. . . . The moment the ridge was gained the work of entrenching was begun under the superintendence of Captain Walker." The balance of the report tells about the fifth parallel and the flying-sap, which took them up to Battery Wagner and the battery renamed Chatfield on Cumming's Point, in order to commemorate Colonel John L. Chatfield, killed July 18th, at Battery Wagner.

FIRING THE BIG GUN CHATFIELD

ONE OF THE MOST POWERFUL GUNS OF THE CONFEDERACY, IN FORT MOULTRIE

This huge gun in Fort Moultrie was designed to throw 600-pound shells. With such defenders Charleston became the best-fortified city on the Confederate sea-coast, and proved a stumbling-block to both the Federal army and navy. Fort Moultrie was on Sullivan's Island, guarding the right-hand entrance to the harbor. Charleston was finally evacuated February 17, 1865, after Sherman's march to the sea.

WAGNER AND GREGG

These two forts (Wagner shown above; Gregg to the right) were captured successively in the slow approach by parallels along Morris Island, preceding the evacuation of Charleston. Both Wagner and Gregg were evacuated September 6, 1863. General Beauregard, the Confederate commander, states that Wagner was an inconsiderable work. General Gillmore, whose forces occupied the place, insists that it was an exceedingly strong fort. Its bomb-proofs would hold 1,500 or 1,600 men, and eighteen pieces of heavy ordnance were captured when it finally fell.

GUNS THAT WERE NOT NEEDED
THE SOUTH BATTERY IN CHARLESTON ITSELF
THE FEDERAL FLEET NEVER GOT BEYOND THE HARBOR FORTS

The upper photograph shows two 10-inch Columbiads in the White Point or "South" Battery, in Charleston. This was situated on the extreme southeast point between the Ashby and Cooper Rivers. It was established for the purpose of affording a last opportunity to stop vessels that might get past Fort Sumter into the inner harbor. Sumter, however, was so far out, and with Moultrie, Gregg, and the others proved so effectual a barrier to the harbor's mouth, that no use was found for the guns here in the city itself. How close they were to the heart of the city is shown by the gun in the lower photograph, emplaced on the battery directly in front of the public square. Charleston was the birthplace of secession, and was prepared to make a stout defense. Sumter almost single-handed held out until inland communications were cut, and the city was evacuated February 17, 1865.

ONE OF THE "SOUTH BATTERY" GUNS
DIRECTLY ON THE PUBLIC SQUARE

WRECK OF THE GIANT BLAKELY GUN AT CHARLESTON

This was an English gun, all steel, to which the principle of "initial tension" was successfully applied. From the breech to the trunnions of the Blakely gun it was pear-shaped, for the purpose of resisting the tremendous power-pressures. By "initial tension" is meant intentional strain in the metal of the gun, scientifically placed, so as to counteract in a measure the strains set up by the powder discharge. There is an inner tube, on the outside of which bands are shrunk so as to set up a strain of extension in the exterior band. By properly combining these strains the extreme tension due to the powder gases at their moment of greatest expansion does not affect the gun as injuriously as if these initial strains were not present. This was among the earliest form of cannon to be successful with this principle of "initial tension," a fundamental element in the scientific design of the best modern built-up guns.

VIEW FROM THE REAR

THE ONLY GUN IN THE LINE OF FIRE

The city of Charleston was fortified up to its very doorsteps, as is evidenced by these three photographs of the wrecked carriage of the immense Blakely gun on the Battery. The only battery in the path of the Federal fire was that containing this monster piece. Under date of January 6, 1864, Major Henry Bryan, Assistant Inspector-General at Charleston, reported that from August 21, 1863, to January 5, 1864, the observer in the steeple of St. Michael's Church counted 472 shells thrown at the city. Of a total of 225 investigated, 145 struck houses, nineteen struck in yards, and sixty-one struck in the streets and on the edge of the burnt district. Only about one third of these burst. The section of the city most frequently struck was bounded on the north by Market Street from East Bay to Meeting, down Meeting to Horlbeck's Alley, and along Horlbeck's Alley to Tradd Street; on the south by Tradd Street from the corner of King to Church Street, down Church Street to Longitude Lane, along that to East Bay; and on the east by East Bay Street.

LOOKING OUT TO SEA

LOOKING NORTHEAST

This view shows the street running at right angles to the one in the adjoining photograph.

THE HEART OF THE CITY

This shows how close to the dwelling houses the Federal shells must have fallen during the bombardment.

These views show the result of the bombardment from August 17 to 23, 1863. The object was to force the surrender of the fort and thus effect an entrance into Charleston. The report of Colonel John W. Turner, Federal chief of artillery runs: "The fire from the breaching batteries upon Sumter was incessant, and kept up continuously from daylight till dark, until the evening of the 23d. . . . The fire upon the gorge had, by the morning of the 23d, succeeded in destroying every gun upon the parapet of it. The parapet and ramparts of the gorge were completely demolished for nearly the entire length of the face, and in places everything was swept off down to the arches, the *débris* forming an accessible ramp to the top of the ruins. Nothing further being gained by a longer fire upon this face, all the guns were directed this day upon the southeasterly flank, and continued an incessant fire throughout the day. The demolition of the fort at the close of the day's firing was complete, so far as its offensive powers were considered." So fared Sumter.

WHERE SHOT AND SHELL STRUCK SUMTER

SOME OF THE 450 SHOT A DAY

THE LIGHTHOUSE ABOVE THE DÉBRIS

VI

THE ORDNANCE OF THE FEDERAL ARMIES

A FEDERAL TRANSPORT IN APRIL, 1865, TAKING ARTILLERY DOWN THE JAMES RIVER. THE VIEW IS NEAR FORT DARLING ON DREWRY'S BLUFF

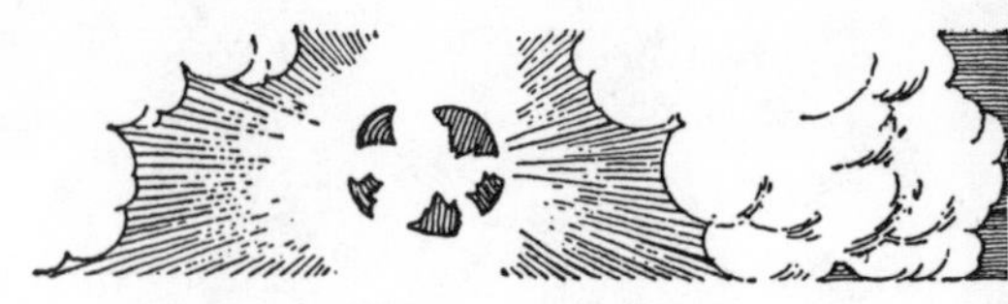

THE ORDNANCE DEPARTMENT OF THE FEDERAL ARMY

By O. E. Hunt
Captain, United States Army

THE provision of muskets and cannon for the vast army of volunteers that flocked to Washington in answer to President Lincoln's call for troops, presented a problem hardly second in importance to the actual organization and training of these citizen soldiers. As the United States had but a small regular army, there were no extensive stores of arms and munitions of war, nor were there large Government manufactories or arsenals adequate to supply great armies. The opening of the Civil War found the Federal War Department confronted, therefore, with an extraordinary situation. From scientific experiment and the routine of a mere bureau, whose chief duties were the fabrication and test of the ordnance required by the small regular army, the Ordnance Department suddenly was called upon to furnish from its all too meager supply, tens of thousands of weapons for the different arms of the service, on a scale quite unprecedented in the military operations theretofore attempted in the United States.

Enjoying a reputation for scientific and painstaking work, especially in the making of large cast-iron cannon, it early became apparent that, in the event of hostilities, there must be a wide extension of the activities of the Ordnance Department. Accordingly, at the outbreak of the war the Ordnance Department was reorganized, and the new organization provided for a chief of ordnance with the rank of brigadier-general, two colonels, two lieutenant-colonels, four majors, twelve captains, twelve first lieutenants, and twelve second lieutenants.

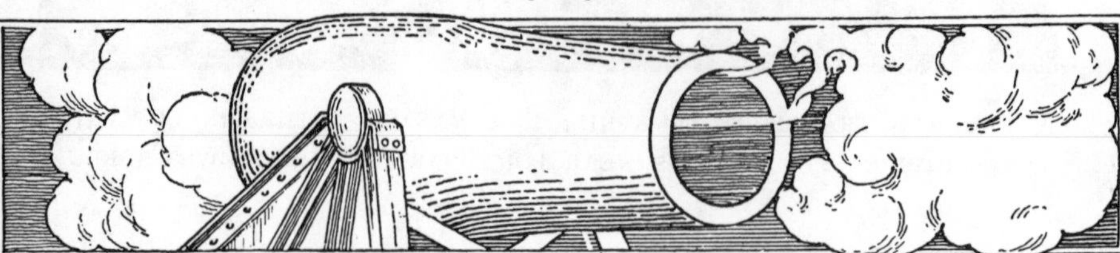

BAYONETS, HOWITZERS AND REVOLVERS OF THE CIVIL WAR DAYS

The soldiers are part of Company L of the Second New York Heavy Artillery. They were armed with rifles provided with musket bayonets This bayonet was a very effective weapon. The blade was made of steel, eighteen inches long. To give lightness and stiffness, its three faces were grooved in the direction of the length, or "fluted." The blade was joined to the socket, which fitted over the muzzle, by a "neck" which, due to the change of direction, had to be made very strong. During the Civil War there was more actual use of the bayonet than since, but the presence of the bayonet still gives a moral effect both to the defender and assailant. The upper photograph shows two 24-pounder smooth-bore guns in Fort C. F. Smith in the defenses of Washington. The carriages are those usually used with siege guns, the heavy scooped-out block on the trail being for the purpose of holding the base of the gun when it was being transported. These 24-pounders were for short range. In the lower photograph "Captain Schwartz, the sharpshooter," is holding a revolver which looks exceedingly clumsy compared to the neat twentieth-century weapons.

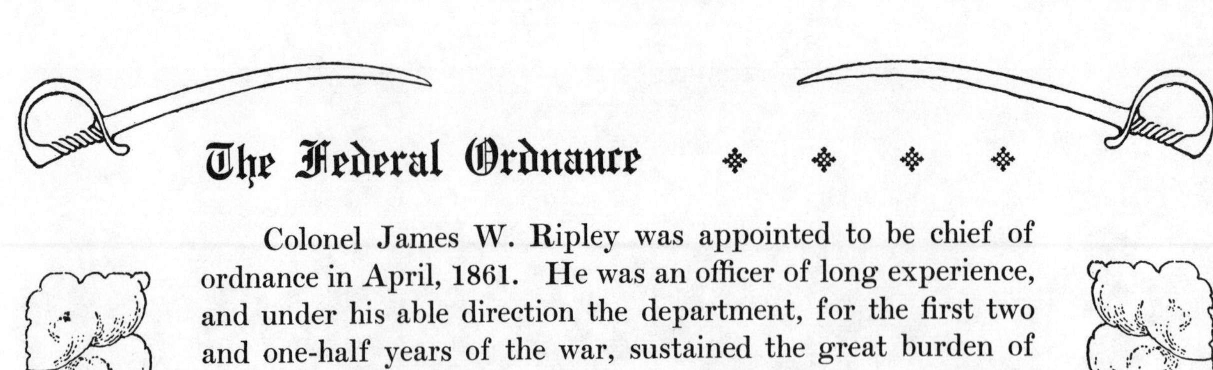

The Federal Ordnance

Colonel James W. Ripley was appointed to be chief of ordnance in April, 1861. He was an officer of long experience, and under his able direction the department, for the first two and one-half years of the war, sustained the great burden of arming and equipping the immense armies that were suddenly raised for the prosecution of the conflict.

During previous years of peace, nearly seven hundred thousand muskets had been ordinarily on hand in the various Government arsenals, but even this number had been allowed to diminish, so that the store of muskets of all kinds, on October 30, 1860, was about five hundred and thirty thousand, distributed among the arsenals of the country, there being at no one place more than one hundred and thirty thousand. As this supply of arms was applicable to the army, the navy, the marine corps, and the militia, it was evidently not great, especially in view of the emergency. Furthermore, there had been a sale of a considerable number of old-pattern muskets, but this sale was stopped, in order not to deplete the supply too seriously.

During 1860, the apportionment of Government arms to the various States for arming their militia was carried on under an old law, that of 1808, but, on account of the small number on hand, only 14,615 were distributed. The allotments were made in proportion to the number of senators and representatives in Congress. Distribution of equipments, other ordnance, and ordnance stores was also made on the same basis to the States.

By the latter part of 1860, there were thirteen arsenals, two armories, and one depot for the manufacture and safekeeping of ordnance and ordnance stores. This was a period of much technical development in the manufacture of cannon, and in consequence of proposed changes in the mode of casting guns, very few were made during the year. Large quantities of iron for gun-carriages, however, were provided, and preparations were made for very active work in the beginning of

IN THE WASHINGTON ARSENAL YARD—A ROW OF "NAPOLEONS"

This type of piece was used extensively during the war, and was usually made of bronze. Its exterior was characterized by the entire bsence of ornament, and was easily distinguished from the older types of field-guns. The weight of the piece was 1,200 pounds. It ired a twelve-pound projectile, also case-shot and canister. The charge for solid projectiles and case was two and a half pounds of owder; for canister, two pounds. This gun had as long range and as accurate as any of the heavier guns of the older models, while he strain of the recoil on the carriage was not nearly so heavy as in the older guns. This yard was always kept in immaculate order.

1861. Likewise, in the manufacture of gunpowder the department had determined there should be an improvement. The sudden strain on the large guns of quick-burning powders had caused some to burst, and the problem confronting the experts was to produce a slow-burning powder that would not cause the great initial strain of the quick-burning kinds, without sacrifice of velocity or range.

As showing the distribution of ordnance supplies at the outbreak of the war, it may be stated there were stored in arsenals in the South about one hundred and thirty-five thousand small arms of all patterns. These fell into the hands of the Confederates, depleting considerably the already small supply for the use of the Union armies.

In verbal reports to the Secretary of War, about the 23d of April, 1861, the chief of ordnance suggested that, in view of the limited capacity of the arsenals, there should be purchased from abroad from fifty thousand to one hundred thousand small arms and eight batteries of rifled cannon. There was no immediate action on this request; on the contrary, efforts were made to encourage the private manufacturers in the Northern States to increase the capacity of their plants. This, it was foreseen, would lead to an endless variety of arms soon being in use in the service, unless special effort was made to provide a uniform pattern. The Springfield model of the United States rifle was then being manufactured at the armories of the Government at a cost of a little less than fourteen dollars, and it was estimated that it could be made in private armories for twelve dollars, so that, with a proper margin of profit, it could be sold to the Government for the cost of manufacture in Government factories. The United States musket then, as nearly always since, had no superior in the world.

The patriotic efforts of the States to assist the general Government were well shown by the action of New York in purchasing, early in 1861, twenty thousand Enfield rifles from England, with an initial purchase of one hundred thousand

LADIES AND OFFICERS IN THE INTERIOR COURT, WASHINGTON ARSENAL

These leisurely ladies and unhurried officers do not betray the feverish activity which existed in the Union Ordnance Department throughout the war. By the latter part of 1860 there were thirteen arsenals, two armories and one depot for the manufacturing and safe-keeping of ordnance and ordnance stores in the United States. There were stored in arsenals in the South about 61,000 small arms of all patterns which fell into the hands of the Confederates. About April 23, 1861, the Chief of Ordnance suggested that, in view of the limited capacity of the arsenals, there should be purchased from abroad from 50,000 to 100,000 small arms and eight batteries of rifled cannon. There was no immediate action on this request. Early in 1861 the State of New York purchased 20,000 Enfield rifles from England, with an initial purchase of 100,000 rounds of ammunition. Efforts were made to encourage the private manufacturers in the Northern States to increase the capacity of their plants, and to provide a uniform pattern. The Springfield model of United States rifle was then the standard. The arsenal was kept in model condition throughout the war. In the yard were stored thousands of heavy and light cannon, with hundreds of thousands of projectiles of every description. Hundreds of extra wheels, besides promiscuous material piled in order, were kept there always ready for issue.

rounds of ammunition. This was followed by an inquiry made of the chief of ordnance to ascertain whether the same ammunition could be manufactured in the Government arsenals, for issue to the troops armed with the Enfield. Necessarily, the answer was "No," and the chief of ordnance, on June 17, 1861, reported to the Secretary of War that the issue of "fancy" arms to troops about to be mustered into the service of the United States was highly undesirable. By the end of December, 1861, however, it was found that the capacity of the various arsenals of the Government was not equal to the great output necessary, and that the practice of buying by contract had to be recognized to a great extent. The States had already sent troops for service armed with numerous patterns of rifles, and it was impracticable to rearm all of them.

On January 25, 1862, the chief of ordnance reported to Secretary Stanton that, under the administration of his predecessor, Secretary Cameron, it had been tentatively decided to have, if possible, but one caliber of rifles, and to cause the necessary changes to be made to accomplish this. It was found that there were in the arsenals but ten thousand rifles of .58-inch caliber, the standard size deemed best for the military service, and it was decided to ream up to that size all arms of less caliber. The Government shops were working to their utmost capacity, and could not make the alterations without serious injury to the necessary business from an interruption of the operations and consequent diminution of the output. Certain private firms took over all the small arms that were to be changed, paid the Government a price almost equal to the original cost price, reamed them to the standard size, put on sword-bayonets, and returned them to the Government at a slight advance, sufficient to cover the cost of the work and give a small margin of profit. Thereby, the service secured a supply of arms that would take the regulation ammunition.

The consensus of expert opinion at the time inclined toward the use of the muzzle-loader in preference to

A 17,000-POUND SEA-COAST MORTAR IN THE WASHINGTON ARSENAL

This leviathan of the shore dwarfs by its size the big guns visible in the background. Some idea of its huge proportions can be gained by figuring its diameter by the height of the man leaning against it. The bore of this mortar was 35.1 inches in length, and the maximum charge was about 75 pounds of powder. It was employed principally for sea-coast fortifications, where it was expected to operate against the decks of vessels, the great weight of the projectiles being exceedingly destructive. These mortars were sometimes used for siege purposes, as at Yorktown, but their great weight made them difficult to move and emplace in temporary works.

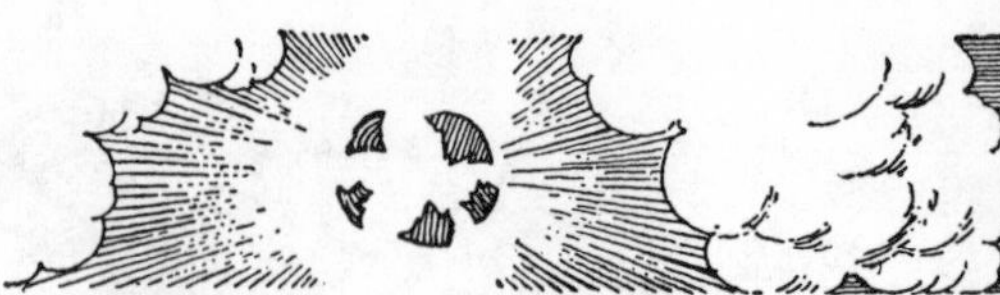

the breech-loading rifle, and the repeaters of the day were considered especially undesirable for military purposes. Those in use were complicated in their mechanism, liable to get out of order, and more difficult of repair than the more simple weapon. Besides, with the repeaters, the ammunition was so heavy and the expenditure so rapid, that the supply was soon exhausted, while, owing to the excessive rapidity of fire, the soldier took less care in aiming, with the net result that the value of his ammunition was much less than by the old method of loading.

The question of a repeating rifle was, however, much discussed. Before the war opened there was no weapon of this type considered altogether suitable for military purposes. Inventors immediately began producing models and improving upon them, and the Government armories afforded favorite places for the work of these men. One of the best models was the Spencer, patented in 1860. This was a very ingenious weapon, which was made at the Harper's Ferry Armory. Compared with a revolver, it was quicker in action and held more cartridges, while having the advantage of the better enclosed rifle construction. In this rifle, for the first time, the problem of a closed breech and barrel, as in a single loader, was successfully solved. Theretofore, rapidity of fire had been associated only with the revolver principle. By operating the lever which formed the trigger-guard, the breech-block was given two motions—one rotary, and the other one of depression. The magazine was a tube in the stock, having a spring which fed the cartridges toward the breech mechanism.

All throughout the war this gun and similar types did splendid service, notwithstanding the fact that the prevailing opinion among ordnance experts was in favor of the muzzle-loader. It is stated that, at Ball's Bluff, one regiment of Confederates was armed with the repeater and did great execution. Due to the use of the Spencer rifle by a part of General Geary's troops at Gettysburg, a whole division of Ewell's corps was

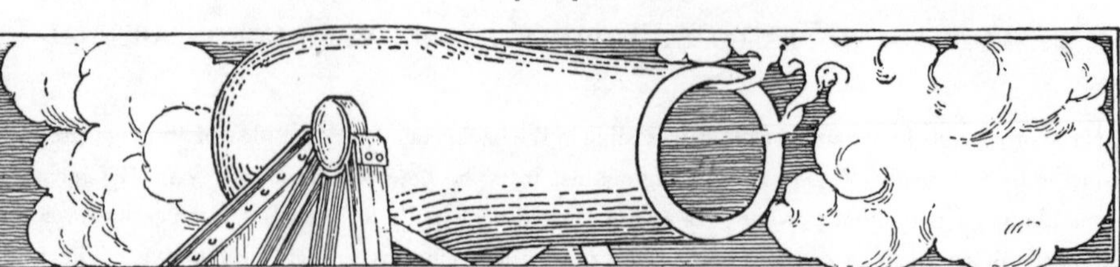

A DAHLGREN 11-INCH SMOOTH-BORE NAVAL GUN, OPPOSITE YORKTOWN

:he Dahlgren guns of large caliber were made of cast iron, solid and cooled from the exterior. The powder-chamber was of the "Gomer" ɔrm—almost a cone with the base forward and of the size of the bore of the gun, so that when the projectile was rammed home it vould not go entirely down to the bottom of the cavity, but would leave a powder-chamber behind it so shaped that the gases had ccess to a greater surface of the projectile than if the bore had been cylindrical to the base. The 11-inch Dahlgren had a bore of 32 inches in length, a maximum diameter of thirty-two inches, and a weight of 16,000 pounds. The service charge of powder was fteen pounds, the maximum twenty pounds, and the weight of the solid shot 170 pounds. It sometimes fired a shell weighing 130 pounds.

A 10-INCH COLUMBIAD IN BATTERY SEMMES

Vith a charge of fifteen pounds of powder this gun, above Farrar's sland on the James River, could throw a shot weighing 123 pounds ,976 yards, or as far as the Dutch Gap Canal, over two miles away.

AN 8-INCH PARROTT AND A RODMAN GUN

In this battery at Yorktown are a pear-shaped Rodman gun and the long slim lines of an 8-inch Parrott in front. The latter is reënforced by an extra part shrunk over the powder chamber.

repulsed by inferior numbers. Of this an eye-witness said, "The head of the column, as it was pushed on by those behind, appeared to melt away or sink into the earth, for though continually moving it got no nearer." In the West, it was found that a regiment armed with the Spencer was more than a match for a division armed with the old Springfield. In 1863, the Winchester was patented, and was an improvement over the former models of repeaters—and from that time to the end of the war these and kindred types were greatly sought after by new regiments going to the front.

During the first part of the war, so great was the demand for muskets that Secretary Stanton approved a recommendation of the chief of ordnance on August 8, 1862, for a somewhat lenient interpretation of the contracts with private establishments delivering small arms. General Ripley stated that it had been found impossible to hold contractors to the literal, strict compliance with all the terms of their contracts. In view of the fact that contractors had expended large sums for equipping their factories, and having in mind the urgent need for great quantities of small arms, as close an inspection at the private factories as in the United States armories was not carried on. Arms were not rejected for small blemishes not impairing the serviceability of the weapon. The main points insisted on were that they should be of standard caliber to take the Government ammunition, and that the stocks, barrels, locks, and other essential parts should be of the strongest quality. Otherwise, the matter of acceptance or rejection was left in the hands of the inspector.

The greatest difficulty was experienced in securing iron for the manufacture of small arms and cannon. Up to August, 1862, a sufficient quantity of American iron could not be procured, and the department was forced to buy abroad. On August 8th of that year, the Secretary of War was informed by the chief of ordnance that the use of American iron was what the ordnance officers were striving for without success.

THE DIVERSITY OF THE FEDERAL ORDNANCE—WIARD GUN BATTERIES

This view of the Washington Arsenal yard shows three batteries of Wiard steel guns. This was only one of many types which added to the complexity of the armaments of the Federal ordnance. It is recorded that the artillery with Rosecrans's army February 8, 1863, included thirty-two 6-pounder smooth-bores, twenty-four 12-pounder howitzers, eight 12-pounder light Napoleons, twenty-one James rifles, thirty-four 10-pounder Wiard steel guns, two 6-pounder Wiard steel guns, two 16-pounder Parrotts, and four 3-inch rifle ordnance guns. Of the batteries here shown, two were rejected on account of reported defects in the guns.

A 6-POUNDER WIARD—A MODERN-APPEARING TYPE

Every inducement had been offered to manufacturers to prepare iron of a suitable quality; the highest prices had been offered, and a great many samples had been tested. Whenever American iron of acceptable quality was presented, it was always used in preference to foreign iron, other things being equal. The chief of ordnance stated that he had no doubt there was a sufficient quantity of good American material, but up to that time the producer had not furnished it, and a resort to foreign markets was a necessity.

The difficulties experienced with small arms were repeated with the ammunition. When the Army of the Potomac took the field in the middle of March, 1862, for the Peninsula campaign, the Ordnance Department held, at the Washington Arsenal, sixteen million five hundred thousand rounds of small-arms ammunition, for five different kinds of arms, in reserve. This ammunition was for smooth-bore muskets, caliber .58; foreign muskets of various makes, caliber .577, and nondescript, unclassified muskets, caliber .54. For carbines and pistols of various kinds, one million rounds were in reserve. For artillery there were sixty-four thousand two hundred projectiles for three kinds of 6-pounders, three kinds of 12-pounders, and one kind each of 10-, 20-, 24-, and 32-pounders. The mere mention of these various classifications is sufficient to indicate the strain under which the department was laboring. But this task was met and well done, for history seldom records a shortage of ammunition that could be traced to the ordnance officers.

In February, 1863, there were on hand in the ordnance armories and arsenals nearly one hundred and thirty-seven million rounds of small-arms ammunition, and up to that time, since the opening of the war, nearly fifty-five million pounds of lead had been purchased for use in making bullets.

The development of rifled cannon was in an experimental stage when the war opened. There had been a decided movement toward the adoption of these guns in 1859, simultaneously

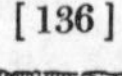

THE BIGGEST GUN OF ALL—THE 20-INCH MONSTER FOR WHICH NO TARGET WOULD SERVE

A photograph of the only 20-inch gun made during the war. It weighed 117,000 pounds. On March 30, 1861, a 15-inch Columbiad was heralded in *Harper's Weekly* as the biggest gun in the world, but three years later this was exceeded. In 1844 Lieutenant (later Brigadier-General) Thomas Jefferson Rodman of the Ordnance Department commenced a series of tests to find a way to obviate the injurious strains set up in the metal, by cooling a large casting from the exterior. He finally developed his theory of casting a gun with the core hollow and then cooling it by a stream of water or cold air through it. So successful was this method that the War Department, in 1860, authorized a 15-inch smooth-bore gun. It proved a great success. General Rodman then projected his 20-inch smooth-bore gun, which was made in 1864 under his direction at Fort Pitt, Pittsburg, Pennsylvania. It was mounted at Fort Hamilton, New York Harbor, very soon afterwards, but on account of the tremendous size and destructive effect of its projectiles it was fired only four times during the war. It was almost impossible to get a target that would withstand the shots and leave anything to show what had happened. These four shots were fired with 50, 75, 100 and 125 pounds of powder. The projectile weighed 1,080 pounds, and the maximum pressure on the bore was 25,000 pounds. In March, 1867, it was again fired four times with 125, 150, 175 and 200 pounds of powder, each time with an elevation of twenty-five degrees, the projectile attaining a maximum range of 8,001 yards. This is no mean record even compared with twentieth century pieces.

THE BIGGEST GUN IN THE WORLD.

We publish on page 205 an accurate drawing of the great Fifteen-inch Gun at Fort Monroe, Virginia; and also a picture, from a recent sketch, showing the experiments which are being made with a view to test it. It is proper that we should say that the small drawing is from the lithograph which is published in Major Barnard's "Notes on Sea-Coast Defense," published by Mr. D. Van Nostrand, of this city.

This gun was cast at Pittsburgh, Pennsylvania, by Knapp, Rudd, & Co., under the directions of Captain T. J. Rodman, of the Ordnance Corps. Its dimensions are as follows:

Total length	190	inches.
Length of calibre of bore	156	"
Length of ellipsoidal chamber	9	"
Total length of bore	165	"
Maximum exterior diameter	48	"

NEWS OF MARCH 30, 1861

with their introduction into the foreign services. Prior to that time, artillerists and inventors had directed their attention to the production of a projectile on the expanding system. This method of making the projectile take the rifling had been more or less successful with the bullet, and it was hoped that a device could be invented which would permit the use of the same principle with larger projectiles. The board of rifled ordnance, in 1859, expressed an opinion that such would be the case, with the exception of one member, who recommended the continuation of experiments with flanged projectiles and similar types. However, the Charrin projectile, an expanding type, was adopted at first, but proved to be unsatisfactory and was withdrawn. The introduction of rifled cannon did not simplify the question of calibers.

Up to the summer of 1862, there were made, in the arsenals of the Government and in certain private establishments, bronze rifled guns of 3.67 and 3.8 inches, and large numbers of iron rifled cannon of 2.9 and 3.0 inches. There had been already both smooth-bore and rifled guns of 4.62 inches, and guns of 4.5 inches were also made. The great objection to the smaller calibers was that the range was needlessly great, and the shell too small to be of practical value. With the system of expanding projectiles at first adopted, the question of exact calibers was not of such great importance, for by the method used for accommodating the projectile to the rifling, the same shot could be used for both the 3.67-inch and the 3.8-inch gun.

Bronze had been adopted as a standard metal for field-guns in 1841, and served the purpose excellently until the introduction of rifled cannon, when the increased strain due to the imparting of the rotary motion to the projectile proved too great, and the metal was too soft to stand the wear on the rifling. It was then found that wrought iron served the purpose best, and of this material 3-inch muzzle-loading guns were made. On the introduction of breech-loaders, forged steel proved to be more satisfactory. However, many Parrott rifled

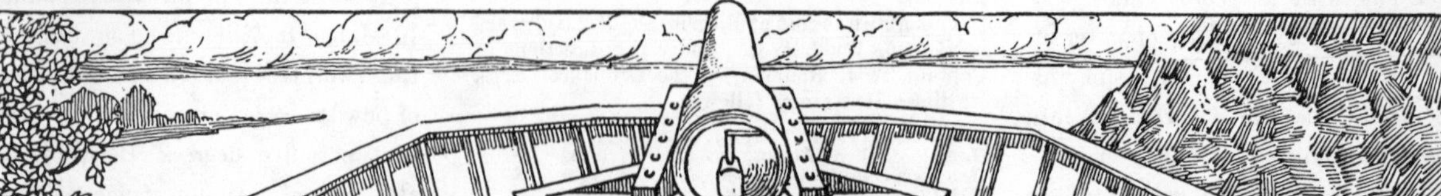

HANDLING HEAVY GUNS—TOWING A PIECE FROM A CONFEDERATE BATTERY ON THE JAMES

It was no slight task to move the heavy ordnance, after the James River was opened and Richmond had fallen. The barge in the upper photograph has sunk deep into the water and lists heavily. A crowd of men are busy handling it. The tripod at Broadway Landing in the lower photograph had legs about as thick as the body of a man, but it looks none too large to handle the big guns lying beneath. Judging from the height of the sentry standing by its left leg, the guns are ten feet long. Both of them are reënforced at the breech.

A TRIPOD SWINGING PARROTT GUNS BY THE APPOMATTOX, AT BROADWAY LANDING

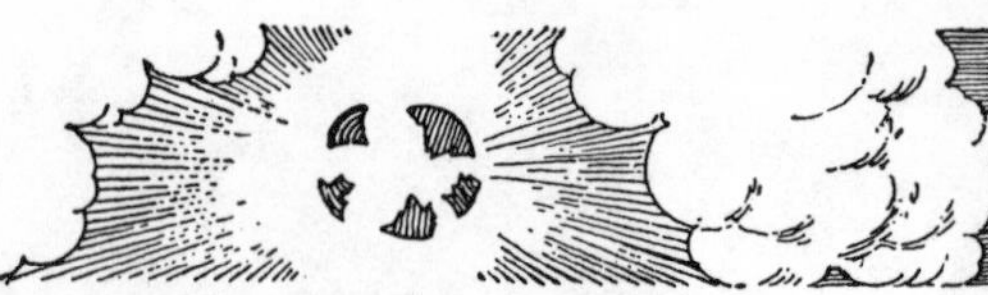

cast-iron field-guns were successfully used. These received a reenforcement of wrought iron shrunk around the base. A considerable number of the bronze Napoleon guns were, however, retained, and did effective service at short ranges.

For heavier ordnance cast iron was early found to be the most suitable material, and proved entirely satisfactory until the adoption of the rifled systems. The American smooth-bore type of ordnance was the best in the world. In 1860, the Ordnance Department adopted Colonel Rodman's method of interior cooling of a hollow cast tube, and in 1863 the extreme effort was made to produce a heavy gun, resulting in a successful 20-inch smooth-bore throwing a shot weighing 1080 pounds. The heavy rifled guns of the Civil War period were somewhat untrustworthy, however, and many accidents resulted. In consequence, their use was limited principally to those built on the Parrott principle, and the great mass of the heavy artillery used by the Union armies was of the smooth-bore type.

The expenditures of the Government on account of the Ordnance Department for the fiscal year ending June 30, 1863, were over $42,300,000. The principal purchases that were made during the year consisted of 1577 field-, siege-, and sea-coast cannon, 1,082,841 muskets, 282,389 carbines and pistols, over 1,250,000 cannon-balls and shells, over 48,700,000 pounds of lead, and over 259,000,000 cartridges for small arms, in addition to nearly 6,000,000 pounds of powder.

These purchases were made necessary by the fact that the arsenals and armories under the direct control of the department were not able to produce all of this immense quantity of war matériel. But the progress toward obtaining greater facilities for the production of these supplies was very great. The Secretary of War, in his report of the operations of the War Department for 1863, made note especially of the tremendous work done by the ordnance officers and the personnel under their direct charge. He stated that the resources of the country for the production of arms and

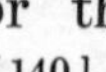

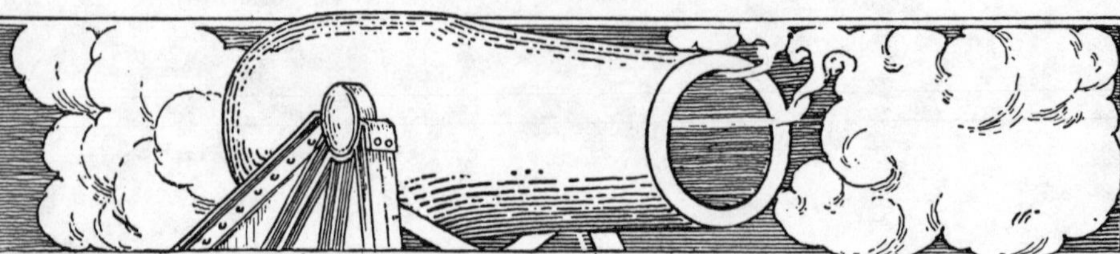

BRINGING UP THE MORTARS AT BUTLER'S CROW'S NEST

So annoying to the Union force at Dutch Gap, digging the canal in 1864, did the fire of the Confederate batteries become, that a battery and lookout were established above the canal. The upper photograph shows the big mortars of the battery being placed in position. They are old style 10-inch mortars and very difficult to handle. A lookout with a crow's-nest on top can be seen in the trees. This is where the signal men did their work. During the imprisonment of the Confederate fleet above Chaffin's Bluff, their crews and officers served ashore. So close were the Confederate batteries that with a spy-glass some naval officers actually recognized some of their former companions in the Federal service. That it was no easy task to install this battery is clear from the gigantic paraphernalia to move big guns, shown in the lower photograph. This was a giant sling-cart used by the Federals in removing captured ordnance from the batteries on the James River below Richmond, after there was no more use for the battery shown above. By means of this apparatus the heaviest siege and sea-coast cannon could be moved. The cart was placed over the piece, ropes run under the trunnions and the cascabel, or knob, on the rear of the gun, and a large pole placed in the muzzle for the accommodation of another rope.

A SLING CART MOVING A HEAVY GUN

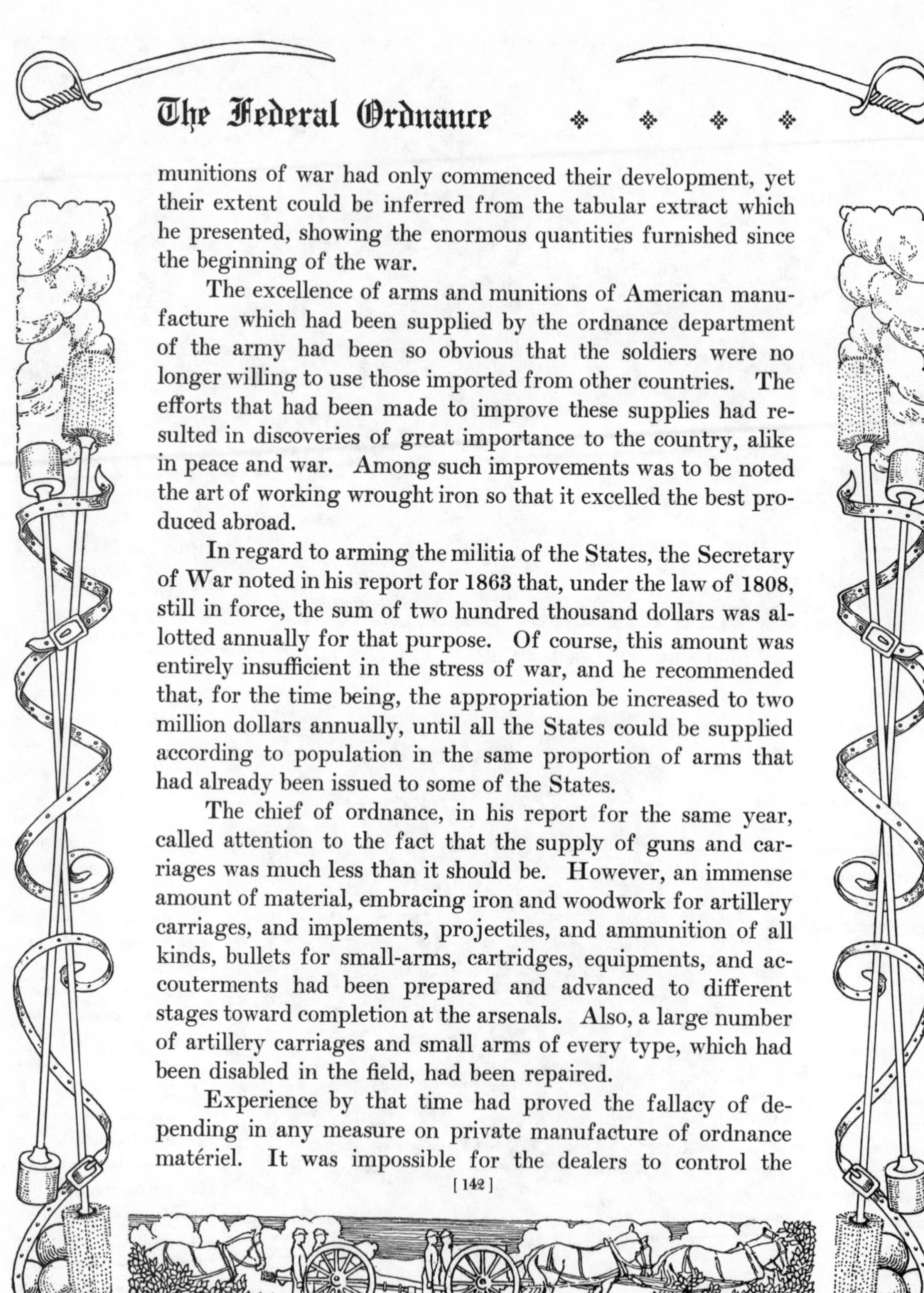

munitions of war had only commenced their development, yet their extent could be inferred from the tabular extract which he presented, showing the enormous quantities furnished since the beginning of the war.

The excellence of arms and munitions of American manufacture which had been supplied by the ordnance department of the army had been so obvious that the soldiers were no longer willing to use those imported from other countries. The efforts that had been made to improve these supplies had resulted in discoveries of great importance to the country, alike in peace and war. Among such improvements was to be noted the art of working wrought iron so that it excelled the best produced abroad.

In regard to arming the militia of the States, the Secretary of War noted in his report for 1863 that, under the law of 1808, still in force, the sum of two hundred thousand dollars was allotted annually for that purpose. Of course, this amount was entirely insufficient in the stress of war, and he recommended that, for the time being, the appropriation be increased to two million dollars annually, until all the States could be supplied according to population in the same proportion of arms that had already been issued to some of the States.

The chief of ordnance, in his report for the same year, called attention to the fact that the supply of guns and carriages was much less than it should be. However, an immense amount of material, embracing iron and woodwork for artillery carriages, and implements, projectiles, and ammunition of all kinds, bullets for small-arms, cartridges, equipments, and accouterments had been prepared and advanced to different stages toward completion at the arsenals. Also, a large number of artillery carriages and small arms of every type, which had been disabled in the field, had been repaired.

Experience by that time had proved the fallacy of depending in any measure on private manufacture of ordnance matériel. It was impossible for the dealers to control the

ROWS OF FEDERAL ORDNANCE AT THE BROADWAY LANDING DEPOT, 1865

In the background are Parrott and Brooke rifles—the former belonging to the Federal army and the latter captured from the Confederates. To the left are lighter field-guns, some rifles, and some smooth-bores. The small, low carriages in front of the field-pieces are for small mortars. Two Rodman smooth-bores are lying dismounted on the ground. There is a marked difference between the heavy Parrott, probably a 100-pounder, in the traveling position on the carriage at the right of the photograph and the howitzer on the small carriage alongside. This photograph gives some idea of the tremendous output of the Union ordnance department during the latter years of the war. In the year ending June 30, 1864, it spent $38,500,000, and the supplies produced included 1,750 caissons and carriages, 802,525 small arms, 8,409,400 pounds of powder, nearly 1,700,000 projectiles for cannon, and nearly 169,500,000 rounds of small-arms ammunition, besides miscellaneous supplies. In the lower left-hand corner are some sling carts to handle the smaller guns.

fluctuation in the market of labor and raw material, even if they so desired, and no private establishment could afford to carry on hand a large stock of ordnance stores such as would meet possible demands from the Government. Warned by repeated failures to procure supplies, the chief of ordnance had taken energetic measures, as far as the funds appropriated would permit, to enlarge the principal arsenals, viz.: Watertown, Massachusetts; Watervliet, West Troy, New York; Allegheny, Pennsylvania; St. Louis, Missouri; Washington, and Benicia, California.

Owing to the development of the resources of the United States, less material had been purchased abroad during the year ending June 30, 1863, than at previous periods of the war, and the Ordnance Department determined that still less should be acquired in Europe in the future. The only articles of which there appeared to be a possible lack were sulphur and saltpeter. During the year the reserve supply of saltpeter had been held intact, and all the powder necessary had been purchased, while the supply of sulphur had been augmented.

In the matter of small arms, the country, by June 30, 1863, was entirely independent. The supply from the Springfield Armory alone was capable of equipping two hundred and fifty thousand troops a year, and the private manufacturers were fully able to supply two hundred and fifty thousand more. Of carbines for cavalry, the capacity of established factories under contract with the Government was at least one hundred thousand annually, and of pistols not less than three hundred thousand.

The duties of officers commanding armories and arsenals and their responsibilities were almost without limitation, involving the control and disbursement of vast quantities of the public money, and the supervision of almost every branch of the mechanic arts. The department, due to the untiring energies of its personnel, both commissioned and enlisted, aided by the large body of civilian employees in service, had been able

A MAMMOTH SEA-COAST CANNON AIMED BY WOODEN WEDGES—1861

This Rodman smooth-bore gun in Port Royal, South Carolina, is mounted on a wooden carriage of a type prevalent during the war. These carriages were sufficiently strong to carry the guns of that time, being made of selected oak, beech, ash, hickory, cypress, or some other durable and resisting wood; but at the close of the war the increased size and power of the guns had surpassed the strength of the old carriages, and the Ordnance Department was confronted with the problem of replacing all the old carriages and making iron carriages for the guns then in process of construction. The elevating device seen on this carriage is primitive, consisting of wooden wedges to be inserted, one on top of another, until the required elevation of the breach was obtained. The recoil on firing sent the piece back, and it was loaded in its recoil position. The piece was returned "in battery" by inserting the bars in the holes in the wheels of the upper carriage. The piece is centered on a pivot, and wheels running on the circular track allow it to be "traversed." This was known as a "center-pintle" carriage. It could be revolved in a complete circle.

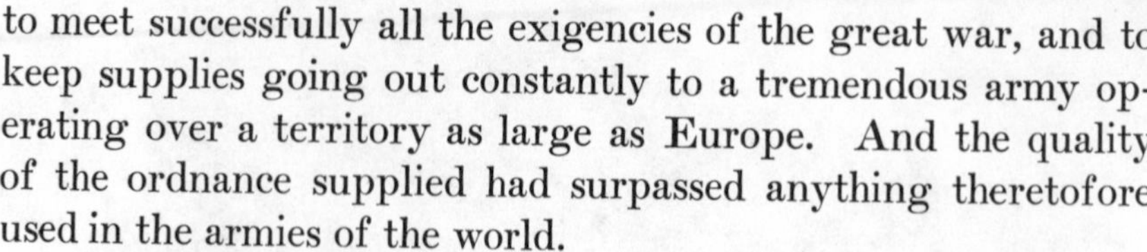

to meet successfully all the exigencies of the great war, and to keep supplies going out constantly to a tremendous army operating over a territory as large as Europe. And the quality of the ordnance supplied had surpassed anything theretofore used in the armies of the world.

During the year ending June 30, 1863, over twenty thousand officers had been accountable to the department for ordnance and ordnance stores, and over eighty thousand returns should have been made to the office of the chief of ordnance. All of the accounts rendered for supplies had to be carefully checked, and this involved an immense amount of labor. Many of the returns that were due were not submitted by officers in the field, however, their time being fully occupied with the sterner duties of war.

The activities of the department required an expenditure for the next year of over $38,500,000. The supplies produced included 1760 pieces of ordnance, 2361 artillery caissons and carriages, 802,525 small arms, 8,409,400 pounds of powder, nearly 1,700,000 projectiles for cannon, and nearly 169,500,000 rounds of small-arms ammunition, besides miscellaneous supplies. In addition to this, large quantities of matériel were repaired after service in the field.

The capacity of the arsenals for the production of munitions was vastly increased, as far as the amount of the Congressional appropriations would permit. By this time, the superiority of the articles fabricated in the Government workshops had received unanimous recognition, and the increased facilities had enabled these factories to reduce the cost below that of private manufacture. The Springfield Armory could, by June 30, 1864, turn out three hundred thousand of the finest muskets in the world, annually, and the arsenal at Rock Island, Illinois, was under construction, and promised a great addition to the capacity of the Ordnance Department. There were, in the hands of troops in the field, one and one-quarter million small arms, and the stock on hand in the armories and

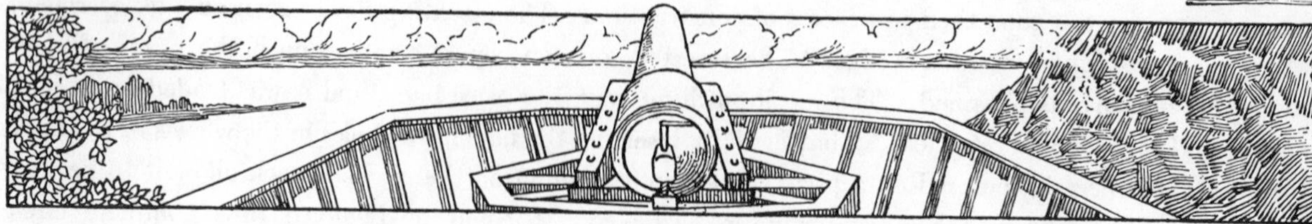

PULASKI'S PARAPETS AFTER THE CAPTURE

ne of the first siege exploits of General Quincy A. Gillmore was the reduction of Fort Pulaski, at the mouth of the Savannah River, hich fell April 11, 1862. The upper photograph shows the Third Rhode Island Artillery at drill in the fort, and the lower shows attery A, looking toward Tybee. Behind the parapet is part of the remains of the covered way used by the Confederates during the ombardment. The parapets have been repaired, all is in order, and a lady in the costume of the day graces the fort with her presence. ulaski mounted forty-eight guns in all. Twenty bore upon Tybee Island, from which the bombardment was conducted. They cluded five 10-inch Columbiads, nine 8-inch Columbiads, three 42-pounders, three 10-inch mortars, one 12-inch mortar, one 24-ounder howitzer, two 12-pounder howitzers, twenty 32-pounders, and two 4½-inch Blakely rifled guns. Against these General Gillmore rought six 10-inch and four 8-inch Columbiads, five 30-pounder Parrotts, twelve 13-inch and four 10-inch siege mortars, and one 8-pounder, two 64-pounder and two 84-pounder James rifles. The most distant of the batteries on Tybee Island was 3,400 yards om the fort, and the nearest 1,650. Modern siege-guns can be effective at a dozen miles. Modern field artillery has a maximum ffective range of 6,000 yards. In the Civil War the greatest effective range of field artillery was about 2,500 yards, with rifled pieces.

arsenals available for issue had been increased to three-quarters of a million.

The introduction of breech-loaders for the military service throughout was now very generally recommended. The success of the Spencer, the Sharp, and some other types of repeaters had brought them prominently to notice. The great objections to the breech-loading small arm, in addition to that heretofore mentioned, were that these pieces were heavier than the muzzle-loaders, did not shoot as accurately, were more expensive, and more liable to get out of repair. Besides, dampness penetrated between the barrel and the breech; there was greater risk of bursting; the cartridges were troublesome to make and expensive to buy; the ammunition was heavier, and the projecting pin of the cartridge, then thought a necessity, was liable to cause an explosion by being accidentally struck.

When the war closed, the activities of the Ordnance Department were at their height. Forty-three million one hundred and twelve thousand dollars were spent during the last year, and the main efforts were directed toward providing the same types of matériel that had theretofore been supplied. The manufacture of arms at the national armories was reduced as rapidly as consistent with the economic interests of the Government. With a view to changing the old muzzle-loaders to breech-loaders, extensive experiments were made, but had not, by that time, produced any satisfactory results. The Secretary of War recognized that the importance of the matter demanded that time be taken in reaching a decision, and insisted that no model which had defects of well-known character be accepted. The department had permitted about five thousand of the Springfields to be altered to suit a plan tentatively adopted, and these rifles were issued to troops, but at the time of the cessation of hostilities these were still undergoing tests, and the plan had not been found satisfactory.

There were one million Springfields on hand in the armories, and about one-half million captured muskets of domestic

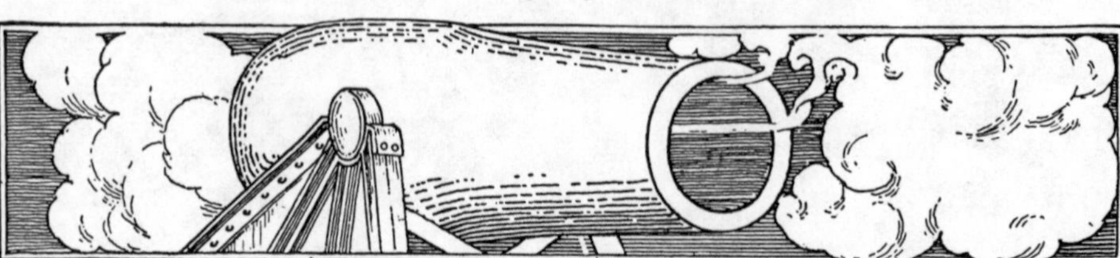

McCLELLAN'S GUNS AND GUNNERS READY TO LEAVE YORKTOWN

This photograph of May, 1862, shows artillery that accompanied McClellan to the Peninsula, parked near the lower wharf at Yorktown after the Confederates evacuated that city. The masts of the transports, upon which the pieces are to be loaded, rise in the background. On the shore stand the serried ranks of the Parrott guns. In the foreground are the little Coehorn mortars, of short range, but accurate. When the Army of the Potomac embarked early in April, 1862, fifty-two batteries of 259 guns went with that force. Later Franklin's division of McDowell's Corps joined McClellan with four batteries of twenty-two guns, and, a few days before the battle of Mechanicsville, McCall's division of McDowell's Corps joined with an equal number of batteries and guns. This made a grand total of sixty field batteries, or 353 guns, with the Federal forces. In the background is part of a wagon train beginning to load the vessels.

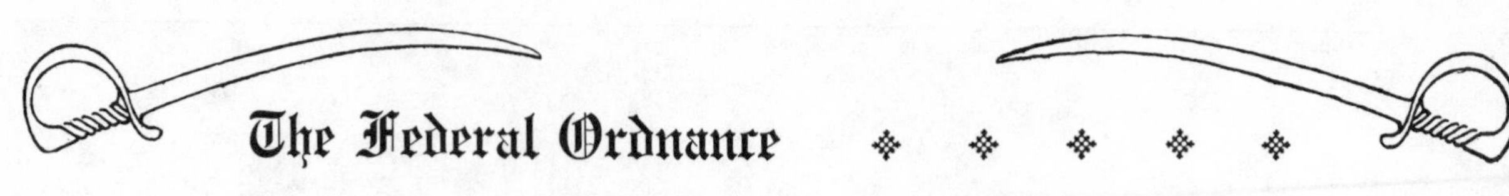

and foreign make. All the latter were being sold as fast as suitable prices could be obtained, and ordnance stores of a perishable nature were also being disposed of.

All the Southern arsenals that had been in the hands of the Confederate forces were reoccupied by the Union authorities, except that at Fayetteville, North Carolina, which had been destroyed. The Confederates also had a powder-mill at Augusta, Georgia, and a laboratory and an unfinished armory at Macon, Georgia. These had been captured, and were occupied by the Federal Ordnance Department.

The evident importance of arming permanent fortifications as fast as they were built, required the construction of cannon and carriages for that purpose as far as the appropriations would permit. The construction of the forts had proceeded faster than the equipment of them, on account of the difficulty in finding suitable cannon to meet the increasingly exacting conditions of warfare. Wooden carriages had been used for many sea-coast guns, but the increased size and power of these weapons had surpassed the strength of the old carriages, and at the close of the war the Ordnance Department was confronted with the problem of replacing all the old carriages and making iron carriages for the guns then in process of construction. Cast-iron smooth-bore cannon of the largest caliber had been found entirely practicable. The rifled guns had not proved as efficient, however. Up to that time no rifled guns had been built that would fulfil all the requirements of service, and many ordnance experts had concluded that the type was impracticable. Wrought-iron guns had been tried and found to be failures, and it was decided that no more of them would be bought or made.

Experiments that were carried on at Fort Monroe to test the power and endurance of 8- and 10-inch rifled guns of cast iron, made by the department, were, however, highly satisfactory, and warranted the belief that cast-iron guns of these calibers might be introduced into the service with safety and

LIGHT FIELD GUNS—A PIECE OF "HENRY'S BATTERY," BEFORE SUMTER IN 1863

Battery B of the First United States Artillery became known as "Henry's Battery" from the name of its young commander, Lieutenant Guy V. Henry (afterward a brigadier-general; later still a conspicuous figure in the Spanish-American War). It took part in the siege operations against Forts Wagner and Gregg on Morris Island, and against Sumter and Charleston, from July to September, 1863. Bronze had been adopted as a standard metal for field guns in 1841, and many of the field batteries were equipped with bronze 12-pounder napoleons. The metal proved too soft to stand the additional wear on rifled guns, however, and it was then found that wrought iron served the purpose best. Later forged steel proved more satisfactory for breech loaders.

AFTER THE ATTEMPT ON SUMTER—THIRD NEW YORK LIGHT ARTILLERY

NAPOLEON GUN IN BATTERY NO. 2, FORT WHIPPLE

The lush, waving grass beautifies this Union fort, one of the finest examples of fortification near Washington. The piece of ordnance are in splendid condition. The men at the guns are soldierly but easy in their attitudes. They are evidently well-drilled crews. The forked pennant of the artillery flies defiantly above the parapet. But there are no longer any Con federates to defy. The nation is again under one flag, as former Confederate leaders proved by leading Union troops to victory in 1898 Fort Whipple was a mile and a half southwest of the Virginia end of the Aqueduct bridge. It was a "semi-permanent" field work completely closed, having emplacements for forty-one heavy guns. The gun in the foreground is a 12-pounder smooth-bore, a Napo-

PEACE AT THE DEFENSES OF WASHINGTON

leon. During four years it has been carefully oiled, its yawning muzzle has been swabbed out with care, and a case has been put over it to keep it from rusting in foul weather. In the case of larger guns, the muzzles were stopped up with tampions. Now the rust may come, and cobwebs may form over the muzzle, for nearly fifty years have passed and Americans have fought side by side, but never again against each other. As splendidly as the Confederates fought, as nobly as they bore themselves during the Civil War, still more splendid, still more noble has been their bearing since under the common flag. Nothing could add more luster to their fame than the pride and dignity with which they not only accepted the reunion of the parted nation, but have since rejoiced in it and fought for it.

advantage. A 12-inch rifle was also under test, and had been fired, by the time the war closed, three hundred and ninety times, with a charge of powder weighing fifty-five pounds, and throwing a 600-pound projectile. This was almost conclusive in favor of the gun. Some of the large Parrott rifles used in the siege of Charleston showed remarkable endurance—one of them, a 4.2-inch 30-pounder having fired four thousand six hundred and six rounds before bursting.

After the great pressure of war was over, the department undertook the duties of cleaning, repairing, preserving, and storing the tremendous quantities of war matériel that had accumulated. Fire-proof warehouses were constructed at Watervliet, Frankfort, and Allegheny arsenals, three great magazines were constructed at St. Louis Arsenal, and one each at Washington and Benicia arsenals. The Harper's Ferry Armory had suffered so much in the stress of war that it was in bad repair, and was abandoned. At the Springfield Armory, the work was confined to cleaning, repairing, and storing the small arms used during the conflict, and to making preparations for the conversion of the old Springfield muskets, the best in the world of their kind, into rifled breech-loaders, the new type which the experience of war had brought into being.

France had sent an army into Mexico. The United States declared this a violation of the Monroe Doctrine, and the issue was doubtful. The Ordnance Department expected further trouble, but was fully prepared for it. The able officers of the department and the devoted personnel under their direction had made an institution unsurpassed in history. Be it for peace or war, no concern was felt for the outcome, for arms, equipments, and miscellaneous stores for nearly two million men were ready for issue, or already in the hands of troops. This was the net result of the great labors of the men of the department. But France realized the power of the United States, withdrew her forces from the support of Maximilian, and the crisis was past.

VII

ORDNANCE OF THE CONFEDERACY

EARLY CONFEDERATE ORDNANCE — WHAT REMAINED IN 1863 OF THE FAMOUS "FLOATING BATTERY" THAT AIDED THE SOUTH CAROLINIANS TO DRIVE ANDERSON AND HIS MEN OUT OF SUMTER IN 1861

THE ORDNANCE OF THE CONFEDERACY

By J. W. Mallet

Lieutenant-Colonel, Confederate States Army, and Superintendent of the Ordnance Laboratories of the Confederate States

And O. E. Hunt

Captain, United States Army

AT the beginning of the Civil War the Confederate States had very few improved small arms, no powder-mills of any importance, very few modern cannon, and only the small arsenals that had been captured from the Federal Government. These were at Charleston, Augusta, Mount Vernon (Alabama), Baton Rouge, and Apalachicola. The machinery that was taken from Harper's Ferry Armory after its abandonment by the Federals was removed to Richmond, Virginia, and Fayetteville, North Carolina, where it was set up and operated. There were some State armories containing a few small arms and a few old pieces of heavy ordnance. There was scarcely any gunpowder except about sixty thousand pounds of old cannon-powder at Norfolk. There was almost an entire lack of other ordnance stores—no saddles and bridles, no artillery harness, no accouterments, and very few of the minor articles required for the equipment of an army. There was a considerable number of heavy sea-coast guns at the fortified seaports, and others were seized on board men-of-war at Norfolk and among the stores of the Norfolk Navy-Yard. The supply of field-pieces amounted to almost nothing. The States owned a few modern guns, but the most of those on hand were old iron guns, used in the war of 1812–15.

CONFEDERATE CANNON—IMPORTED, MANUFACTURED, ADOPTED AND INVENTED

IMPORTED FROM FRANCE

"RIFLES" INVENTED BY JOHN M. BROOKE, C. S. N.

AN OLD COLUMBIAD IRON BANDS ADDED

The French 12-pounder bronze field-guns in the top photograph were made by Le Place Frères in Paris. They weighed 1,200 pounds and fired a projectile weighing 25¼ pounds with a charge of 2½ pounds of powder. The Southern output was large, of the bronze 12-pounders known as Napoleons. During 1863 and 1864, no less than 110 of these were manufactured at the Augusta arsenal under the direction of General George W. Rains of the Confederate ordnance service. In the lower photograph is an old cast-iron Columbiad, strengthened at the Tredegar Iron Works at Richmond, by the addition of iron bands, after the manner of the Brooke heavy artillery invented by John M. Brooke, formerly of the United States navy, the designer of the ironclad *Virginia*—better known as the *Merrimac*. The gun in the middle of the second photograph is a light Brooke rifle—a 3-inch gun. Its length was about seventy inches, the diameter of the barrel at the muzzle was eleven inches, and the piece weighed nearly 900 pounds. The weight of the projectile was ten pounds with a powder charge of one pound. The maximum effective range of these guns was 3,500 yards, and the time of flight fifteen seconds, with an elevation of fifteen degrees.

In the arsenals captured from the Federals, there were about one hundred and twenty thousand muskets of old types, and twelve thousand to fifteen thousand rifles. In addition to these, the States had a few muskets, bringing the total available supply of small arms for infantry up to about one hundred and fifty thousand. With this handicap, the States entered the greatest war in American history. President Jefferson Davis said that "it soon became evident to all that the South had gone to war without counting the cost."

At first, all the ordnance and ordnance supplies of the United States in the Southern arsenals and armories were claimed by the States in which they were found. This caused no little delay in the acquisition of necessary ordnance stores by the Confederate Government, due to the necessity for negotiating for their transfer. The first steps toward provision for ordnance needs were taken while the Government was still at Montgomery, Alabama. An Ordnance Department was organized. Colonel Josiah Gorgas, a graduate of the United States Military Academy in the class of 1841, was appointed chief of ordnance about the end of February, 1861. The department immediately sent out purchasing-officers. Of these, Commander Raphael Semmes (afterward Admiral Semmes) was sent to New York, where, for a few weeks, he was able to buy ordnance stores in considerable quantity and ship them to the South; and Colonel Caleb Huse was soon afterward sent to London to act as general purchasing-agent in England and on the European continent. He remained on this duty throughout the war, and did invaluable service to the Confederate cause.

The seat of the Confederate Government having been moved to Richmond, Colonel Gorgas there proceeded to organize the center of activity of the Ordnance Department. There were four main sources of supply: arms on hand at the beginning of the war, those captured from the United States, those manufactured in the Confederacy, and those imported

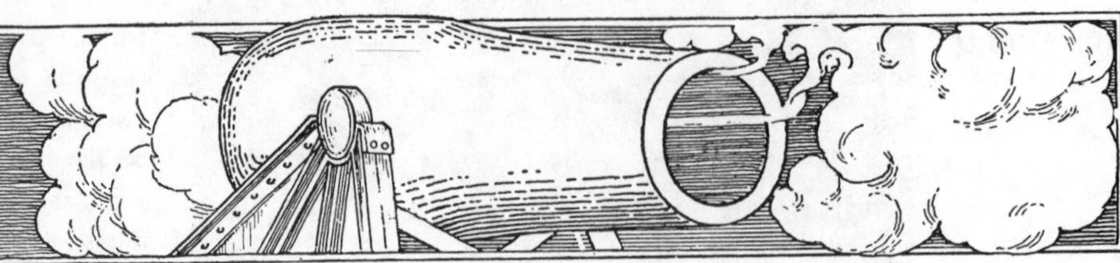

GUNS JUST SEIZED BY CONFEDERATES—1861

he photograph of the cannoneers in their hickory shirts, and the long line of cannon, was taken by J. D. Edwards of New Orleans. his is one of the Confederate sand-bag batteries bearing on Fort Pickens. The Northern administration not only failed to take steps ; the outset of the war to protect the great navy-yard at Norfolk, but it also surrendered that at Pensacola. The former could have een retained had the incoming administration acted more promptly. With the loss of these two great establishments to the Union ent some thousands of cannon which aided immensely to arm the Southern batteries. This was one more source from which the onfederacy secured her guns. All of the big guns in the coastwise forts were old-time Columbiads placed there in 1856.

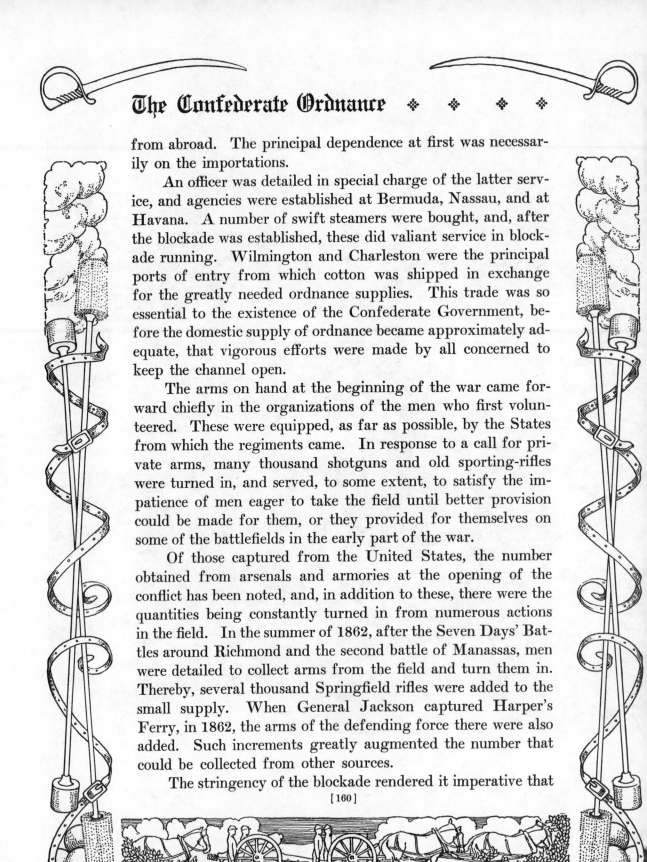

from abroad. The principal dependence at first was necessarily on the importations.

An officer was detailed in special charge of the latter service, and agencies were established at Bermuda, Nassau, and at Havana. A number of swift steamers were bought, and, after the blockade was established, these did valiant service in blockade running. Wilmington and Charleston were the principal ports of entry from which cotton was shipped in exchange for the greatly needed ordnance supplies. This trade was so essential to the existence of the Confederate Government, before the domestic supply of ordnance became approximately adequate, that vigorous efforts were made by all concerned to keep the channel open.

The arms on hand at the beginning of the war came forward chiefly in the organizations of the men who first volunteered. These were equipped, as far as possible, by the States from which the regiments came. In response to a call for private arms, many thousand shotguns and old sporting-rifles were turned in, and served, to some extent, to satisfy the impatience of men eager to take the field until better provision could be made for them, or they provided for themselves on some of the battlefields in the early part of the war.

Of those captured from the United States, the number obtained from arsenals and armories at the opening of the conflict has been noted, and, in addition to these, there were the quantities being constantly turned in from numerous actions in the field. In the summer of 1862, after the Seven Days' Battles around Richmond and the second battle of Manassas, men were detailed to collect arms from the field and turn them in. Thereby, several thousand Springfield rifles were added to the small supply. When General Jackson captured Harper's Ferry, in 1862, the arms of the defending force there were also added. Such increments greatly augmented the number that could be collected from other sources.

The stringency of the blockade rendered it imperative that

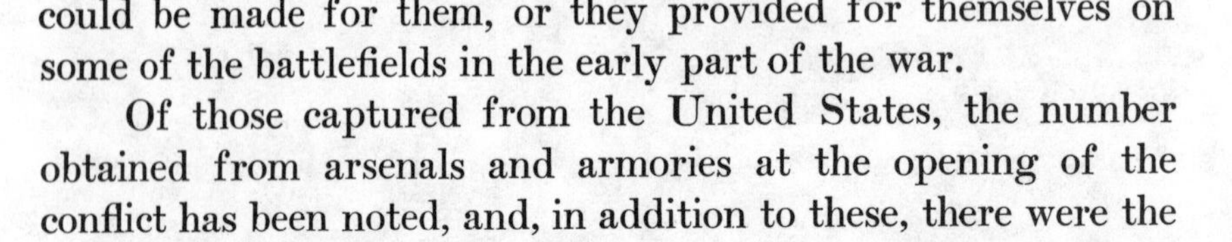

CHIEF OF THE

CONFEDERATE

ORDNANCE

DEPARTMENT

Colonel (later Brigadier-General) Josiah Gorgas served as chief of ordnance of the Confederate States Army throughout the war. He it was who sent Colonel (later Brigadier - General) George W. Rains to Augusta to build the great powder-plant. Facing an apparently insuperable difficulty, in the matter of ammunition, Rains resorted to first principles by collecting 200,000 pounds of lead in Charleston from window-weights, and as much more from lead pipes in Mobile, thus furnishing the South essential means of prolonging the war.

BRIGADIER–GENERAL JOSIAH GORGAS

Julius A. de Lagnel was made captain of the Artillery Corps on March 16, 1861, and major of the Twentieth Battalion of Virginia Artillery, July 3, 1862. He was appointed brigadier-general of the provisional Army of the Confederate States, April 15, 1862, but declined the appointment. During most of his service he was in the ordnance bureau at Richmond, Virginia, ably seconding Colonel Gorgas.

MAJOR JULIUS A. DE LAGNEL

AN ORDNANCE

OFFICER

OF HIGH

RESOURCEFULNESS

every effort be made to increase the domestic manufacture of all kinds of ordnance and ordnance stores. In arranging for the manufacture of arms and munitions at home, establishments of two different kinds were placed in operation: those which were intended to be permanent, built and equipped for their special purpose and intended to concentrate work on a large scale, and those of a more temporary character, capable of yielding results in the shortest time, and intended to meet the immediate demands of the war, with such resources as the country then afforded.

The first of the permanent works undertaken was a first-class powder-mill, the erection and equipment of which were placed in charge of Colonel George W. Rains, of North Carolina, a graduate of the United States Military Academy in the class of 1842. The mill was placed at Augusta, Georgia, and its construction was commenced in September, 1861. The plant was ready to begin making powder in April, 1862, and continued in successful operation until the end of the war, furnishing all the gunpowder needed, and of the finest quality. Competent critics say of this mill, that, notwithstanding the difficulties in the way of its erection and maintenance, it was, for its time, one of the most efficient powder-mills in the world.

Another permanent work erected was a central ordnance laboratory for the production of artillery and small-arms ammunition and miscellaneous articles of ordnance stores. This was decided on in September, 1861, placed in charge of Lieutenant-Colonel J. W. Mallet, and located at Macon, Georgia. It was designed to be an elaborate establishment, especially for the fabrication of percussion-caps, friction-primers, and pressed bullets, in addition to heavier ordnance supplies. Special machinery was made in England and shipped, but did not reach its destination in time for use. A large instalment including a most powerful pair of engines, had reached Bermuda when blockade running practically came to an end, near the close of the war.

A CONFEDERATE GUN THAT RAN THE BLOCKADE

RICHMOND
1865

Beside the home-made guns, which were all muzzle-loaders, a umber of guns of various makes, Whitworth, Armstrong, James, Blakely, and Hotchkiss, were rought in through the blockade. The gun in this photograph is a nodified 12-pounder breech-loading Whitworth. The breech was open when the picture was taken. The breech mechanism was adopted from the British Armstrong type and from the French system. In the Armstrong breech-loading gun the breech-block has the full screw that is seen here. The item taken from the French system was the manner of swinging the block back after the screw had become disengaged. The large ring through which the breech-block passes is hinged to the right side of the breech of the gun. Two Whitworths were sent to the Army of Northern Virginia. One of them was used in an attempt to knock over General Benjamin F. Butler's famous signal-tower. They had a great reputation for range and accuracy of fire, but beyond the shelling of distant columns and trains proved a disappointment. The length and weight of the gun were above the average, making it difficult to transport, and the care and length of time consumed in loading and handling impaired its efficiency for quick work. The cross-section of this gun was a hexagon with rounded corners. The twist was very rapid, and the projectiles were made long. The diameter of the bore was 2.75 inches, its length 104 inches, its weight 1,092 pounds, and it fired a 12-pound projectile with a usual load of 1.75 pounds of powder.

BRIGADIER–GENERAL
GABRIEL J. RAINS

Gabriel J. Rains of North Carolina was a colonel in the infantry corps March 16, 1861, and was appointed brigadier-general September 23d of that year. He was in charge of the bureau of conscription till December, 1862, and was made chief of the torpedo service June 17, 1864.

The third establishment projected to be permanent was a large central armory, equipped with a complete plant of machinery for the fabrication of small arms, and to which the Harper's Ferry machinery, which had been temporarily installed at Richmond and Fayetteville, was to be removed. This was put in charge of Lieutenant-Colonel J. H. Burton, who had gained experience at the factory in Enfield, England. It was determined to locate this armory at Macon, also. The buildings were begun in 1863, but they were not so far advanced toward completion as the laboratory when the end of the war arrested the work.

As a consequence of the necessity for immediate supply of arms and munitions to enable the armies to keep the field, resort was had to temporary arsenals and armories—at least they were designated as "temporary," although they were actually permanent, as far as the purposes of the war which the Confederacy waged was concerned.

The work was scattered among a number of available places throughout the South. Herein entered the problem of transportation by rail. The railroads were not very amply equipped at the outbreak of the war, and were overburdened in operation to such an extent that it would have been impossible to transport material to any single point from great distances, or to secure similar transportation for finished products over long lines. It was, moreover, uncertain how far any one place could be depended upon as secure from molestation by the foe. And there was not time for the removal of the plants from the localities in which they were when the Confederacy took possession of them, and various temporary ordnance works grew up about existing foundries, machine-shops, and railroad repair-shops, and at the various United States arsenals and ordnance depots. The chief localities that were thus utilized were Richmond, Virginia; Fayetteville, North Carolina; Charleston, South Carolina; Augusta, Savannah, and Macon, Georgia; Nashville and Memphis, Tennessee; Mount Vernon

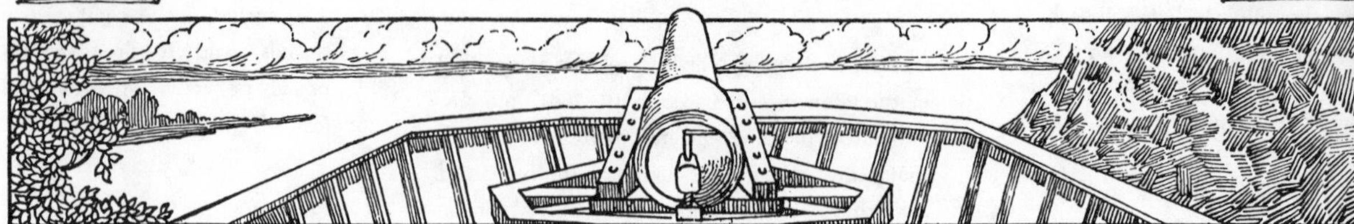

COPYRIGHT, 1911, REVIEW OF REVIEWS CO.

CONFEDERATES AND THEIR SMALL ARMS IN 1861

'his remarkable photograph of the encampment of the Perote Guards of New Orleans was found in the Major Chase home in Pensacola, lorida, in 1862, after the city was evacuated by the Confederates. The comparison is striking between the careless garb of the men nd the business-like small arms stacked and carried by the sentry. "Bright muskets" and "tattered uniforms" went together. oldiers could be found all through the camps busily polishing their muskets and their bayonets with wood ashes well moistened.

THE BOWIE KNIFE—CONSIDERED BY THE NORTHERN PRESS OF '61 AN IMPORTANT WEAPON

n article "concerning fire-rms" published in *Harper's Veekly* of August 2, 1861, tates that "the bowie knife is sually from ten to fifteen iches in length, with a blade bout two inches wide. It is iid to owe its invention to an ccident which occurred to 'olonel Bowie during a bat-e with the Mexicans; he roke his sword some fifteen iches from the hilt, and after-ard used the weapon thus roken as a knife in hand-to-and fights. This is a most ormidable weapon, and is ommonly in use in the West nd Southwest." As much pace is devoted to the de-cription of the bowie knife as is given to siege artillery. An illustration in the same journal for August 31, 1861, shows "Mississippians practising with the bowie knife." The Mississippians are engaged in throwing the knives. The heavy blades are seen hurtling through the air and burying their points in a tree. Grasping his bowie knife in the above photograph stands E. Spottswood Bishop, who started out as a private, was promoted to captain in the Twenty-fifth Virginia Cavalry, wounded five times, and elected colonel of his regiment by its officers. On the right is David J. Candill, who was transferred from the Twenty-fifth to the Tenth Kentucky Cavalry, and was promoted to lieutenant-colonel of his regiment. He was severely wounded in active service in his native State.

and Montgomery, Alabama; New Orleans and Baton Rouge, Louisiana; Little Rock, Arkansas, and San Antonio, Texas. The events of the war soon compelled the abandonment of some of these, and from time to time others were added to the list, as, for instance, Columbia, South Carolina; Atlanta and Columbus, Georgia; Selma, Alabama, and Jackson, Mississippi. Of these, Atlanta and Selma became most important.

Heavy artillery at the beginning of the war was manufactured only at Richmond at the Tredegar Iron Works. Later in the war, excellent heavy artillery was produced at Selma, first in conjunction with the naval officers, and later by them alone.

Field-artillery was made and repaired chiefly at Richmond and at Augusta, small arms at Richmond and Fayetteville, caps and friction-primers at Richmond and Atlanta, accouterments to a great extent at Macon, while cast bullets and small-arms cartridges were prepared at almost all of the works.

After the Federals took possession of the copper mines of Tennessee, there was great anxiety as to the future supply of copper, both for bronze field-guns and for percussion-caps. The casting of bronze guns was immediately stopped, and all the available copper was utilized in the manufacture of caps. It soon became apparent that the supply would be exhausted and the armies rendered powerless unless other sources of supply were discovered. No reliance could be placed on the supply from abroad, for the blockade was stringent, although large orders had been forwarded. Of course, the knowledge of this scarcity of copper was kept from the public as much as possible. In this emergency, it was concluded to render available, if possible, some of the copper turpentine- and apple-brandy-stills which were in North and South Carolina in large numbers. This work was entrusted to Lieutenant-Colonel Leroy Broun, commanding the Richmond Arsenal.

In spite of the difficulties to be overcome and the constantly increasing pressure for immediate results, the Confederate Ordnance Department was able to boast of some useful

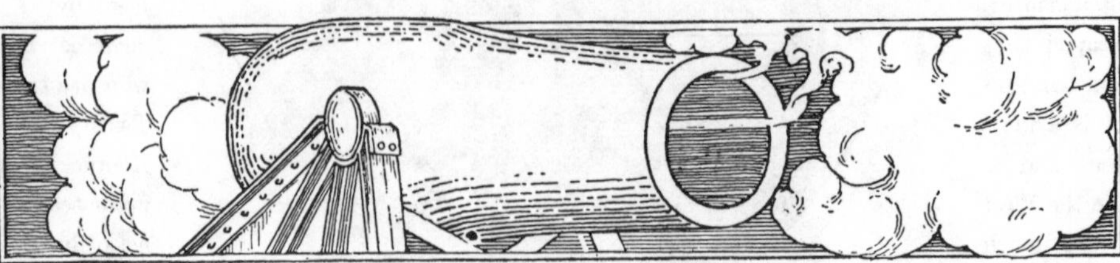

CONFEDERATE GUNS—PRACTICALLY EVERY TYPE USED IN THE CIVILIZED WORLD IN 1865

n the collection of captured Confederate artillery on the wharves f Richmond awaiting shipment North in April, 1865, might be ound practically every type of gun made and used by the ivilized nations of the world, besides some patterns entirely obsolete. The first ources of Confederate artilery were the captured navyards and arsenals. Purhasing agents were sent to urope and some guns were mported from abroad. This vas eventually checked by he Federal blockade. One f the principal places of nanufacture was the Tredear Iron Works in Richnond. Large quantities of rdnance were also obtained rom all battlegrounds of he war where the Conederates held the field for a ime following the battle. Due to these various sources of supplies the ordnance material was varied and incongruous. The wagon in the foreground is a tool-wagon, but observe the light wheels. Just over the top of this wagon is visible a caisson, complete, with the fifth, or spare wheel, on the back. In the chests of the caisson are stored projectiles and powder which cannot be carried in the limber of the gun. Below several brass mountain-howitzers appear. Mountain artillery must be light enough to be carried on the backs of pack animals if necessary. The howitzer used for this purpose was a short, light 12-pounder, weighing 220 pounds. When a carriage was used, it was mounted on a low, two-wheeled one. The projectiles were shell and case-shot, and the charge was half a pound of powder.

CONFEDERATE BRASS HOWITZERS

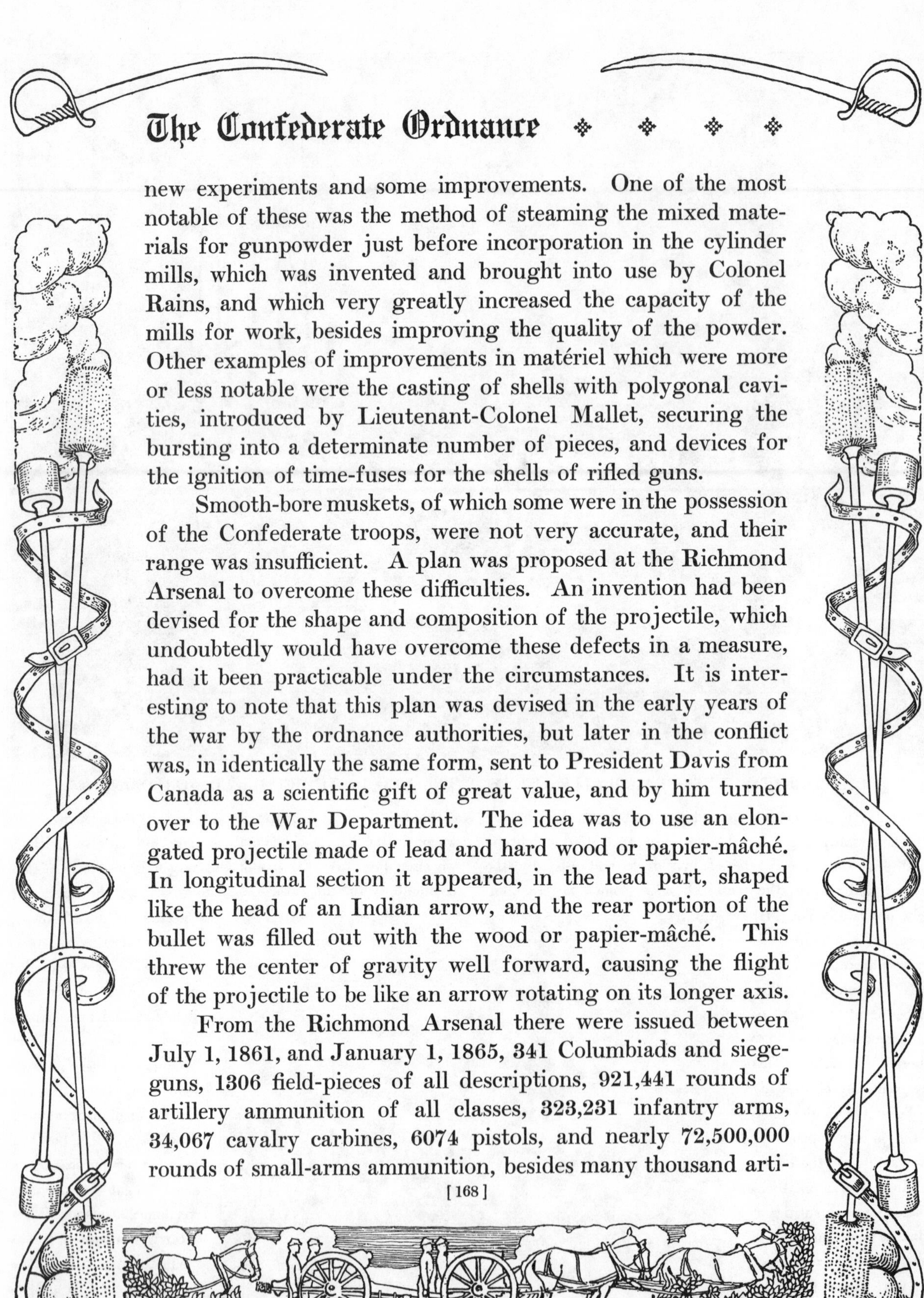

new experiments and some improvements. One of the most notable of these was the method of steaming the mixed materials for gunpowder just before incorporation in the cylinder mills, which was invented and brought into use by Colonel Rains, and which very greatly increased the capacity of the mills for work, besides improving the quality of the powder. Other examples of improvements in matériel which were more or less notable were the casting of shells with polygonal cavities, introduced by Lieutenant-Colonel Mallet, securing the bursting into a determinate number of pieces, and devices for the ignition of time-fuses for the shells of rifled guns.

Smooth-bore muskets, of which some were in the possession of the Confederate troops, were not very accurate, and their range was insufficient. A plan was proposed at the Richmond Arsenal to overcome these difficulties. An invention had been devised for the shape and composition of the projectile, which undoubtedly would have overcome these defects in a measure, had it been practicable under the circumstances. It is interesting to note that this plan was devised in the early years of the war by the ordnance authorities, but later in the conflict was, in identically the same form, sent to President Davis from Canada as a scientific gift of great value, and by him turned over to the War Department. The idea was to use an elongated projectile made of lead and hard wood or papier-mâché. In longitudinal section it appeared, in the lead part, shaped like the head of an Indian arrow, and the rear portion of the bullet was filled out with the wood or papier-mâché. This threw the center of gravity well forward, causing the flight of the projectile to be like an arrow rotating on its longer axis.

From the Richmond Arsenal there were issued between July 1, 1861, and January 1, 1865, 341 Columbiads and siege-guns, 1306 field-pieces of all descriptions, 921,441 rounds of artillery ammunition of all classes, 323,231 infantry arms, 34,067 cavalry carbines, 6074 pistols, and nearly 72,500,000 rounds of small-arms ammunition, besides many thousand arti-

A GIANT CONFEDERATE SLING-CART TO CARRY SIEGE-GUNS

This giant sling-cart was built by the Confederates for the purpose of handling the two 12-inch guns that were cast at the Tredegar Iron Works, in Richmond, just before the evacuation. These guns weighed nearly fifty thousand pounds each. The size of the cart can be estimated by comparing it with the man visible through its spokes in the upper photograph. The wheels are more than eleven feet high. The cart required twelve mules and one hundred and fifty men with drag ropes to move it, when carrying only an 8-inch rifle or a heavy Columbiad over bad roads. The big guns were slung underneath the cart by ropes so as to clear the ground by a few inches. It was captured by the Federals, and used in the removal of the ordnance from Drewry's and Chaffin's bluffs.

cles of other ordnance and ordnance stores. The enormous number of pieces of artillery issued were, of course, not all made at the arsenal, but had been obtained by manufacture, by purchase, or by capture. The Richmond *Enquirer,* on the day after the evacuation of Richmond, said that, assuming the issues from the Richmond Arsenal to have been half of all the issues to Confederate troops, which was approximately true, and that 100,000 of the Federals had been killed, it would appear that about 150 pounds of lead and 350 pounds of iron were fired for every man killed, and, furthermore, assuming that the proportion of killed to wounded was about one to six, it would appear that one man was wounded for every 200 pounds fired. These figures exaggerated the form of the old belief that it took a man's weight in lead to kill him in battle.

Considering the general lack of previous experience in ordnance matters, the personnel of the corps, both at the arsenals and in the field, deserved great praise for intelligence, zeal, and efficiency. Many names of officers deserve to be remembered. Among the most prominent were Lieutenant-Colonels J. H. Burton, superintendent of armories; T. L. Bayne, in charge of the bureau of foreign supplies; I. M. St. John, at the head of the niter and mining bureau; Lieutenant-Colonel J. W. Mallet, in charge of the Central Laboratory at Macon, Georgia; Lieutenant-Colonel G. W. Rains, of the Augusta powder-mills and Arsenal; Lieutenant-Colonel Leroy Broun, commanding the Richmond Arsenal; Major M. H. Wright, of the Atlanta Arsenal; Lieutenant-Colonel R. M. Cuyler, of the Macon Arsenal; Major J. A. De Lagnel, of Fayetteville; Major J. T. Trezevant, of Charleston Arsenal; Lieutenant-Colonel J. L. White, of Selma Arsenal; Lieutenant-Colonel B. G. Baldwin, chief of ordnance, Army of Northern Virginia; Lieutenant-Colonel H. Oladowski, chief of ordnance, Army of Tennessee, and Major W. Allen, chief ordnance officer, Second Corps, Army of Northern Virginia.

VIII

AMMUNITION

13-INCH SHELLS FOR THE SEA COAST MORTARS

These missiles, filled with explosive, and trailing a fiery fuse, shrieked like lost souls in their flight, that covered nearly two and a half miles from the gaping mouths of the tremendous mortars looking like huge bullfrogs with their muzzle elevation of forty-five degrees. The shells seen in this photograph show the larger hole where the time fuse was inserted, and the indentations which enabled the gunners to handle them with a sort of pincers carried by two men. The mortars were manned by the famous First Connecticut Heavy Artillery, prominent in many important engagements from the Peninsula to the Petersburg Campaign. Companies served on the Bermuda Hundred lines in 1864, also at Fort Fisher.

THE AMMUNITION USED IN THE WAR

By O. E. Hunt
Captain, United States Army

UNTIL the middle of the nineteenth century there was but little improvement in cannon or gunpowder. One reason for this was that bronze and iron were used for making guns, and these metals could not withstand the exceedingly great pressures of heavy charges of powder unless the cannon were cast so large as to be unmanageable. No scientific treatment of the subject of gun-strains had been attempted previous to this time, because it was assumed that all the powder in a charge was converted instantaneously into gas.

Powder and ball for small arms were originally carried loose and separately. Gustavus Adolphus, King of Sweden, first made an improvement by providing separate receptacles for each powder charge; these were called cartridges (Latin *carta*, or *charta*) from their paper envelopes. He subsequently combined the projectile with the powder in the paper wrapper, and this, until about 1865, formed the principal small-arms ammunition.

However, not all of the ammunition used in the Civil War was prepared in this form, and from the fact that powder and ball were carried separately arose the danger of inadvertently loading the piece with more than one charge at a time. Even in the use of the two in one package, inasmuch as there was usually nothing to prevent the reloading of the gun before the previous cartridge had been fired, there still remained this danger. As a consequence, it was reported that nearly half of the muskets abandoned on the field of Gettysburg were found to contain more than one load, and some of

AMMUNITION IN FEDERAL FORT No. 9, ATLANTA

While Sherman rested his soldiers before their march to the sea, this view was taken of Federal Fort No. 9, looking northwest toward Forts Nos. 8 and 7 at Atlanta. Bags of charges for the 12-pounders in the embrasures are ranged along the parapet in exposed positions that they never would have occupied if there had remained any danger of an assault. The bags are marked "12 Pdr. Model. 1857." These were for the brass Napoleons, the most popular guns for field-artillery during the war. In the lower photograph of Confederate works near Petersburg appear boxes in which the cartridges for rifles had been served out. Evidently, they have been hastily ripped open and cast aside. On the further box, lying upside down, are the words "ball cartridges." Beside lie a few shells for field-guns, although the guns themselves have been withdrawn. The photograph was taken after these works passed into the hands of the Federals, and the silent witnesses of a feverish moment under fire tell their own story. The order at drill was, "tear cartridge." The ends of them were usually bitten open, especially in action. At one end of the cartridge came the bullet, then the powder, and the other end was torn open in order to free the powder when it was rammed home.

AFTER THE FIRING

them had three or four. In the excitement, men were observed to load, make a motion mechanically as if to fire the piece, fail to notice that it had not been discharged, and then hasten to put another load on top of the first.

The state of the arts required the first breech-loading ammunition to be in a paper or cloth package. However, as it was impossible to prevent the escape of the gas, the joint required for rapid loading was generally placed in front of the chamber, from which position the soldier suffered least from the discharge. To facilitate loading, the mechanism of the gun was so arranged that, the paper or cloth cartridge having been broken or bitten open, the bullet acted as a stopper to hold the powder in place until the piece was closed.

The next improvement in ammunition was the introduction of the metallic cartridge-case. This was invented in France, and was first used by troops in our Civil War. It contained all the components of the ammunition in a case that protected them from the weather, and thus prevented the deterioration of the powder. The principal purpose of the case, however, has been to act as a gas-check, to prevent the escape of the gases to the rear and to permit the use of an easily operated breech-mechanism.

Being rigid and of fixed dimensions, the metallic cartridge was first used extensively in magazine rifles. There was, at first, a great objection, however, limiting the use of these rifles for military purposes, and that was the rapid consumption of ammunition, which soon exhausted the supply on the person of the soldier. The caliber of the guns was large and the ammunition heavy; hence only a small amount could be carried.

A fulminate, or firing-composition, has always been required for the ignition of the powder, in whatever form it has been used. For loose powder and for paper or cloth cartridges, a percussion-cap, fitted over a vent communicating with the powder in the breech of the gun, served the

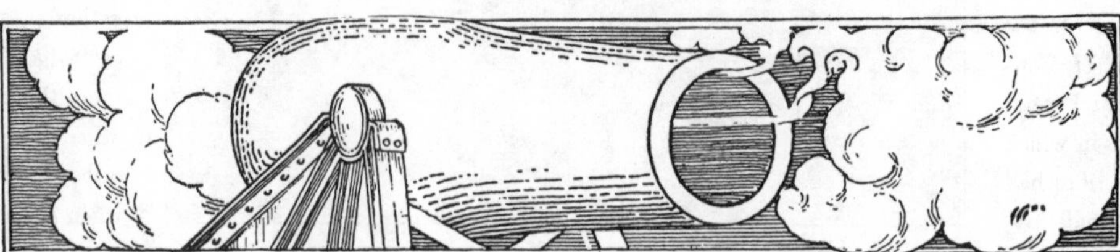

AMMUNITION STORED IN THE WASHINGTON ARSENAL—1864

An essential factor in the winning of pitched, open battles was a plentiful supply of ammunition. At Gaines' Mill, in June, 1862, the Union soldiers found it difficult to cheer convincingly when they had shot away all their cartridges, and found themselves separated from their ammunition wagons by the fast-swelling Chickahominy. The ammunition train always took precedence on the march.

SCHOONERS PILED WITH CARTRIDGE-BOXES—HAMPTON ROADS, DECEMBER, 1864

By 1864, the problem of getting ammunition expeditiously to the front had been solved, and there were no more such shortages as at Gaines' Mill. In this photograph, the harbor of Hampton Roads swarms with ammunition schooners, transports, coal barges, and craft of every sort. The decks of the schooners in the foreground are piled high with cartridge-boxes.

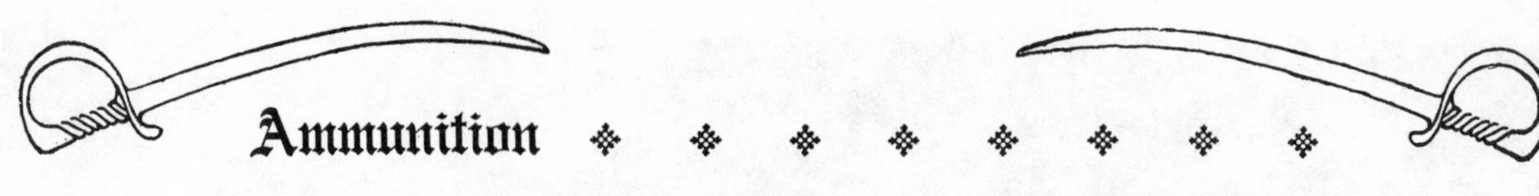

purpose. In the first practicable form of metallic cartridge, the composition was placed in the rim which formed the base of the cartridge, and which enabled it to be withdrawn after discharge—the rim thus serving two purposes. These rim-fire cartridges answered very well until the powder charges became heavier, when it was discovered that the weakening of the metal by folding to make the rim caused it to sheer off at the edge of the chamber of the gun, and the copper, of which they were made, would expand and render it almost impossible to extract the shell. And since the fulminate had to be placed entirely around the rim, a greater quantity was used than necessary for firing, and the distribution was imperfect, thus causing misfires. A pin-fire cartridge was invented, but proved unsatisfactory. A pin projected from the rim and was intended to be struck by the hammer of the gun; but, of course, any object striking it would cause an explosion, and it was dangerous. Neither the pin-fire nor the rim-fire cartridges could be reloaded.

On June 25, 1864, the chief of ordnance of the United States army reported that among the most important changes in firearms evolved from the experience of the war was the metallic cartridge-case. Linen had been in use, but copper was much superior. The case formed a perfect gas-check; it gave the benefit of allowing a fulminate to be used in the case itself, which was an advantage over the former method of using a cap; there was a gain of time in that the piece did not have to be recapped with each new load; there was greater ease of loading, and the ammunition was waterproof.

For the field-artillery of both services there were supplied solid shot, case, and shell with time-fuses and with percussion-fuses. Solid shot were designed for destroying the heavy walls of fortifications, or for some similar purpose, but were used also in the field. The other forms of ammunition were used against troops. Case was of two kinds—canister, which separated at the muzzle of the piece in consequence of the shock

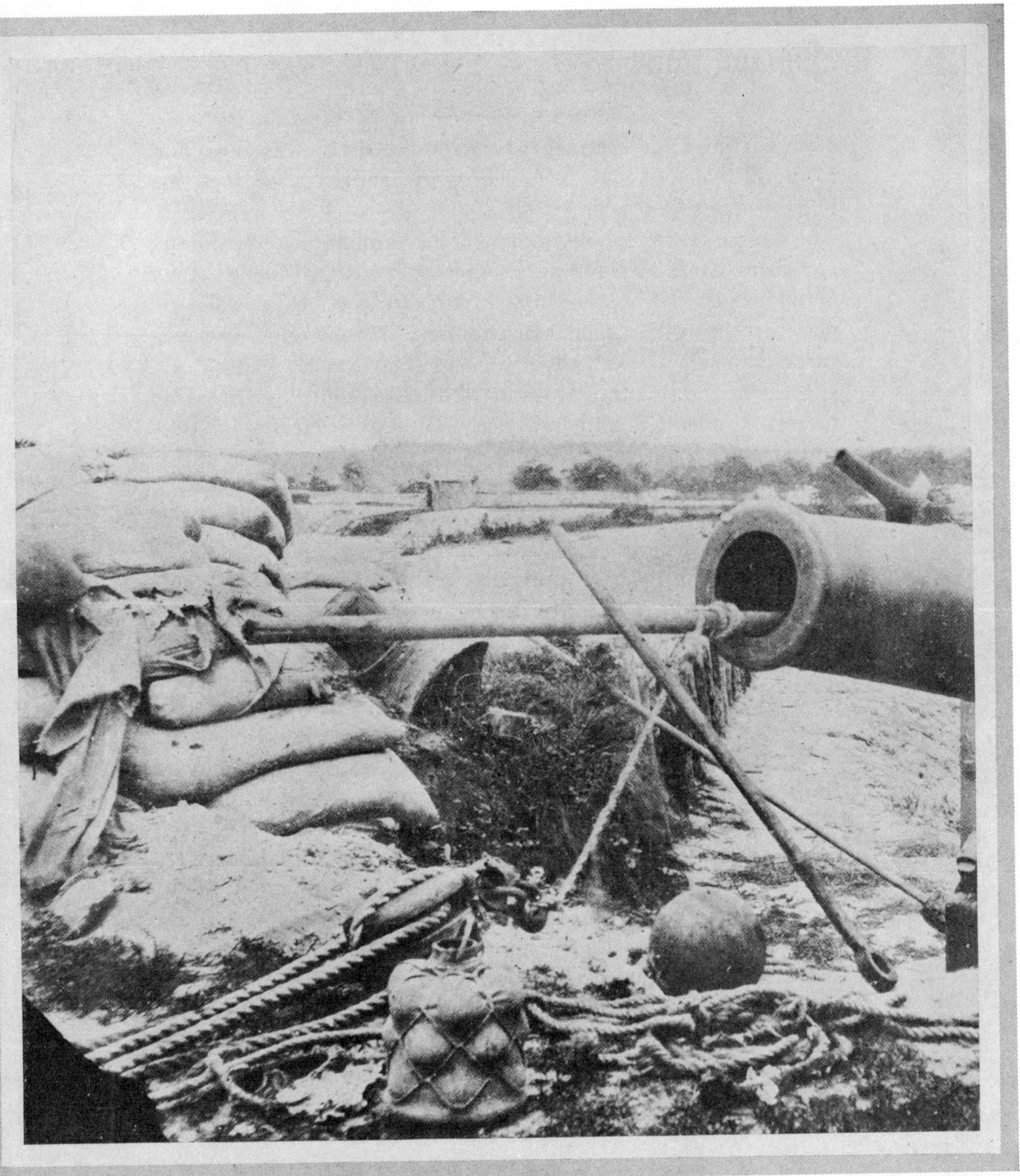

CONFEDERATE AMMUNITION—SOLID SHOT AND A CHARGE OF GRAPE

This view of the Confederate works at Yorktown, in 1862, shows an 11-inch Dahlgren smooth-bore naval gun. Several of these were taken from the Norfolk Navy-Yard. On the ground is a solid shot and a charge of grape. Grape-shot consisted of a number of small projectiles secured together by a series of iron plates containing holes in which the shot is held. In addition to the common cast-iron shells not intended to pierce iron, forged steel shells were used. In the days of smooth-bore guns, bar shot, chain shot, grape-shot, hot shot, shrapnel and canister were in use. Shrapnel are shaped like shell, but have thinner walls and are filled with lead or iron balls. A small bursting-charge breaks up the case in the air and the balls scatter like shot from a shotgun. In canister the balls, larger than those in shrapnel, are sunk in soft wood disks piled up to form a cylinder and the whole covered with a tin case; or, in small calibers, the balls are simply pushed in sawdust and enclosed in a cylindrical tin case. Grape, shrapnel and canister were all three known as case-shot.

of discharge, and shrapnel, which separated at a distance, due to the presence of a bursting charge which scattered the contents of the receptacle.

The shell was a hollow projectile, containing also a bursting charge, intended for destructive effect at a distance. One of its principal purposes was in the destruction of walls of masonry and other solid construction. By using percussion-fuses the shell would penetrate, and then burst, opening out a breach; and by the addition of further shots in the same place, an opening could be made through which assaulting troops could pass.

The ammunition used by the Federal siege-artillery was of prime importance in the conduct of the war. The siege-guns consisted of mortars, smooth-bore guns, and rifles. All the ammunition received preliminary tests at the factories, and a great portion of it also by target practice in the defenses of Washington. The records of this practice were the most complete ever compiled regarding artillery ammunition, and covered all features of the firing; therefore, when it was issued to the troops in the field, they were informed of the proper results to be expected, as far as the target practice could be simulated to field firing. Experiments were also made at Washington with the Confederate ammunition that had been captured, and certain of the features of that ammunition received very favorable notice from the Federal ordnance officers.

The mortars were designed to throw a shell containing a bursting charge, and carrying either a time-fuse or a percussion-fuse. The time-fuse was ignited by the propelling charge, before leaving the gun. At times this fuse was uncertain in its action, as it would become extinguished during flight or on striking, and the bursting charge, which was intended to cause the damage, would not explode. The percussion-fuse was not ignited by the propelling charge in the mortar, but contained a fulminate that was ignited by a plunger of some description which moved when the shell was fired or when it

SHELLS IN FORT PUTNAM, SOUTH CAROLINA

PROJECTILES IN THE SEA-COAST FORTS

The guns of the parapet of Fort Putnam were siege guns of heavy caliber. Shells with metal rims made soft to take the grooves of the rifling are stacked up in the foreground. The projectiles by the chassis in Battery Magruder were 8.5-inch Armstrong rifle-shot, which could be used as shell or solid shot at pleasure. They had a cavity for the insertion of a bursting charge, which, with its percussion-fuse, was not inserted unless it was desired to fire the projectile against advancing troops as shell. These had a terrific effect, bursting at times into more than 200 pieces. The view of Fort Johnson reveals both spherical solid shot and oblong shell. The latter are slightly hollowed out at the base, in order to secure a better distribution of the gases generated when the pieces were discharged. The stack of projectiles around the two 100-pounder Parrott guns in the lower view of Fort Putnam are for these rifles. Their weight was eighty-six pounds—although the guns were known as 100-pounders—and the powder charge was ten pounds. The projectile for the 3-inch field-gun on the top of the parapet weighed ten pounds, and the powder charge was one pound.

PROJECTILES IN MAGRUDER BATTERY, YORKTOWN

INTERIOR OF FORT JOHNSON, MORRIS ISLAND

INTERIOR OF FORT PUTNAM, MORRIS ISLAND

struck, thereby communicating the flame to the bursting charge. Of course, these were not always sure.

Whether the one or the other form of fuse was used, depended on the purpose of the firing. If against troops, it was desirable to cause the shell to burst in their midst, and not to allow it to penetrate the ground. If desired for the destruction of earthworks or magazines, it had to be exploded after the penetration. In the former case the time-fuse, and in the latter the percussion-fuse was used.

At Fort Scott, near Washington, in October, 1863, an experiment was tried to test the value of spherical case-shot when fired from mortars. The 10-inch shell was filled with 12-pound canister-shot, and the bursting charge was loose. The capacity of the shell was thirty-eight of that size balls, but twenty-seven only were used. They were inserted through the fuse-hole, and two and a half pounds of bursting powder placed on top of them. The shell weighed ninety pounds and each of the balls forty-three hundredths of a pound, making a total weight of about one hundred and four pounds. A charge of one pound six ounces of mortar-powder gave a range of eight hundred yards with a time of flight of thirteen seconds.

The experiments showed that the fragments scattered a great deal and the balls had ample power to kill. They penetrated the ground from three to seven inches in a turf where, when thrown by a man with his whole strength, they entered less than one inch. A little calculation showed that the velocity must have been over two hundred feet per second, and as the projectiles weighed nearly half a pound each, there was easily sufficient force to disable a man or a beast. The practicability of the shot having been fully determined, a field-trial was given which proved conclusive.

The projectile was used in the battle of the Petersburg mine, where General Hunt's orders for the artillery were to use every exertion to quiet the batteries of the foe bearing on

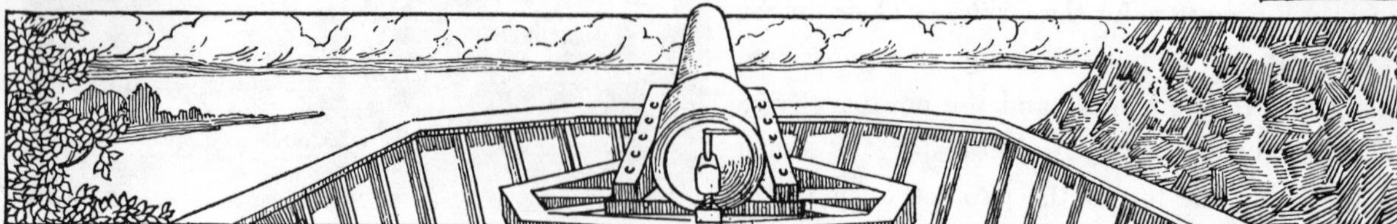

COPYRIGHT, 1911, REVIEW OF REVIEWS CO.

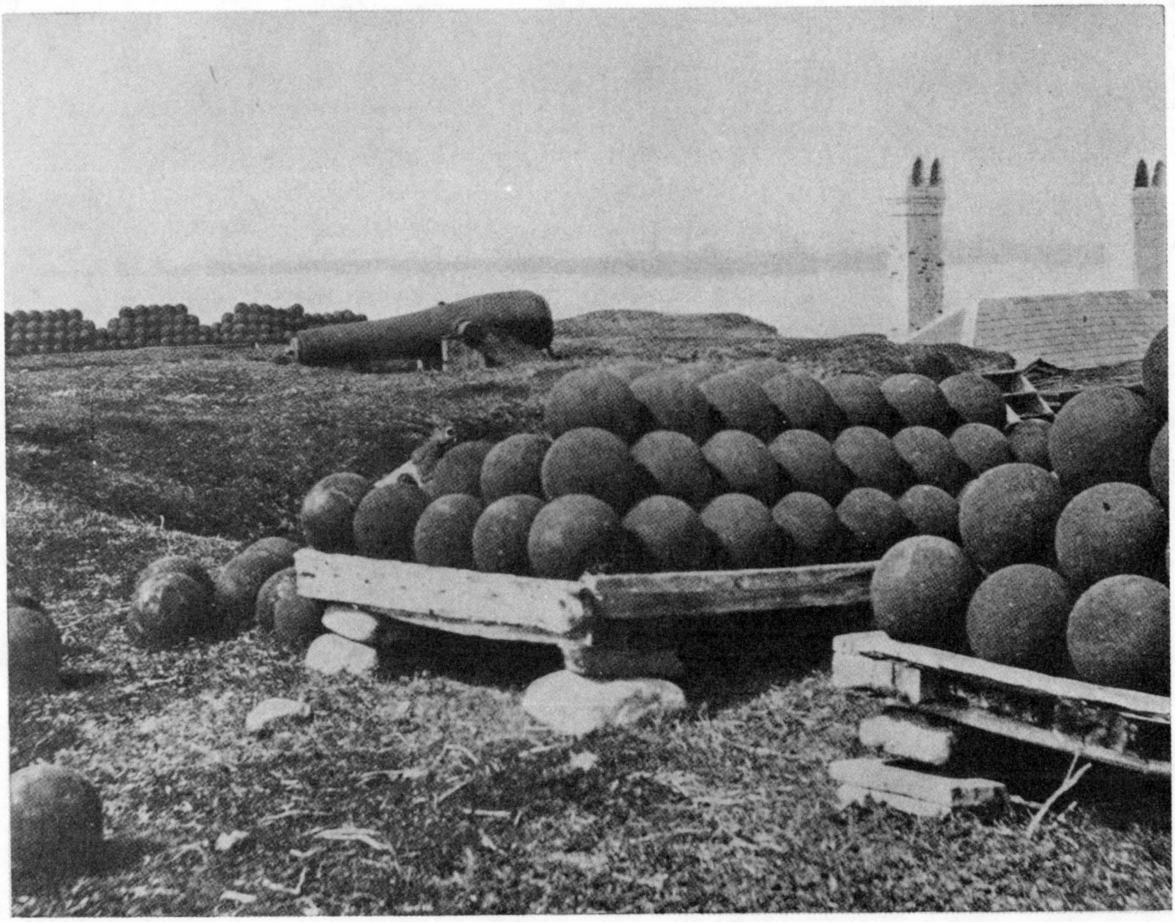

IN CASTLE PINCKNEY—428-POUND PROJECTILES

A BIG GUN IN CASTLE PINCKNEY

The gun overlooking the parapet of Castle Pinckney is a 15-inch Columbiad which used a powder charge of 40 pounds. The projectile weighed 428 pounds. A large number of these projectiles are stacked in the foreground. With an elevation of twenty degrees, the maximum range of this gun was 3,787 yards, or a little over two miles. This fort was used as a prison for Union captives in 1861. In Battery Rodgers, within the corporate limits but nearly half a mile below the wharves and populous portion of the city of Alexandria, there were two magazines, one twelve by thirty feet and the other twelve by eighteen feet interior dimensions. These were sunk entirely below the *terre plein*, and protected by a cover of earth seventeen and a half feet thick, armed with five 200-pounders.

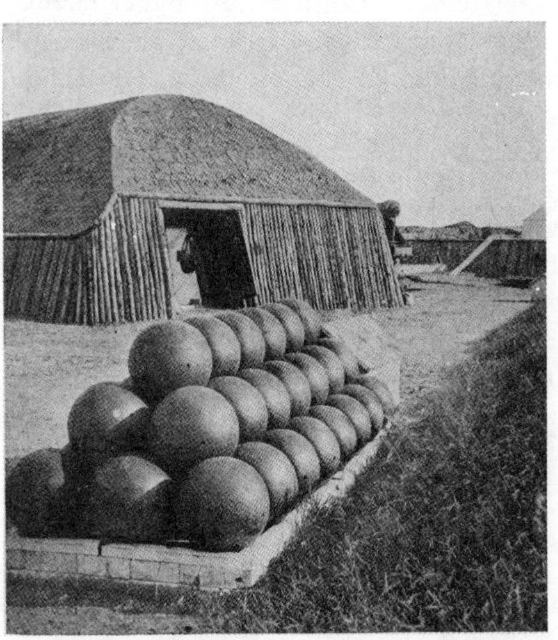

POWDER MAGAZINE IN BATTERY RODGERS

the point of assault. A battery of 10-inch mortars was placed near the subsequent location of Fort Rice, and directed its fire, at a range of eight hundred yards, upon a salient battery of the Confederates, from which much trouble was anticipated. Not a shot was fired from the Confederate battery after its range was obtained, and from information received afterward from a Southern officer, it was found that the men could not remain at their guns after the showers of balls began falling, every thirty seconds, around them.

The ordinary mortar-shell was the one used largely in all the operations. At Yorktown, the Confederates had an 8-inch mortar with which they did rather indifferent shooting, but the moral effect on the Federal soldiers of the screeching shells was great. Accordingly, the Federals thereafter paid close attention to the training of men for the use of a similar type of mortar, and at Petersburg there was a good opportunity to reply in kind. The Confederate gunners, now feeling the effect of the fire from the other side, and having for a time no bombproofs in which to take shelter, were appalled by the sudden opening of the Federal mortars. The lines were so near together that the soldiers were under the necessity of keeping their works closely guarded to prevent their being taken by assault, and the moral effect was very depressing. One case is related of a Confederate soldier having been blown entirely over the parapet of the work by the explosion of one of the Federal 8-inch mortar-shells, and his body lay out of reach of his friends, who were compelled to keep under cover by the Federal sharpshooters.

As soon as the Confederates could place mortars in position at Petersburg, they opened on the besiegers, and thereafter the fire was severe. The Federal expenditure of mortar ammunition was over forty thousand rounds, and that of the Confederates was estimated to have been not much less.

The incident of the so-called " Petersburg Express," when the Federals mounted a 13-inch sea-coast mortar on a railroad

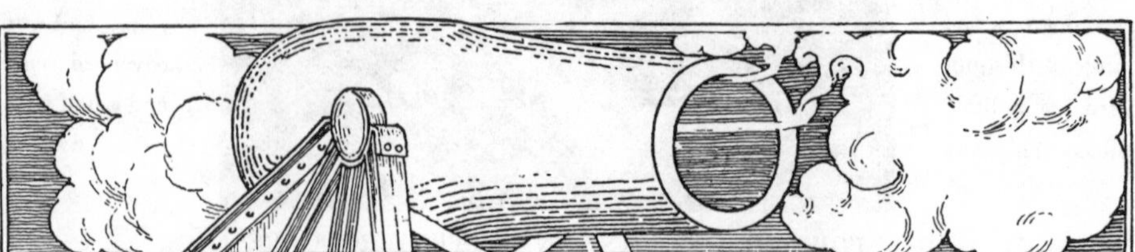

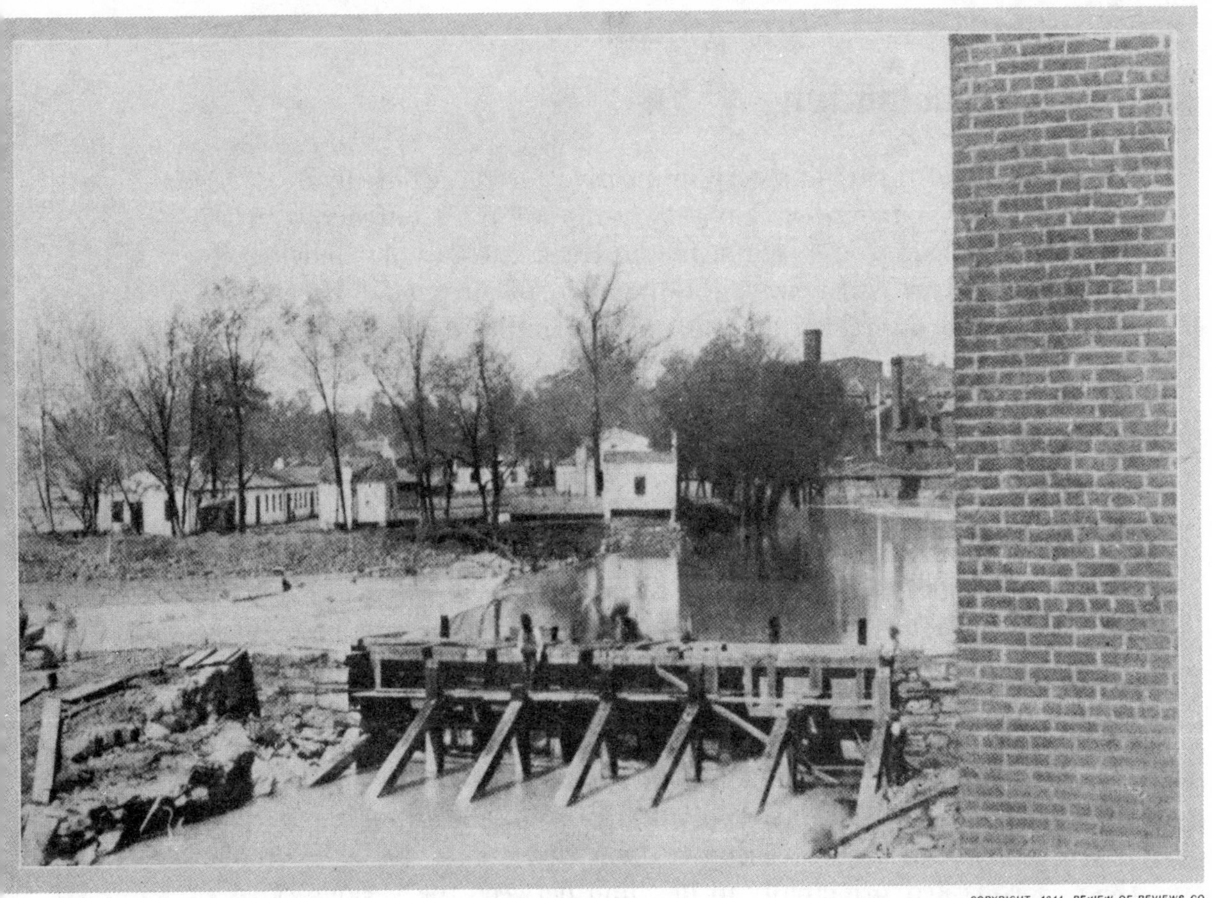

THE LABORATORY FOR SMALL AMMUNITION AT RICHMOND

This photograph was taken the day the new flag of the Confederate States of America was thrown to the breeze on top of Libby prison. The entire supply of gunpowder in the Confederacy at the beginning of the conflict was scarcely sufficient for one month of active operations. Not a pound was being made throughout its limits. The comparatively small amount captured at the Norfolk navy-yard, with that on hand from other sources, was promptly distributed to the army gathering on the Potomac, to Richmond, Yorktown, Pensacola, Mobile, and New Orleans. Scarcely any remained for the force assembling under the command of General Albert Sidney Johnston in Kentucky. In the face of these difficulties, Colonel (later General) George W. Rains was given *carte blanche* to take charge of the manufacture of gunpowder. He established immense works in Augusta, Georgia. So extensive were they that at no time after their completion were they worked to their full capacity. They were never run at night. They satisfied in little more than two days the urgent call of General Ripley at Charleston for cannon-powder, to replace the twenty-two thousand pounds consumed during the action with the iron-clad fleet. The Richmond laboratory made 72,000,000 cartridges in three and a half years, nearly as much as the others in the Confederate States combined.

platform car, was very impressive for the Confederates. The car was moved within easy range of the Confederate works, and halted at a curve in the track, so that, by moving it a few feet either way, the direction of fire could be changed. Much apprehension was excited in the defenders' works by the huge missiles, and observers reported that one of the shells, on explosion, threw a Confederate field-gun and carriage above the parapet of the works. The range was about thirty-six hundred yards.

Although the first really successful application of rifled cannon to warfare occurred in the Italian campaign of Napoleon III, in 1859, the problem of a projectile that would satisfactorily take the rifling of the gun had not been solved, and up to the outbreak of the Civil War in America the employment of such guns was, on this account, an uncertain undertaking. During the years from 1861 to 1865, there was continual trouble in finding a projectile that would take the rifling successfully without injury to the gun, but developments were such during the war that, at its close, the problem consisted principally in deciding between the various types of projectiles. Both belligerents devoted much time to the solution of these difficulties. Many inventions had temporary vogue, and then gradually were laid aside, so that even experienced ordnance officers could not, at the close of the conflict, tell exactly what the prevailing opinion as to types was at any particular date.

In the Federal service, experience caused the rejection of a number of varieties of rifled projectiles. For the siege of Petersburg there were used those of Parrott, Schenkl, and Hotchkiss. The first was fired by the Parrott guns, and the others by the ordnance guns. Case-shot and shell were used with all the systems, and solid shot in the Parrott and Hotchkiss. The guns were also supplied with canister not designed to take the rifled motion.

Observations made throughout the war by the Federal

REMOVING POWDER FROM CONFEDERATE TORPEDOES

1864

In this photograph is one of the stations established for extracting powder from the torpedoes dredged up by the Federal gunboats in the James. When the activities of the Army of the Potomac centered about the James and the Appomattox in 1864 and 1865, it became the paramount duty of the coöperating navy to render the torpedo-infested streams safe for the passage of transports and supply vessels. The powder in these channels helped to guard Richmond from the Union gunboats. In the foreground sit two old salts discussing ways and means of rendering one of the deadly infernal machines harmless, while all about in this quiet nook lie remains of the dreaded submarine menaces that were constantly being placed in the channel by the Confederates.

artillery officers, supplemented by data collected elsewhere, showed that the penetrations of the elongated rifled projectiles were variable, depending largely on the direction maintained by the axis of the projectile. When the axis remained coincident with the trajectory or nearly so, the penetration exceeded that of the round shot of the same weight by about one-fourth, even at the shortest ranges, though greater charges were used for the guns firing the latter shot. Whenever the axis of the projectile was turned, as the slightest obstruction would cause it to do, the penetration was greatly reduced. There was a noticeable tendency to curve upward after entering an earth embankment. The percussion shells, which were designed to explode on impact, attained usually about three-fourths of their entire penetration before bursting, and time-fuses, prepared to burn a certain number of seconds after leaving the gun, frequently became extinguished on entering the dirt.

With ordinary clay-loam, parapets and magazines required at least a thickness of sixteen feet to resist the 6.4-inch projectile (100-pounder) and twelve feet to resist smaller calibers. In new earth not well settled, those thicknesses had to be increased. Earthen parapets of the proper dimensions could not be injured greatly by rifled shells of any caliber less than 6.4 inches, and not permanently by those if the garrison were active in repairing the damage.

The moral effect of the shells as they went shrieking over the heads of the troops was frequently great. In describing an engagement, a Confederate private soldier said that the reports of cannon were incessant and deafening; that at times it seemed as if a hundred guns would explode simultaneously, and then run off at intervals into splendid file-firing. No language could describe its awful grandeur. Ten thousand muskets fired in volleys mingled in a great roar of a mighty cataract, and it seemed almost as if the earth were being destroyed by violence. The shells howled like demons as they sailed over the heads of the troops lying close to their impro-

THE DAY AFTER THE EXPLOSION THAT REACHED GRANT'S QUARTERS

DANGER EVER PRESENT WITH MILLIONS OF POUNDS OF POWDER

On the 9th of August, 1864, the quiet of noon at City Point was shattered by a deafening roar. Shot and shell were hurled high in the air. Fragments fell around the headquarters of General Grant. Only one member of his staff was wounded, however—Colonel Babcock. "The lieutenant-general himself," wrote Major-General Rufus Ingalls in his official report, "seems proof against the accidents of flood and field." A barge laden with ordnance stores had blown up, killing and wounding some 250 employees and soldiers, throwing down over 600 feet of warehouses, and tearing up 180 feet of wharf. Seventy men were killed and 130 wounded, according to contemporary report. This view was taken the next day.

vised shelter, and caused the men to crouch into the smallest possible space and wish for the little red cap of the fairy story, which would make the wearer invisible.

But it was the Hotchkiss shell that made the infernal noise which caused the bravest to duck his head. Though no more destructive than the others, its mere sound worked on the men's nerves, and the moral effect was powerful. The tremendous scream of the missile was caused by a ragged edge of lead which remained on the shell as it left the gun. When the light was favorable, and with the observer standing behind the gun, a peculiar phenomenon was often observed. The projectile seemed to gather the atmosphere as it sped along, just as our globe carries its atmosphere through space, and this apparently accounted for the statement that sometimes men were killed by the wind of a cannon-ball.

Hand-grenades were sometimes used with great effect when the troops were close. The grenade was ignited by the act of throwing, and had the peculiar value that, due to the arrangement of the fuse, the enemy could not utilize the same missile to throw back. It could be thrown about one hundred feet, but as the fragments scattered nearly two hundred yards, the assailant had to seek cover himself to prevent injury from his own grenade.

The variety of rifled projectiles used by the Confederates was very great. This was due to the fact that their ordnance had to be procured from whatever source possible, and the differences in ammunition were, of course, greater than those of the guns. About seventy different kinds of projectiles were in use at one time.

One of these devices was a cupped copper plate, fastened to the shell by a screw, and held firm by radial grooves. It was used principally for the larger calibers, and took the rifling very well. However, one objection to it was that the copper plates often became detached and were liable to cause damage to troops in front of the guns.

CONFEDERATE TORPEDOES, SHOT AND SHELL COLLECTED IN THE CHARLESTON ARSENAL

Conical-ended torpedoes, as well as several different kinds of shot and shell, make up the heterogeneous collection in the yard of the Charleston Arsenal. The breech and several pieces of the huge Blakely gun used in the defense of the city also appear. In two years, the powder and ordnance works at Augusta turned out among other things 110 field-guns, mostly bronze 12-pounder Napoleons, 174 gun-carriages, 115 caissons, 343 limbers to field artillery, 21 battery wagons, 31 traveling forges, 10,535 powder-boxes, 11,811 boxes for small-arm ammunition, 73,521 horseshoes, 12,630 pounds of nitric acid, 2,227 ounces of fulminate of mercury, 2,455 complete saddles, 2,535 single sets of artillery harness, 2,477 signal rockets, 85,800 rounds of fixed ammunition, 136,642 artillery cartridge-bags, 200,113 time-fuses, 476,207 pounds of artillery projectiles, 4,580,000 buckshot, 4,626,000 lead balls, 1,000,000 percussion caps, and 10,760,000 cartridges for small-arms. General Rains, who was in charge of these works, was able to supply these records for 1863 and 1864 only.

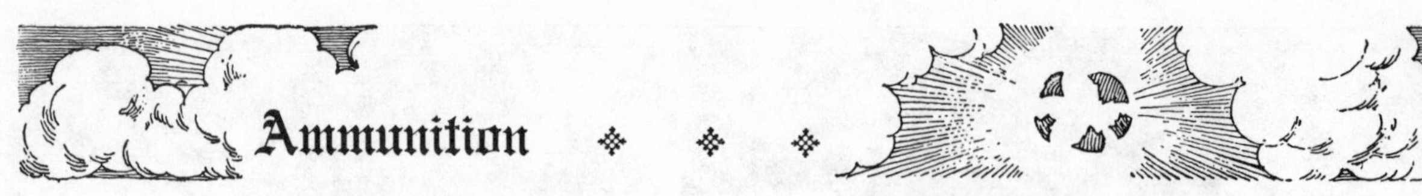

Another device consisted of making the projectiles of wrought iron, with the base cup-shaped like the lead bullet for the small arms. There were also systems resembling the Federal Parrott projectiles, and a type that had a sabot like the Schenkl of the Federal service, except that most of the sabots were made of lead. The Whitworth, Hotchkiss, Armstrong, and Blakely types were very effective.

Lieutenant-Colonel J. W. Mallet, who was in charge of the Confederate States Central Laboratory at Macon, Georgia, devised a shell having a polyhedral cavity, instead of a conical or spherical one, in order to provide for a definite number of pieces when it burst. In explanation of his improvement, Colonel Mallet said that it obviously was not a matter of indifference into what number of pieces the shell might separate on bursting; that if the pieces were very small the destructive effect of each would be insignificant, while, on the other hand, if the pieces were large and few in number, the chance of objects in the neighborhood being hit would be slight. With the size of the fragments known, in order to produce a certain effect, it was clearly desirable that the shell should burst into as many pieces of that size as possible, and the fragments should be projected as equally as possible in all directions about the center of explosion. As ordinary shells then made were either spherical or elongated, it was almost impossible to tell along which lines the case would break, since the interior surface was symmetrical and parallel to the exterior. To effect the desired object, Colonel Mallet proposed to cast shells with the polyhedral cavity, so that there would be certain lines of least resistance, along which the shell would be certain to separate.

Prior to the invention of this device, the efforts to cause the shell to burst into equal parts had been confined to the "shrapnel shell" and the "segment shell." In both of these types the walls of the case were thin, and enclosed a definite number of pieces of metal which would scatter as the shell

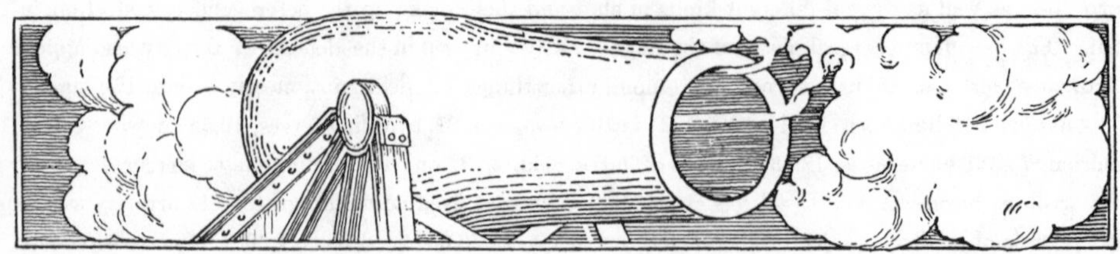

SOLID SHOT, MORTAR SHELLS AND GRAPE IN RICHMOND RUINS

In this photograph piles of solid shot, mortar-shells, and boxes of ammunition are seen lying amidst the ruins of the Tredegar Iron Works. The foreground is covered with a miscellaneous collection of grape and débris. The shot held together by two, three, four, and in some cases five plates, are grape. All these missiles, made to be hurled in the faces of the advancing Union armies, now lie on the ground, helter-skelter, at their mercy. They will never cleave the Virginia air, shrieking their messages of death. The war is over, and every true American, South and North, is proud that it was fought so well, glad to be a citizen of the reunited nation, and more than happy that no more lives are to be sacrificed to the preservation of those principles of brotherhood and unity which make it the greatest Republic in the world and that such a scene as this will never be repeated.

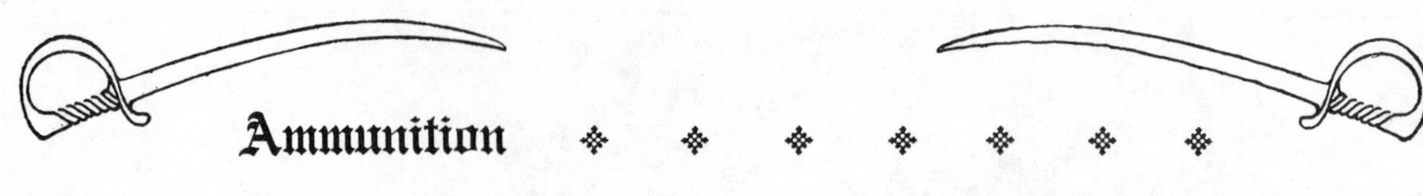

burst. It was a matter of indifference as to how large or how small the pieces of the case became.

In the use of this new form of shell for the 6-, 12-, 24-, and 32-pounders, the cavities were completely filled with powder. Musket or rifle powder always gave the best results with the 6-pounder, and fine-grained cannon powder was suitable for the others.

The Federal artillery paid the Confederate service the compliment of appreciating the improvements in shells, and in 1867, General Henry L. Abbot, of the Corps of Engineers, in a report on siege-ordnance used during the war, stated that there were two improvements in mortar-shells introduced by the Confederates which, in his judgment, should be adopted into the United States service. He did not state who was responsible for the innovations in the Confederate service, but the reference was to the shells perfected by Colonel Mallet and to the providing of certain mortar-shells with ears, to permit greater ease of handling.

Many failures of the Confederate artillery were attributed by their officers to defective ammunition, yet they unanimously pronounced the service of their Ordnance Department, which supplied it, to be the best possible under the circumstances. To illustrate the difficulties under which the department labored, it may be remembered that all the operations had to be organized from the foundation. Waste had to be prevented, and a system of accounting established. The raw troops had no conception of the value of ammunition, and frequently it was lost or damaged through neglect. Although the Confederate armies were never in condition to use ammunition as lavishly as the Federals, the supply never failed in great emergencies, and no disaster has been attributed to its scarcity; and, in fact, whatever scarcity there was must be attributed principally to the inability of the army to carry it, and not to the inability of the Ordnance Department to supply it in sufficient quantities.

IX

ENTRENCHING AND FORTIFICATION

CONFEDERATE ABATIS—COLLECTED AT PETERSBURG, TO BE PLACED IN POSITION AGAINST GRANT'S ATTACK

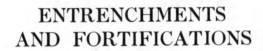

ENTRENCHMENTS AND FORTIFICATIONS

By O. E. Hunt
Captain, United States Army

THE development of the use of earthworks in war between civilized nations has been due to the adoption and increase of power of long-range firearms. The introduction of the breech-loading rifle, of comparatively recent date, has served to give a still greater impetus to the subject of field-works for the protection of the forces engaged, and to-day the spade is second in importance only to the rifle. "Hasty entrenchments," as they are known by soldiers, were first used largely in the American Civil War.

Even at that time, General Sherman expressed his belief that earthworks, and especially field-works, were destined to play a conspicuous part in all future wars, since they enabled a force to hold in check a superior one for a time, and time is a valuable element in all military operations.

At the beginning of the Civil War, the opinion in the North and South was adverse to the use of field-works, for the manual labor required to throw them up was thought to detract from the dignity of a soldier. The opinion prevailed in some quarters that masked batteries were not devices of civilized warfare; and the epithet of "dirt-diggers" was applied to the advocates of entrenchments. Expressions were heard to the effect that the difference ought to be settled by "a fair, stand-up fight, in the open."

"Self-preservation" as a law of nature, and "necessity," as the mother of invention, soon impressed themselves, however, on the officers and men confronting one another in the field—

HOW THE PIONEER PHOTOGRAPHER HELPED TO FORTIFY

The lettering on the wagon curtain, "Photographic Wagon, Engineer Department," explains how the problem of preserving the visual teachings of war was solved for the Union Government. Vast strides in photography were being made by the pioneers Brady, Gardner, and Captain Poe. Diagrams and sketches gave place to actual reflections of the engineering problems which were overcome. Here is the first instance of field-photography for a war department. This photograph reveals the interior of Union Fort Steadman, in front of Petersburg, and its bomb-proof quarters in traverses. On the right is a photographic wagon of the Engineer Corps. The attendant is taking his ease in its shade. This photographic outfit was maintained for the purpose of keeping an official record of matters of professional engineering interest, and good use was made of it. In the West, Captain O. M. Poe was performing a similar service as chief of photography of the United States Engineer Corps. General John Gross Barnard was General Grant's chief of engineers in the East. The accompanying set of photographs of fortifications is largely from these sources.

the first maxim dictating that it was better to dig dirt than to stand up and be shot at, and the second quickly pointed the way to make dirt digging effective. Great necessity and the stern experience of war drove erroneous notions from the heads of the combatants, and before the conflict had progressed far, we find both armies digging trenches without orders, whether in the presence of the enemy or not.

One of the historians of the war has stated that they waited neither for orders, deployment of skirmishers, nor even for formation of lines. The standing rule, adopted by common consent without a dissenting voice, was that they should proceed with this work without waiting for instructions. It mattered not that their lines might soon be moved. A little labor and effort on the soldiers' part at the opportune time often saved a life later.

It was the good common sense of the troops that led them to understand the value of even slight protection. The high intelligence of the individual American soldier made it a simple matter for him to grasp this fundamental truth of his own accord. He did not need to be educated to it by his officers; he knew it by instinct as soon as the enemy began firing at him. Nor was the initiative in the matter of seeking both natural and artificial protection caused by his knowledge of the art of war. Certain features of the art came to him instinctively, and this was one of them.

The Confederates made great use of earthworks, and by their aid were able to hold the Federals, in superior numbers, at half-rifle-shot distance on many hard-fought fields. On many occasions they extemporized protection and dug themselves into rifle-pits, hid their artillery in gun-pits and behind epaulments on the flanks of their infantry lines, and thus made their positions impregnable.

The rapidity with which adequate protection from rifle fire could be obtained by the use of bayonets, tin cups, knives, and other parts of the equipment which the soldier always had

THE ENGINEER PHOTOGRAPHER BEFORE ATLANTA, 1864—A CAPTURED CONFEDERATE FORT

A CLOSER VIEW OF THE ENTANGLEMENTS ON MARIETTA STREET—CHEVAUX-DE-FRISE

with him, early became a surprise to everyone; and it did not take long to discover that a short additional time and a little more work rendered that same pit safe from ordinary direct artillery fire. In loose soil, a few minutes sufficed to throw up a mound of earth a foot high and fifteen inches in thickness, by about two feet in length, for cover against bullets, and this was often topped by a knapsack. It was not believed when the war broke out that a man could save his life by lying behind such a slight cover, but before the campaign on the Peninsula was over, every man of both armies knew it.

The Confederates threw up works on the field of Manassas immediately after their victory. The position was well chosen and the entrenchments were very well constructed. To increase the appearance of strength a number of embrasures were filled with "quaker guns," so-called by the Federals—being simply logs shaped to resemble cannon and placed in position to deceive the foe. These lines were located and the works thrown up, not with the object of assuming the offensive, but to hold the advantage they had gained until it should be decided what further operations should be undertaken. Consequently, their entrenchments were for defensive purposes only, as the quaker guns indicated.

The Federal plan of campaign having been decided on, the information reached the Confederates before the Union army was started for the Peninsula, and Manassas was evacuated immediately. The quaker guns were still in position when the Federals took possession of the Manassas works. When McClellan arrived on the Peninsula, he found that the Confederates were there ahead of him in sufficient force to place works across from Yorktown, utilizing, in a large measure, the trace of the old Revolutionary works of Lord Cornwallis, and strengthening the parapets to fulfil the more modern conditions of warfare. The Yorktown works were built for the same general purposes as the Manassas lines—for defense. And they served the purpose admirably, for

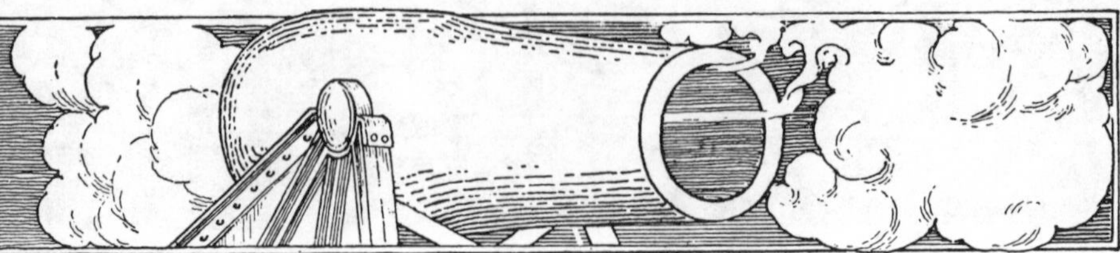

CLOSER STILL TO THE ATLANTA FORT

PICKET FENCES TO STOP SHERMAN'S ATTACK

Picket fences with shaped and molded points, dangerous to the small boy's breeches in times of peace, have been utilized by the Confederates to delay Sherman's men for that fatal instant which loses many lives to a charging line. These seem proportionately as effective as the *chevaux-de-frise*, in the rear—logs pierced by sharpened spokes and the elaborate ditches and embankments, and palisades constructed in the works all about Atlanta. Historians have declared that no clear conception of Sherman's remarkable campaign to Atlanta can be had unless the difficult character of the country and the formidable nature of these artificial defenses are remembered. Practically every foot of the way from Ringgold to Atlanta was entrenched.

McClellan's army was delayed a month before the Confederates evacuated.

The preliminary reconnaissances by the Federal engineers persuaded McClellan that a regular siege of Yorktown was necessary, and accordingly strong works were erected opposite those of the Confederates. Emplacements for heavy guns and parapets to protect them were pushed to completion. Regular siege-works, consisting of "parallels" and "approaches," were projected. The Confederates held the position until the last moment, and just as fire was about to be opened on them they abandoned the lines. By that time the works of defense had assumed almost the proportions of a fortress. Enormous labor was required to effect this, and, correspondingly, the labors of the besiegers were great. The low-lying ground of the Peninsula was under water part of the time from the tremendous rains, and the heavy guns of both armies sank into the mud, and it required tremendous exertions to extricate them. Yet, without fighting, the purpose of the Confederates was attained—that of delay; and, while many guns had to be abandoned, the expense was compensated for by the increased preparations of the main Confederate army.

But, notwithstanding the lessons in fortification given both combatants by these operations, the individual soldier did not appreciate, to any great extent, his own responsibility in the matter of entrenchments, since these Yorktown works were on a large scale and used by the entire masses of men of the hostile armies. It was in the campaign to follow that the important instruction in the art was to come.

The progress of the Federals was energetically disputed by inferior numbers in field-works at Williamsburg, which was not so solidly fortified as Yorktown. A large fort with six redoubts barred the road into the town, but, with the flanks not well protected, the position could be turned, and the Union troops did not wait to undertake a siege. At Mechanicsville, Gaines' Mill, Seven Pines, Malvern Hill, and Harrison's

FEDERAL FORTIFICATIONS AT ALLATOONA PASS, GEORGIA

When Sherman's army passed this point—early in June, 1864—entrenching was becoming a fine art with the American armies. From the battle of New Hope Church, on May 25th, almost every advanced line on either side entrenched itself as soon as its position was taken up. Not to be outdone by their Western comrades, the great armies operating in Virginia also got down and "dug dirt." In timber, huge logs were placed in position and covered with earth. Without timber, the parapets were often made as much as fifteen feet thick, to stop artillery fire. Even on the march the Western armies found time to make gabions of wattles with marvelous celerity.

THE TYPICAL HEAD-LOG WITH SKIDS—SHERMAN'S DEFENSE BEFORE ATLANTA

If a shell drove back one of the head-logs in this photograph, it might crush and maim the soldiers in the trenches but for the skids across the trenches. The head-log was placed on top of the earth parapet, with a space left under the log to permit the men to fire.

Landing, the works thrown up by the Federals were increasingly strong, and the private soldier gradually learned his own individual responsibility in preparing the earth-and-log protection.

In the Seven Days' Battles, while they were on the defensive, the Union troops took advantage of all sorts of protection —woods, rail fences, trees, irregularities of the ground, and houses, but made little use of earthworks. There were so many of the other forms of protection and time was so precious that earthworks did not figure much in their calculations.

The last scene of the Peninsula campaign was placed at Malvern Hill, and Harrison's Landing, which was strongly fortified. There was thrown up an improvised fortress where, after several days of victorious pursuit of the Federals, the Confederates were checked.

The system of fortifications in this first campaign paralyzed the offensive movements on both sides, saving first the Confederates and then the Federals probably from total defeat, and proving beyond doubt that entrenchments of even the slightest character gave excellent results in defensive operations, but also that they must be constructed "with a celerity that defied the rapid march of the opposing army and with an ability and aptitude that enabled a defender to transform an entire field of battle into an improvised fortress."

Yet, despite the experiences of this campaign, the lesson was not fixed in the minds of the combatants. The former schools of military teaching still showed their effects. In the campaign between Lee and Pope, in 1862, but little use was made of field-works, and at Antietam Lee fortified only a part of his line, though strictly on the defensive. But Antietam evidently taught the lesson anew, for we find that same Confederate army at Fredericksburg with lines that defied the efforts of the assailants as effectually as permanent fortifications could have done.

The manner of construction of these works of hasty entrenchment usually was this: The men, deployed in a line of

"GUNS"

THE CONFEDERATES

ABANDONED

AT MANASSAS

These are some of the earliest Confederate fortifications. The works were thrown up on the field of Manassas immediately after their victory. The position was well chosen and the entrenchments very well constructed. As seen in the upper photograph, the time was before the soldiers had learned to "dig dirt"; the works are rather thrown up than dug down. A happy combination of the two was later adopted by both the Confederate and Union armies. To increase the appearance of strength in 1861, a number of embrasures were filled with "quaker guns," so called by the Federals on account of the unwarlike nature of the followers of that faith. These were simply logs shaped to resemble cannon and placed in position to deceive the foe. The end projecting from the fortifications was painted black to make the deception more complete. This was a particularly amusing subterfuge on the part of the Confederates, so destitute of cannon. They had captured a few pieces at the first battle of Manassas, but their supply was still woefully inadequate.

A

"QUAKER GUN"

AT CENTREVILLE

skirmishers, would dig, individually, shallow trenches about four or five feet by two, with their longest dimension toward the foe, and throw up the earth in a little mound of a foot or fifteen inches in height, on the side toward the opponent. This would result in a line of such excavations and mounds, each individually constructed and without any communication with its neighbors. Then the neighbors would dig out the ground between them and throw it to the front, thus forming a continuous line of earthern parapet; but, if their antagonists were firing, or danger was near, it was preferable to deepen the trenches and throw up a larger earth protection before joining the individual trenches. In the rear of such hasty works, heavier lines often were constructed by large forces working with spades.

Semi-permanent works were used both in the East and in the West. Island No. 10, Forts Henry and Donelson, and other small works were all of a permanent or semi-permanent character, having more or less of the scientific touch that followed the old school of fortification. But little was known in the West of the art of hasty entrenchments for some time. At Shiloh, the Federal camps were not entrenched, although the foe was known to be somewhere in the vicinity. General Sherman said that the reason for the lack of field-works was that their construction would have made the new men timid. As a matter of fact, the value of them was not realized by anyone, except that it was known, of course, that heavy works were capable of withstanding an attacking body several times the strength of the defending force.

But, after Shiloh, Halleck took command and erected earthworks nearly every foot of the way from Pittsburg Landing to Corinth, Mississippi, a distance of at least twenty miles, and then prepared for a regular siege of the latter place, where his army outnumbered that of Beauregard about two to one. His approach took a month, at the end of which time Beauregard evacuated Corinth without loss.

This cautious advance marked the first use of

A CONFEDERATE WATER BATTERY THAT DEFENDED VICKSBURG

The natural fortifications around Vicksburg rendered it well-nigh impregnable, and it was made completely so by S. H. Lockett, chief engineer of the defenses under General Pemberton. Only starvation finally reduced the beleaguered force. In two unsuccessful assaults thousands of Federal soldiers were shot down. An instance of the spirit in which Americans fight is related by Lieutenant Roswell Henry Mason, who led his company of the Seventy-second Illinois Infantry into the city. The soldiers started in with three full days' rations in their haversacks. The gaunt and hungry Confederates lined the road on either side. "Hey, Yank, throw us a hardtack," they called; or "Hey, Yank, chuck us a piece of bacon." When Mason's company halted in the city not a haversack contained a morsel of food.

CONFEDERATE WORKS BEHIND VICKSBURG

WHERE GRANT'S ARMY WAS HELD FOR OVER SIX WEEKS

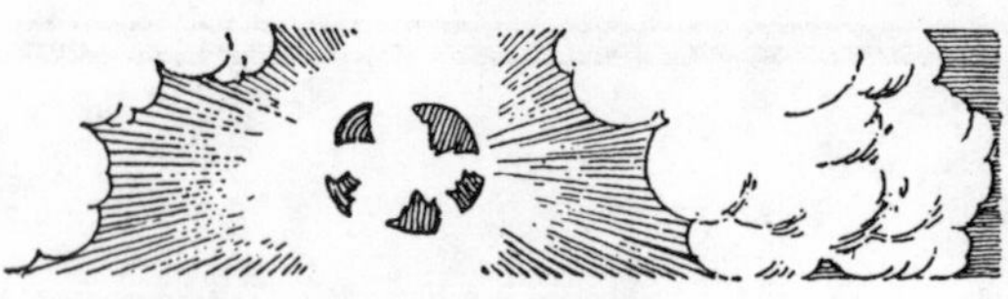

entrenchments at every halt. In at least two of the great battles during the preceding period of the war—Bull Run and Shiloh—no entrenchments to speak of had been used. Now, Halleck, going to the extreme in the other direction, lost valuable time constructing trenches for which a little effort at reconnaissance would have told him there was no use. With such good preliminary preparation we should be prepared to see field-fortifications used everywhere more lavishly. And we are not disappointed in finding that both parties to the controversy had now learned their lesson.

At Stone's River, or Murfreesboro, the Federals entrenched a part of their extreme left and the Confederates their right and center before the battle. On the first day, the Federal right was driven back, and during the following night the Confederates entrenched practically all of the remainder of their line. The net result of the battle was a drawn fight, the opponents not daring to attack each other's works seriously. A wholesome respect had grown for hasty entrenchments. The " dirt-diggers " were coming to the front.

The defensive warfare carried on to the end by the Confederates in the West placed them most of the time behind their temporary or semi-permanent works. All the forts along the Mississippi were, necessarily, of the strongest character, assuming the importance of permanent fortifications, armed with heavy guns and manned by small permanent garrisons and, during Grant's and Banks' campaigns, by larger garrisons, pushed in from the field. All of these stronger places had to be taken by the process of regular siege.

When Bragg retired from Murfreesboro, he entrenched several lines between that place and Chattanooga, but Rosecrans, by consummate strategic skill, turned him out of all of them without fighting serious battles. On the battlefield of Chickamauga, the infantry and artillery of Thomas' wing of the Federal army stood " like a rock " behind entrenchments and barricades of earth, fence rails, and logs. Bragg, attacking

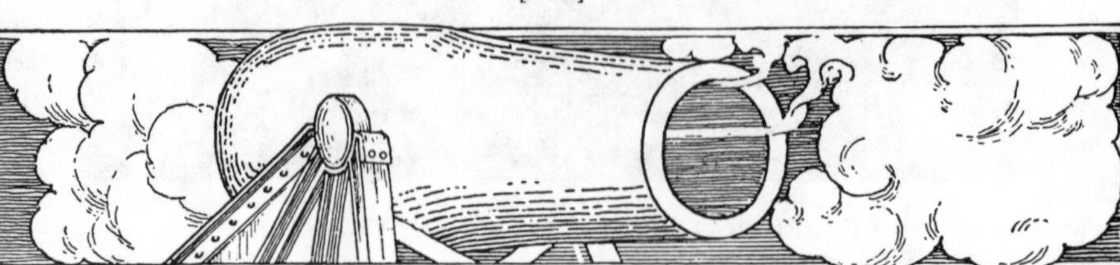

CONSTRUCTING GABIONS FOR GRANT'S ATTACK ON PETERSBURG

The basket-like objects in this photograph are gabions. On the top of one row lie sand-bags. The soldier is seated on three short fascines, and in the background are some long fascines on another row of gabions. A gabion is a cylindrical basket with no bottom, which may be placed in a fortification and filled with earth. Gabions make an exceedingly strong defense, since the dirt remains even if the baskets are smashed. Thousands of gabions were used in the entrenchments of both attacking and defending forces at Petersburg. Fascines consist of small branches or twigs tied by wire or rope or thongs of some tough vine. They vary in length according to whether they are to be used in the construction of works or filling in a ditch. They hold the earth at a steeper slope than the natural slope when the earth is loose. Gabions are also useful for revetments from their perpendicularity; through sand-bags, a foot or two might be added to their height.

in the open, was repulsed, but later sat down behind entrenchments in front of Rosecrans at Chattanooga, and almost starved out the Federal army before it could be relieved.

Grant attacked Bragg to drive him off. Hooker was successful at Lookout Mountain, but Sherman did not make any headway against the right of the Confederate army, being checked before the heavy trenches. Grant ordered Thomas' men to take the works at the foot of Missionary Ridge and halt. Because of the Federal defeat at Chickamauga, it is reported that Grant feared that the men of Thomas' army could not be trusted to stand under heavy pressure, and he did not want them to go farther than the foot of the ridge. He ordered that they stop there, after driving the Confederates from the trenches. But the lines kept on, higher, higher, and the clouds of battle became larger as they ascended. Seeing the line disobeying orders, Grant turned to Thomas, who was near, and inquired by whose orders the men had gone beyond the foot of the mountain, to which Thomas is said to have replied, "By their own, I think." Grant's rejoinder was: "If they succeed, all right. But if they don't, some one will suffer for this." The works at the top were heavy; but Thomas' troops succeeded, and no one suffered except the gallant men of both sides who fell.

Grant went East, turning over the command of the Western Federal armies to Sherman, who prepared to attack Johnston, entrenched around Dalton, in northern Georgia. Buzzard's Roost formed the strongest portion of Johnston's line, which consisted of heavy fortifications on the heights, in front of which lighter lines had been placed. Sherman felt this position, found it almost impregnable, made a flank movement, and turned Johnston out of his stronghold. In the retaining attack on the works, the Federal troops took a portion of the lower lines of entrenchments, but found the upper works too strong. The turning movement having succeeded, the Union troops withdrew from the front, and Johnston retired to

THE "SAP" AND THE "COONSKIN" TOWER AT VICKSBURG, 1863

In the center rises "Coonskin" Tower, a lookout and station for sharpshooters. It was built under the direction of Lieutenant Henry C. Foster of the Twenty-third Indiana Infantry. In honor of his raccoon-fur cap, the soldiers nicknamed him "Coonskin." The sap-roller, shown in the illustration below, was used for construction of a sap or trench extending toward the defenders' works in a siege. A famous sap appears in the upper photograph—that built by Logan's busy men, winding its way toward the strong redan of the veteran Third Louisiana Regiment on the Jackson Road. First a parallel is opened—that is, a trench is constructed parallel to the besieged entrenchments. From this are constructed several approaches, or saps, to enable an approach to be made under cover to a position where a second parallel may be. These are built in a zigzag direction, so that the defender cannot enfilade the trench, except when very close to the opposing works, when it is frequently necessary to approach directly. Here is where the sap-roller comes into play. It is rolled at the head of the trench in such a manner as to protect the workmen from their opponents' fire. It must therefore be thick enough to stop bullets. To construct a sap-roller in the form shown, two cylindrical baskets of the same length are made, a small one to form the interior wall, and a larger one for the outer wall.

A SAP–ROLLER READY FOR SERVICE

Resaca, and thence to succeeding positions until Atlanta was reached. Direct assaults on entrenchments nearly always failed with heavy loss.

By this time it was thoroughly understood that the function of breastworks, whether of earth, logs, rails, or other material, was to give the advantage to the defense, and consequently everyone recognized that good troops behind such protection could hold off three or four times their number of equally good troops making the assault. This was the proportion depended on, and the calculations of the commanding generals were made accordingly. It was usually considered that troops in the works were inferior to the assailants if they did not succeed in withstanding the attack of several times their own strength.

Naturally, also, the character of the works changed somewhat with increasing experience. With rifles, an entrenched line was almost certain to be able to dispose effectually of an approaching force which had eight hundred yards over which to advance in the open, or over ground partially open. In woods, an abatis, or entanglement, was an effectual aid in stopping the advance before it reached the works, since it delayed the line, and enabled the defenders to get a close-range fire on the assailants.

Beginning with the battle at New Hope Church, on the 25th of May, 1864, almost every advanced line, of either side, entrenched itself as soon as the position was taken up. Whenever an organization was moved, its commander sent out a skirmish line ahead of the new position, for the protection of the men engaged in entrenching; caused an inspection of the ground to be made by competent officers to determine the location of the trenches, and then ordered his men to work. The workers stacked their arms, took tools from the wagons or availed themselves of those carried by the troops, and each small organization—company or battalion—entrenched its own part of the line. In timber, huge logs were placed in position and

"SOFT" WALLS BETTER DEFENSES THAN "HARD"—FORT SUMTER

In 1863, the stone walls of Sumter were soon breached by the guns of the Federal fleet, but behind the breaches rose many feet of gabions filled with earth. These were replaced as fast as the guns of the fleet dislodged the soft earth. General G. T. Beauregard wrote in his official report of February 8, 1863: "The introduction of heavy rifled guns and iron-clad steamers in the attack of masonry forts has greatly changed the condition of the problem applicable to Fort Sumter when it was built, and we must now use the few and imperfect means at our command to increase its defensive features as far as practicable." This beautiful view of Fort Sumter in 1865, clear in every detail, one of Barnard's photographic masterpieces, shows the battered parapets of the fort strengthened again and again by gabions. The humble baskets not only served this purpose, but kept flying pieces of the more solid construction which they reënforced from maiming the garrison. One would hardly imagine that the declivity in the center of the mass of gabions had once been a well-chiseled flight of steps. This kind of fortification deteriorated very rapidly unless constantly repaired. In Sumter the work of repairing was particularly heavy, following one bombardment after another throughout the four years of the war. It was not until February 17, 1865, after Sherman's great march, that the fort was evacuated.

covered with earth. Without timber, the parapets were often made as much as fifteen feet thick, to stop artillery fire. A head log, under which the men could fire, was frequently utilized. When struck by a large projectile, of course a log in that position was liable to be thrown backward and injure a number of men. Various methods were used to prevent its coming back, and one device, to prevent injury to the men in case it did come back, was to place skids under it, perpendicular to the line of the parapet, and extending back across the trench so that it would slide over the heads of the men.

Except for special works, all these lines were constructed by the enlisted men with very little direction from the officers, and foreign officers visiting the troops are quoted as being astonished very often at seeing troops of the line performing what, to them, seemed technical engineering duties which, in their services, would be done by trained officers and men.

The Confederates, on their part, occasionally were able to erect their works beforehand, for, when it was decided to retire, the decision was always arrived at deliberately, and time taken to survey the ground more thoroughly than was possible on the side of the assailants. These works having been erected with more thoroughness than those in the immediate vicinity of the foe, more elaborate preparations frequently were made to defend the works. Devices such as *chevaux-de-frise,* consisting of logs pierced by sharpened spokes, were sometimes resorted to, and palisades were constructed in the ditches of strong works. One historian has remarked that no clear conception of the remarkable campaign to Atlanta can be had unless the difficult character of the country and the formidable nature of these artificial defenses are remembered.

Returning to the armies of the Potomac and of Northern Virginia, we find that, at Chancellorsville, Hooker lost precious time by stopping, after attaining Lee's flank, and entrenching, instead of making an immediate attack; and another entrenched line—this time of value—was taken up after Howard

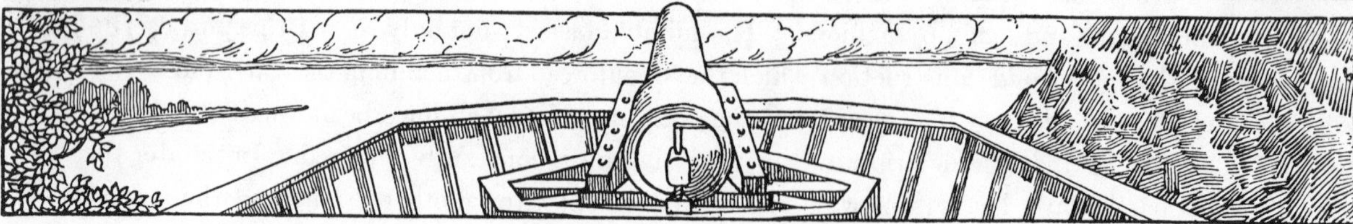

FIGHTING WITH SHARPENED STICKS—PRIMITIVE BUT EFFECTIVE PROTECTION

For its murderous artillery fire every dawn and dusk during the nine months' siege of Petersburg, Union Fort Sedgwick was named by the Confederates "Fort Hell." It was located some three miles south of Fort McGilvery on the southern end of the inner line of Federal entrenchments, east of Petersburg. "Hell" feared invasion in this instance, as the bristling row of slender sharpened sticks planted in the salient witnesses. They were simply light palisades, held by putting poles through holes in a sill, and then fixing the whole in a horizontal position. They look absurdly ineffectual, these sharpened sticks designed to stop the onslaught of an assaulting column, but when another row of them and another and yet another awaited the assailants, their movements were retarded so that they became exposed to fire.

MAJOR-GENERAL D. P. WOODBURY

THE ENGINEER WHO BUILT THE PONTOON BRIDGES AT FREDERICKSBURG

Under the command of regular officers the volunteer engineers soon reached a high point of efficiency. On the Peninsula a brigade, consisting of the Fifteenth and Fiftieth New York Volunteer Engineers, was commanded by Brigadier-General Daniel Phineas Woodbury, a West Point graduate of the class of 1836, and a captain of engineers at the outbreak of the war. In the Peninsula campaign the engineers were active in constructing fortification and building bridges. "Woodbury's Bridge" across the Chickahominy did notable service. Gallant and meritorious conduct in this campaign secured General Woodbury the rank of colonel in the United States Army. At Fredericksburg similar service connected with the work of the pontoon trains brought for him the rank of brigadier-general. He was brevetted major-general August 15, 1864.

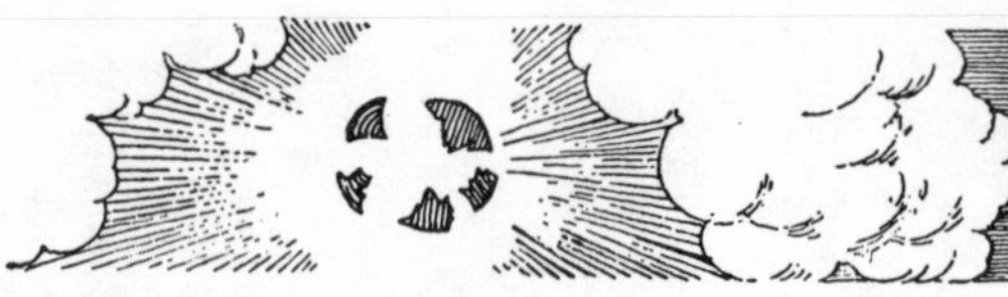

had been driven in by Jackson's flank march and attack. At Gettysburg, the Army of the Potomac made no concerted effort to entrench, but relied largely on natural obstacles.

But a decided change in the record of events commenced when the final campaign started from the Rapidan under Grant, in 1864. We already have noted how, in the Western armies, the art of entrenching had been highly developed. Not to be outdone by their Western comrades, the great armies operating in Virginia now got down and systematically "dug dirt." Each force hugged the ground with bulldog tenacity. The end was coming. Everyone saw that the war must stop, and neither army felt that it was the one that was going to meet defeat.

The great battles of the Wilderness, Spotsylvania, and Cold Harbor, on the way to Petersburg, were but a succession of attacks upon improvised fortresses, defeats for the assaulting troops, flank movements to a new position, new entrenchments, new assaults, new flank movements, and so on continuously. The stronger Northern army never overcame the weaker Southern legions so long as the latter remained in the trenches. The preponderance of numbers enabled the Federal armies to extend ever to the left, reaching out the long left arm to get around the flank of the Confederate positions. This was the final operation in front of Petersburg. To meet the continuously extending left of the Federals, Lee's lines became dangerously thin, and he had to evacuate his works. He was not driven out by the foes assaulting the works themselves until his lines became so thin that they were broken by weight of numbers. Here the principle that already had been demonstrated was again shown to be true—one American in the trench was worth several Americans outside—for all Americans are intrinsically equal.

While these stirring events of the East were occurring, Schofield at Franklin, Tennessee, attacked by Hood, proved again that the increasing faith in hasty field-works was not ill

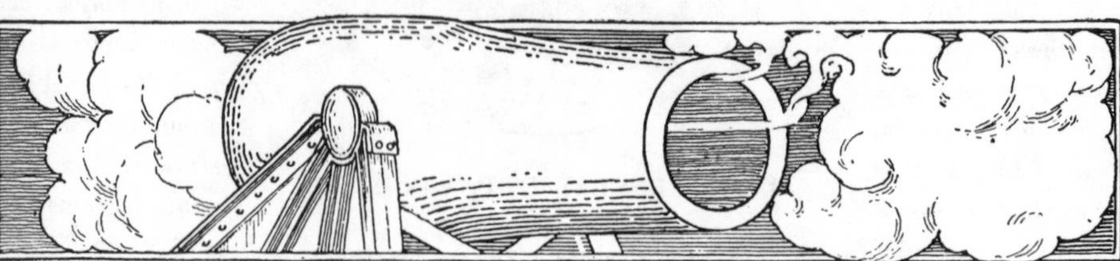

FORT SEDGWICK, WHERE THE GARRISON HELD ITS GROUND

Although the Union Fort Sedgwick before Petersburg was not as elaborate a piece of engineering as the bastioned Forts Wadsworth and Dushane, which commanded the Weldon Railroad, it was nevertheless an exceedingly well-constructed example of field-works. It had to be so in order to stand up against the vindictive fire of Fort Mahone. From this fastness the determined Confederates incessantly tried to render Sedgwick susceptible to assault, thus enabling them to break through and relieve the Army of Northern Virginia from its predicament. The Petersburg campaign was not exactly a formal siege, but the operations of two armies strongly entrenched, either of which at any moment was likely to strike a powerful blow at the other. An abatis, or entanglement, lies to the right in front of the thick earthworks with their revetments of gabions. The Confederates never dared to attempt to carry this huge field fort. They finally selected the far weaker Fort Stedman as the point for their last dash for liberty. Below is another section of the gabion entrenchments of Fort Sedgwick, heightened by sand-bags. These fortifications, very effective when occupied and kept in repair, began to fade away under the weather, and the depredations of the residents of the locality in search of fire wood. A few years after the war hardly a vestige of them remained. Rainstorms had done more damage than the tons of Federal shells.

SEDGWICK—GABIONS HEIGHTENED BY SAND-BAGS

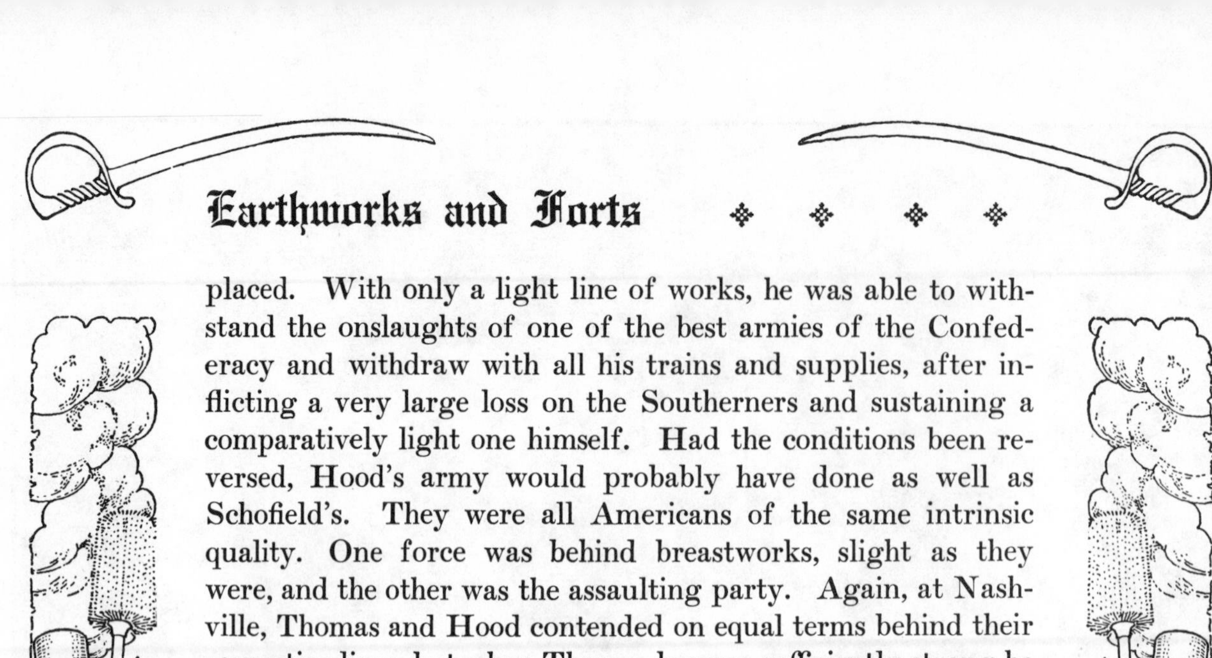

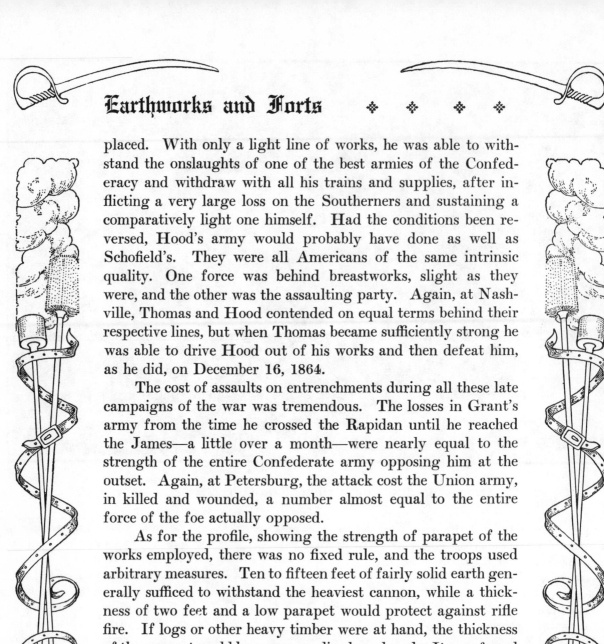

placed. With only a light line of works, he was able to withstand the onslaughts of one of the best armies of the Confederacy and withdraw with all his trains and supplies, after inflicting a very large loss on the Southerners and sustaining a comparatively light one himself. Had the conditions been reversed, Hood's army would probably have done as well as Schofield's. They were all Americans of the same intrinsic quality. One force was behind breastworks, slight as they were, and the other was the assaulting party. Again, at Nashville, Thomas and Hood contended on equal terms behind their respective lines, but when Thomas became sufficiently strong he was able to drive Hood out of his works and then defeat him, as he did, on December 16, 1864.

The cost of assaults on entrenchments during all these late campaigns of the war was tremendous. The losses in Grant's army from the time he crossed the Rapidan until he reached the James—a little over a month—were nearly equal to the strength of the entire Confederate army opposing him at the outset. Again, at Petersburg, the attack cost the Union army, in killed and wounded, a number almost equal to the entire force of the foe actually opposed.

As for the profile, showing the strength of parapet of the works employed, there was no fixed rule, and the troops used arbitrary measures. Ten to fifteen feet of fairly solid earth generally sufficed to withstand the heaviest cannon, while a thickness of two feet and a low parapet would protect against rifle fire. If logs or other heavy timber were at hand, the thickness of the parapet could be correspondingly reduced. It was found that even a slight work, if held by strong rifle fire, always prevailed against the advancing force, unless the latter attacked in overwhelming numbers.

Of the stronger fortifications on each side, those exemplifying the best types were the defenses of Washington, of Richmond and Petersburg, of Vicksburg, Port Hudson, and New Orleans, and the works at Mobile, Fort Fisher, Fort Pulaski,

BURROWS OF GRANT'S SOLDIERS BESIEGING PETERSBURG

In these bomb-proof quarters of Fort Sedgwick, and many others, the Federals sought protection. When the artillery fire was not making it "Fort Hell" in fact as well as in name, the bullets of the Confederate sharpshooters were singing over the salient and the breastworks. A cap on a stick thrust above the breastworks was invariably carried away. Many a man taking a hasty glance over the parapet to note the effect of his own fire was killed. Barrels and gabions were used to lengthen the chimneys needed for heating the underground huts. The distance between the main lines, at Fort Sedgwick, was about fifteen hundred feet, and between the pickets only two hundred.

CONFEDERATE ENTRENCHMENTS AS FAR AS THE EYE COULD REACH

The Confederate fortifications in defense of Petersburg were among the most substantial and strongest erected during the war. These tremendous works were built with a degree of skill that has since made them a wonder to military men. They were undermined and blown up by Union troops at the famous "Crater," but were never carried in a front attack till the final assault after which Lee withdrew.

and Charleston. These were all elaborate and designed to sustain sieges and assaults of the heaviest character.

There were also other strong fortifications that fulfilled the requirements of modern warfare absolutely. The improvements in weapons necessitated changing and, in some instances, entirely abandoning the older conceptions of fortresses, and American ingenuity devised works far better adapted to the powerful weapons of destruction that had been secured and developed by both parties to the conflict.

The habit of making themselves secure at all times became so much second nature that it was not confined to the field of battle. This fact excited the very great interest of foreign observers. In the latter part of the war, whenever the troops halted for whatever purpose, if for nothing more than a short rest on the march, they instinctively entrenched themselves. Even before a fire was built, food prepared, or camp necessities provided for, they frequently set to work to provide a shelter from the foe, and the rapidity with which a serviceable cover could be erected was always a cause for remark. These improvised works were abandoned with the same unconcern with which they were erected. It was entirely a matter of course.

Even by casual inspection and comparison of results, the trade-mark of the American soldier will be found on many of the devices used by the other armies of the world to-day for hasty protection in the field, from the inclemencies of the weather, the disagreeable features of camp-life, and from the enemy. In common with the mark left by the individuality of his civilian comrade, the soldier's initiative has so impressed foreign observers that the effect on other nations is evident. In no profession has the American type stood out more preeminent than in that of soldiering, and in no feature of the military art has that same individuality impressed itself more than in the construction of devices for protection against the winged messengers of death loosed so lavishly by the enemy.

X

THE FEDERAL ENGINEERS

PONTONIERS ON THE DAY OF BATTLE

ROWING THE PONTOONS INTO PLACE, FOR SEDGWICK TO CROSS TO THE REAR OF LEE'S ARMY—RAPPAHANNOCK RIVER, MAY 3, 1863

THE
ENGINEERS DIG
A ROAD FOR THE ARMY

The rapid movement of an army and its supplies wins victories and makes possible the execution of effectiv strategy. Road-making is no less essential to the success of a soldier than the handling of a musket. Th upper photograph shows Major Beers of the Fiftieth New York Engineers, on horseback, directing his battal ion at road-making on the south bank of the North Anna River May 24, 1864. A wagon-train of the Fifth Corps is crossing the bridge by Jericho Mills, constructed on the previous day by Captain Van Brocklin' company of the Fiftieth New York Engineers. In the lower photograph Major Beers has apparently ridde away, but the soldiers are still hard at work. The wagon-train continues to stream steadily over the bridge

50TH N. Y
HARD AT WORK IN
GRANT'S ADVANCE, MAY, 186

A
CLOSER VIEW
MAKING THE DIRT FLY

Iere the reader comes closer to the line of sturdy engineers exerting their muscles in behalf of the Union. The train is over the bridge by this time; only a single wagon is seen, probably attached to the engineer corps. 'arther up the river a number of the men not on this detail have gone in swimming. A couple of tents are 'isible on the bank near the end of the bridge. The busy diggers do not even glance at the men floating on he river below. They are making a road where an army has to pass. Many new ways had to be contructed to enable the supply trains to reach their various commands. South of the river Sheridan's cavalry vas operating. There were continuous engagements on the line of the North Anna River from May 22d to 26th, and at any moment the Confederates might appear from the woods and open fire on the engineers.

ENGINEER CORPS OF THE FEDERAL ARMY

By O. E. Hunt
Captain, United States Army

In modern military operations, no more striking examples of the importance of engineer troops and their work can be found than in the American Civil War. For much of the country over which this great struggle was waged, proper maps were wanting, and frequently roads and bridges had to be built before military movements could be executed. Rivers had to be bridged by pontoons and semi-permanent structures; entrenchments and fortifications had to be constructed when camp was made or a definite position taken for defense or siege, and finally, the men doing this had always to consider the laying-aside of axe and spade, and, shouldering the musket, take their place on the firing-line, where they gave an account of themselves second to none of the combatant organizations. Such conditions of warfare were in striking contrast to those under which the great wars of Europe had been fought, for in the campaigns of Frederick, of Napoleon, and of Moltke, practically every inch of the territory was known and mapped. Military operations took place where well-built roads made travel easy; where permanent forts and walled cities were found, and fighting in swamps or on mountain-tops was unknown. In short, with the formal military science of the day, the American engineers so combined characteristic ingenuity and the lessons of civil life that the progress and success of the battling ranks were made possible under conditions never before encountered in a great war.

The inception of the present Corps of Engineers in the

WHEN THE BRIDGE WAS FINISHED AT FRANKLIN'S CROSSING
APRIL 29, 1863

Hopeful and proud these pontoniers of Hooker's engineer battalion stand upon their just-completed bridge —rushed across in one hour and ten minutes. The bridge "train," wagons and boats, had been masked about a mile from the river in dense woods. Then the boats were carried to the river at night and were actually launched before the Confederates were aware of the enterprise. Troops were ferried across in the face of musketry fire from the opposite bank, and the Confederates were driven off. Captain A. J. Russell, who took this photograph, followed close upon this action. In photographs of Franklin's Crossing taken subsequently, the trees have been chopped down, but here the earth, freshly upturned to make an approach to the bridge, and the little pup-tents just going up across the river, both indicate that the soldiers have just arrived. They were not aware that Jackson was to circle Hooker's right in the woods, take him in reverse and cut him off from United States Ford—and that he was to be huddled into a corner in the Wilderness, hurrying messages to Sedgwick's corps to come to his relief. This bridge, three hundred and ninety feet long, was moved bodily to Fredericksburg and there placed in position on the following Sunday during the battle of Fredericksburg Heights, where Sedgwick finally stormed the position that four months before had cost Burnside nearly 13,000 men. This was one of the most successful exploits of the engineer corps during the entire war.

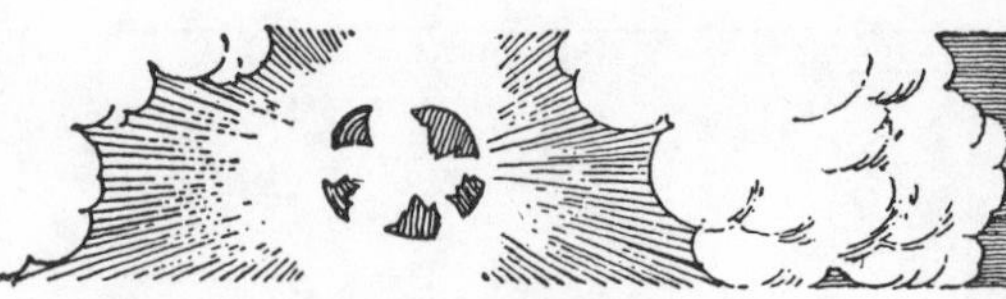

United States army was in 1802. By the act of Congress, of the 16th of March of that year, it was established to consist of one engineer, with the rank of major; two assistant engineers, with the rank of captain; two assistant engineers, with the rank of first lieutenant; two assistant engineers, with the rank of second lieutenant, and ten cadets. The same act authorized the President to make promotions on account of merit whenever he deemed fit, so that the corps, as finally constituted, should not exceed one colonel, one lieutenant-colonel, two majors, four captains, four first lieutenants, and four second lieutenants. The act also provided that the corps, thus constituted, should form a military academy at West Point.

The charge and superintendency of the Military Academy remained in the hands of the Corps of Engineers until July 13, 1866, when, by act of Congress of that date, control passed to the War Department at Washington, and the direct management of the academy to such officers as might be detailed by the President from any of the branches of the service. The Corps of Engineers was thus responsible for the instruction of the officers whose services were invaluable to both the Federal and Confederate armies during the memorable four years of the Civil War.

When the war between the North and South began, there were two organizations of engineers, the Corps of Engineers and the Corps of Topographical Engineers. They were merged in 1863, and thenceforth existed as one organization.

By the act of Congress of August 3, 1861, the Corps of Engineers was reorganized to consist of one colonel, two lieutenant-colonels, four majors, twelve captains, fifteen first lieutenants, fifteen second lieutenants, forty sergeants, forty corporals, eight musicians, two hundred and fifty-six artificers, and two hundred and fifty-six privates—a total of forty-nine commissioned officers and six hundred enlisted men. At the same time the Topographical Engineers were constituted with a total of forty-two commissioned officers. At the end of the

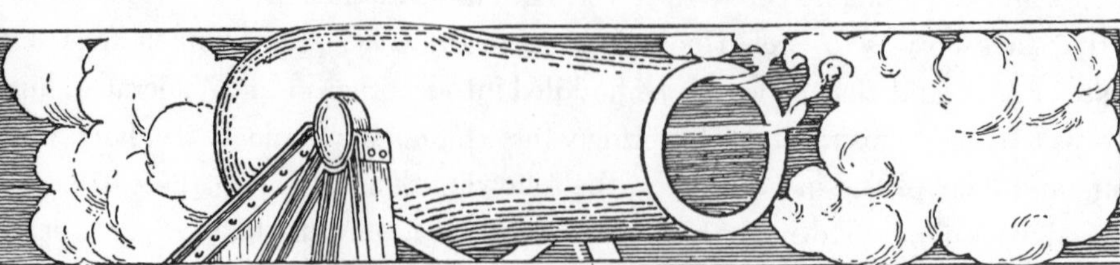

AMATEURS OF '61—UNITED STATES ENGINEERS

This photograph exhibits some unformed engineers the first year of war, with all their experience before them. They had built no bridges at that time, and were not inured to turning from their work to grasp a musket or tranquilly to continue their labor while the dead and wounded from the Confederate sharpshooters' bullets fell thick about them. The uniforms and accouterments are new.

PROFESSIONALS OF '64—GROUP OF COMPANY B, UNITED STATES ENGINEERS

These veterans of Company B as they sit in their camp outside of Petersburg are no longer amateurs, but professionals. Their close-set mouths and steady eyes tell the story of Yorktown, Fredericksburg, along the Potomac and the James; of mighty siege works around Petersburg. They are no longer spick and span as in 1861, but they look much more efficient in their army shirts and loose blouses.

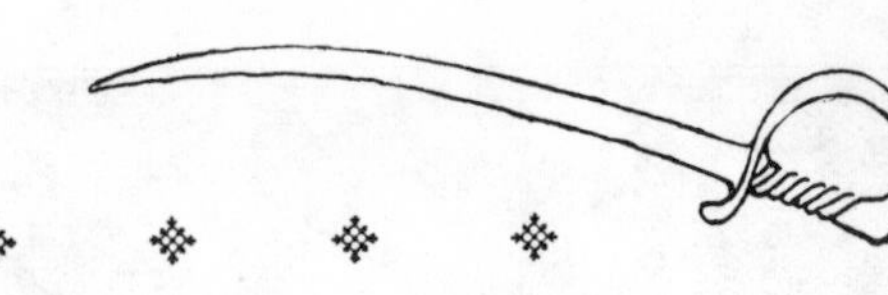

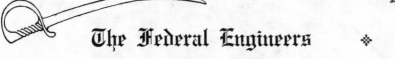

Civil War, the corps consisted of a total of one hundred and five commissioned officers and seven hundred and fifty-two enlisted men.

The duties required of the corps during the war were multitudinous, but consisted principally in planning, tracing, and superintending the construction of all fortifications, of whatever nature, needed in military operations, whether these works were of a temporary or a permanent character; and also in planning, laying-out, and constructing all works needed for the attack or the defense of fortifications. The corps was charged with the duty of securing and reporting upon the topographical features of the country through which the armies were operating, to the extent of furnishing maps and detailed descriptions sufficiently clear and accurate to permit the commanding generals to order the movement of troops with certainty as to the ground over which these troops were to maneuver.

On the field of battle, the exact knowledge of the terrain often decided the result, and the advantage was with the officers who had the best maps. On both sides these were furnished by the engineer officers. They were frequently charged with the duties of selecting positions for camps, either fortified or otherwise, and of reconnoitering the positions of the foe. They had charge of the bridge-equipage of the armies, and under their supervision were built the great structures used for the passage of immense bodies of men over the rivers of the South. Engineer troops were instructed in the arts of sapping, mining, building pontoon bridges, and quickly constructing "hasty entrenchments." Engineer officers not on duty with troops were utilized on the staffs of the commanding generals.

At the outbreak of the war, there were practically no engineer troops—only one small company, which had been organized during the Mexican War. By the act of Congress of August 3, 1861, already referred to, a battalion of four

BLOCKHOUSE BUILT FOR THE DEFENSE OF THE ORANGE & ALEXANDRIA RAILROAD

This blockhouse was near Hunting Creek, close to the Orange & Alexandria Railroad, and covering the bridge over the creek on the Telegraph Road. The walls were built of large logs from sixteen to eighteen inches in diameter. Loop-holes for musketry were cut through the walls, just above the earthern bank, and were "splayed," or widened, toward the inside to permit a greater field of fire. Embrasures for 12-pound howitzers were cut on every face. Two such guns were placed in each blockhouse of this type. Each was provided with a magazine below the floors, arranged for a garrison of sixty men. The lower cut shows a square blockhouse near the Virginia end of Aqueduct Bridge. This structure had two stories, with the upper projecting over the lower, and loop-holes in the floor of the upper story to permit the defenders to fire down on the heads of assailants near the walls. The entrance was through the door in the upper story, to which access was gained over the drawbridge from the top of the trestle. These blockhouses had not much strength, and were useful chiefly for moral effect, although, in case of necessity, a stubborn resistance could have been put up by defenders.

BLOCKHOUSE NEAR AQUEDUCT BRIDGE, ARLINGTON HEIGHTS, VIRGINIA

companies was provided for, and was assigned to the Army of the Potomac. It was utilized in constructing the defenses of the city of Washington in the winter of 1861–62, and during that time received instruction in the duties which it afterward performed so well in the field.

On February 24, 1862, the battalion was sent to Harper's Ferry, Virginia. There, under the greatest of difficulties, it constructed a pontoon bridge across the Potomac. The river was a raging torrent, the water being fifteen feet above the normal level, and filled with huge cakes of drifting ice and quantities of débris. It was with the utmost exertions that the pontoons could be pulled into position, and, once placed, they had to be secured with ships' anchors and chain-cables. But the structure was completed in about eight hours, and General Banks' corps, with all its trains and artillery, crossed safely and without delay. For a time the battalion was engaged in keeping the bridge in position and in good repair. General McClellan, himself an engineer of renown, stated in a letter to Secretary of War Stanton that it was one of the most difficult operations of the kind ever performed.

Immediately after returning to Washington from Harper's Ferry, the engineer troops, with their bridge-equipage, were sent to Fort Monroe, in Virginia, and were moved thence, on April 4th, to a camp near Yorktown, in preparation for the Peninsula campaign. In front of Yorktown the battalion was engaged in constructing trenches and lines of communication, and in superintending and instructing details of soldiers who were unfamiliar with methods of modern warfare. At this period of the war (1862), the troops of the infantry and the cavalry had received no training in the construction of field-fortifications. Consequently, the duty fell heavily on this battalion of men who had received such instruction.

Orders to construct a bridge across the Chickahominy River were received late on the afternoon of the 31st of May. The river was rising rapidly, and the night was extremely dark.

THE MEN WHO MADE MAPS—TOPOGRAPHICAL ENGINEERS BEFORE YORKTOWN

This photograph of May, 1862, affords the last chance to see the Topographical Engineers at work as a distinct organization. At the time this view was taken they still existed as a separate branch, their duties were the compilation of maps and other topographical data for the use of the army; but by act of March 3, 1863, the Corps of Topographical Engineers was abolished and merged into the Corps of Engineers. Time and again on the field of battle the exact knowledge of locality decided the result. Great advantage lay with the officers who had the most reliable and detailed maps. None such existed of the theater of war in Virginia, and on this corps fell the duty of providing all topographical data necessary for the Army of the Potomac. The officers were all highly trained in engineering work, especially in the surveys necessary for their maps, and in their preparation. In this photograph is a surveyor's level, and on the table a map in process of preparation. The enlisted men in this corps were of very high caliber and their work was of inestimable value.

Consequently, the work had to be postponed until daylight, but communication was opened with the opposite bank by 8:15 A.M. Soon another span was built, and the troops were engaged in road-making in the vicinity of the two river-crossings, to keep open the passages across the low, swampy lands through which the river runs. A third structure, of combined cribwork and trestle, was then constructed, some distance below the two pontoon bridges. Of this last passageway, General Barnard, chief engineer of the Army of the Potomac, remarked that it was an excellent structure, capable of bearing all arms and affording direct communication, in place of that by the inconvenient roads across the pontoon bridges.

At Mechanicsville and Gaines' Mill, the engineer troops did valiant service in the construction of trenches and other field-works. By this time the other troops were gaining the necessary experience, and toward the end of the Peninsula campaign the hastily constructed entrenchments of the entire army were models of completeness and speed in building. Road-work, in this desolate region, was of the most fatiguing kind, but was well and thoroughly done. The few men available from the engineer battalion aided as the instructors of the other troops engaged, and, by the time the movement began toward Malvern Hill, nearly all the troops of the Army of the Potomac had become accomplished in the arts of road-making, bridge-building, and entrenching. At Malvern Hill, the engineer battalion was posted as infantry, after preparing the front of the line by "slashing" or felling trees, to impede the advance of the Confederates and to afford an open field of fire to the defending troops.

After leaving Harrison's Landing on the withdrawal from the Peninsula, the battalion was sent to Fort Monroe to replenish its matériel, and thence to the mouth of the Chickahominy, where, in a short time, a fine pontoon bridge was constructed for the passage of McClellan's entire army.

This bridge was 1980 feet long, and for the most part was

THE CHIEF ENGINEER OF GENERAL GRANT

THE FORTIFIER OF NEW YORK

MAJOR-GENERAL JOHN GROSS BARNARD

ENGINEERS, EAST AND WEST

When the war broke out, General John Gross Barnard had just published "Dangers and Defences of New York" (1859) and "Notes on Sea-Coast Defence" (1861). He was immediately summoned to Washington as chief engineer in charge of constructing the defenses. Later he became chief engineer of the Army of the Potomac with the rank of brigadier-general and chief engineer of General Grant. General Barnard had graduated from the Military Academy at West Point in the class of 1833, fought through the Mexican War, where he fortified Tampico, and was for four years in charge of the defenses of New York. At the close of the war he was brevetted major-general. General O. M. Poe did for Sherman in the West what General Barnard did for Grant in the East. He labored constantly in the construction of defenses for the numerous bridges along the line of railroad, fortified many strategic points, made surveys and issued maps, and secured an invaluable photographic record of the engineering in Sherman's campaigns. Many examples are reproduced in this History.

BRIGADIER-GENERAL O. M. POE

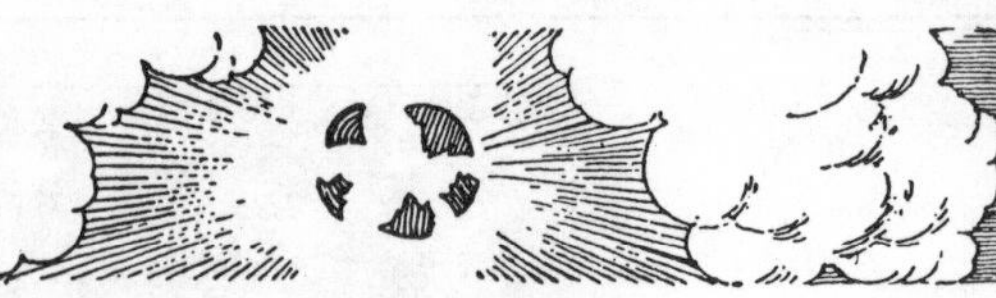

built by successive pontoons—placing the boats in the bridge, one at a time. A portion was built by rafts—i. e., by building a long section separately and placing it in position when complete. The floor was covered with straw to prevent wear. Competent authorities characterized this structure as one of the most extensive known to military history.

On August 18th, after the army had crossed the river, dismantling was begun, the parts being placed in the pontoons, and, within five hours after the work was commenced, rafts of pontoons had been made up, and the whole was on the way to Hampton, near Aquia Creek, on the Potomac.

These troops rendered invaluable service at the battle of Antietam. The night before the conflict they made three of the fords of Antietam Creek possible for artillery, by cutting down the banks and paving the bottom, where it was soft, with large stones. After the battle, by request of its officers, the battalion was assigned to duty as infantry, and it supported one of the batteries in the advance, when the Federals moved away from the Antietam, several weeks later.

On December 11th, a bridge was thrown across the Rappahannock, under fire, at a point known as Franklin's Crossing. Troops embarked in pontoons and were ferried across. Then they stormed the Confederate rifle-pits on the river bank and held them until the passageway was completed. After the battle of Fredericksburg the pontoons were removed.

The following winter, in 1863, a reorganization took place, and the Corps of Topographical Engineers was merged into the Corps of Engineers.

During the Chancellorsville campaign, April and May, 1863, the battalion again constructed a bridge across the Rappahannock at Franklin's Crossing. The bridge train was massed about a mile from the river, in dense woods. At night the boats were carried by infantrymen to the river, without the Confederates being aware of the movement until the boats were actually in the water. Troops were ferried across in the

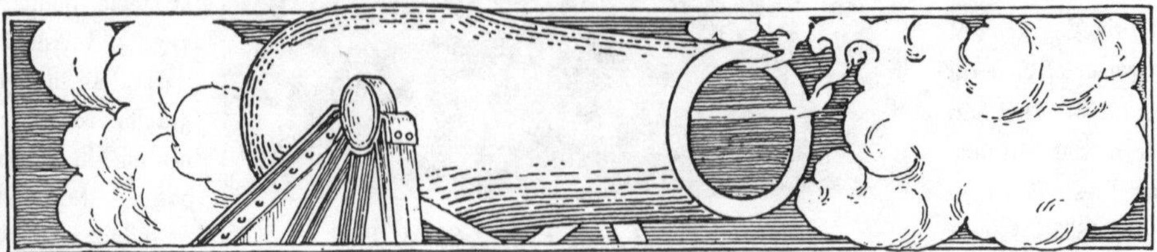

A FEW WEEKS BEFORE THE WILDERNESS—THE FIFTIETH NEW YORK ENGINEERS IN CAMP

The tents in this winter camp at Rappahannock Station, March, 1864, are substantial and roomy wooden huts roofed with tent canvas. To the left is the park of the train. The pontoon-boats are ready on their wagons. All the bridge material awaits transportation.

TWO MONTHS LATER IN 1864

THE ENGINEER CORPS AT WORK

Lee's army, in retiring across the North Anna River before Grant's army in May, 1864, destroyed the permanent bridge at this point. By the summer of 1864 half an hour sufficed for the experienced engineers to lay a bridge like this, after the arrival of the bridge train.

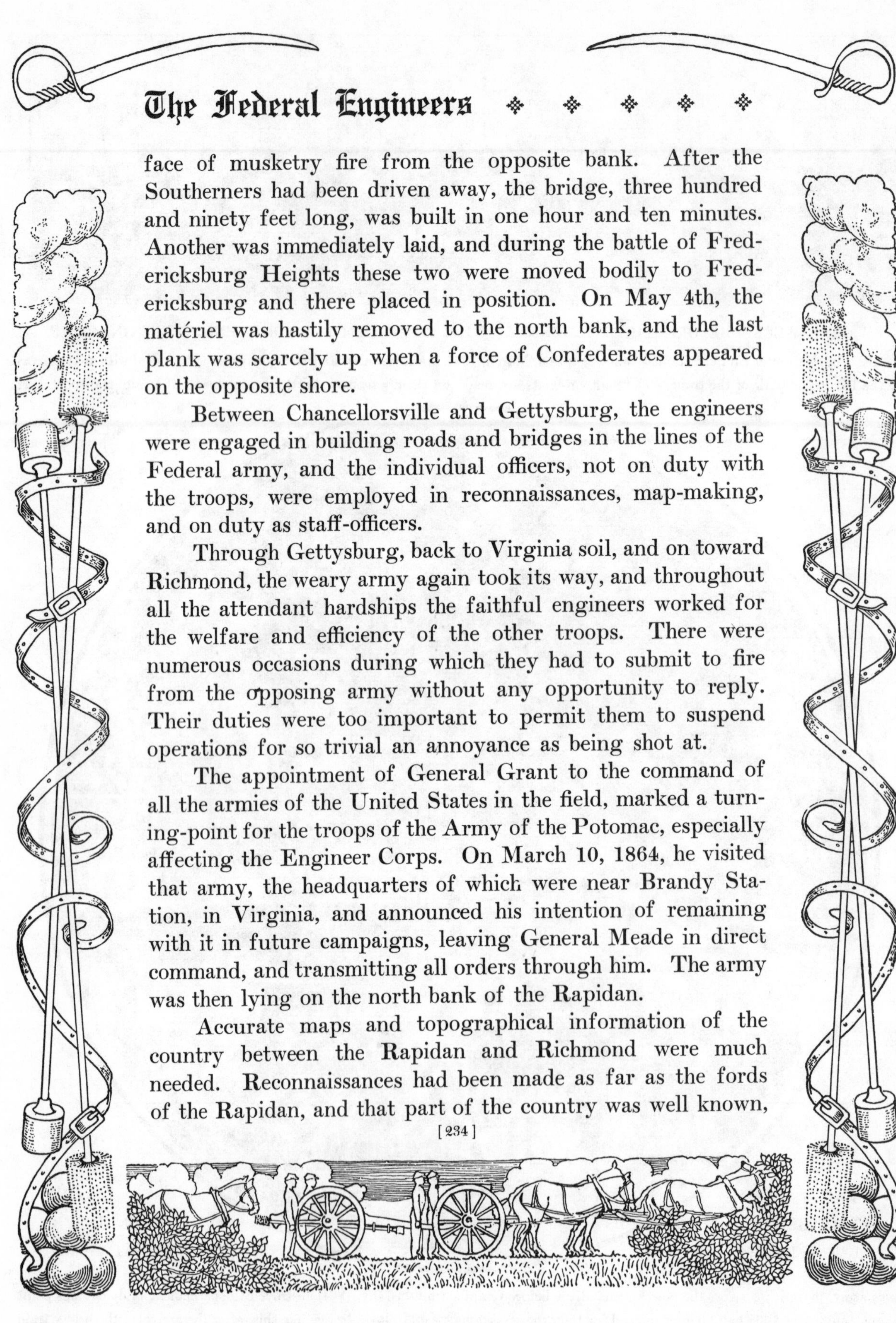

face of musketry fire from the opposite bank. After the Southerners had been driven away, the bridge, three hundred and ninety feet long, was built in one hour and ten minutes. Another was immediately laid, and during the battle of Fredericksburg Heights these two were moved bodily to Fredericksburg and there placed in position. On May 4th, the matériel was hastily removed to the north bank, and the last plank was scarcely up when a force of Confederates appeared on the opposite shore.

Between Chancellorsville and Gettysburg, the engineers were engaged in building roads and bridges in the lines of the Federal army, and the individual officers, not on duty with the troops, were employed in reconnaissances, map-making, and on duty as staff-officers.

Through Gettysburg, back to Virginia soil, and on toward Richmond, the weary army again took its way, and throughout all the attendant hardships the faithful engineers worked for the welfare and efficiency of the other troops. There were numerous occasions during which they had to submit to fire from the opposing army without any opportunity to reply. Their duties were too important to permit them to suspend operations for so trivial an annoyance as being shot at.

The appointment of General Grant to the command of all the armies of the United States in the field, marked a turning-point for the troops of the Army of the Potomac, especially affecting the Engineer Corps. On March 10, 1864, he visited that army, the headquarters of which were near Brandy Station, in Virginia, and announced his intention of remaining with it in future campaigns, leaving General Meade in direct command, and transmitting all orders through him. The army was then lying on the north bank of the Rapidan.

Accurate maps and topographical information of the country between the Rapidan and Richmond were much needed. Reconnaissances had been made as far as the fords of the Rapidan, and that part of the country was well known,

A CANVAS PONTOON BOAT ASSEMBLED READY FOR BUSINESS—MARCH, 1864

When dismantled, the canvas pontoon boats occupied a surprisingly small space. Thus the capacity of a train for bridge material of this kind was very much greater than for that of the wooden pontoons. The latter, however, gave better and more lasting service. The canvas became water-tight if well soaked. These pontoon boats were "knocked down" to be transported; the canvas was folded into a compact bundle and stowed in one of the wagons of the train. The parts of each boat were always kept together, so that they could be assembled at any time. The canvas, all in one piece, was laid out smooth on the ground, the bottom pieces of the frame put in place, the tenons of the uprights and the braces inserted in their corresponding mortises, the gunwales together with the end-pieces placed on the top, and the canvas then brought up over the sides and lashed tightly over the gunwales, by ropes eye-spliced into the eyes of the sides. The inside end-pieces were then carried around the bow and stern and lashed, and the outer pieces brought up over the ends and lashed in the same manner as the sides. The boat was then allowed to soak in the water for a time. Each boat was twenty-one feet long, five feet wide, and two and a half feet deep.

CANVAS PONTOON BRIDGE, NORTH ANNA RIVER

THE BRIDGE FROM UPSTREAM, JERICHO MILLS

BENHAM'S WHARF AT BELLE PLAIN

ONE MONTH BEFORE HIS FAMOUS BRIDGE ACROSS THE JAMES

"Belle Plain, Upper Wharf, erected by Engineer Corps, General Benham, Chief, May 15, 1864." So reads the inscription made by the photographer on his negative. The few words recall important events. At this time Grant was in the midst of his unsuccessful attempt to circumvent Lee and the Army of Northern Virginia at Spotsylvania. The work shown in this photograph was but child's play compared with the undertaking just one month later, when Grant finally decided to cross the James. One hour before noon on June 15th, General Benham received orders to prepare a pontoon-bridge across the James River for the passage of the entire army. In anticipation of this order, pontoons had been sent from Fort Monroe, and the work was started under Major Duane. General Benham reported to General Meade at the position selected, and was directed to proceed at once with the construction. General Meade smiled at the enthusiasm of Benham when he remarked that he would not sleep till the bridge was finished. About five and a half hours after Benham's arrival, a telegram was received from General Meade inquiring about the progress of the work. The indefatigable engineer was able to reply that the last bolt was in position, and that the troops could begin to move when they wished.

and the movements of the army between that river and Mine Run in Virginia, in November and December, 1863, had furnished considerable information concerning that region. The latter experience had proved that the existing maps of the country to be traversed were valueless for the purposes of marching and fighting an army. The country was of the worst topographical nature possible, and, although in one of the oldest States of the Union, there were but few reliable maps. Consequently, this information had to be obtained in advance of the army.

A party composed of regular and volunteer officers and soldiers, under Colonel N. Michler, of the Engineer Corps, was directed to undertake this work. Their labors commenced after crossing the Rapidan. Every road within the lines of the army had to be surveyed and mapped, and the work extended as far as possible to the front and the flanks. The maps were immediately reproduced on the field and distributed as far as time would permit. Revised editions of the maps were published as often as new information was collected. In this way, several editions of eleven maps were arranged and issued, comprising surveys covering an area of seven hundred and thirty square miles. These were also corrected by instruments carried by the supply train and by maps captured from the Confederates.

Before the army started from its winter quarters on the north of the Rapidan, in the spring of 1864, for the last great campaign, there had been twelve hundred maps made and issued. After the start, and before the end of the siege of Petersburg, about sixteen hundred were issued from new surveys.

In addition to the duties of surveying the country and making and distributing maps, the officers of the corps were charged with the work of selecting positions and directing their fortification. On the morning of the 3d of June, a gallant assault by the whole Union army was directed against

PONTOON-BRIDGE WHERE GRANT CROSSED THE JAMES IN JUNE, 1864

Strips of water a few hundred feet wide often nullify the plans for entire armies. This page of pontoon-bridges gives some idea of the inestimable services of the Engineer Corps. In the upper photograph is one of the pontoon-bridges across the James, at Powhatan Point, near Harrison's Landing, which was used by part of General Grant's army in the march from Cold Harbor to Petersburg. Below to the left is shown a pontoon-bridge over the James with a movable draw, to let vessels pass through. On the right is the pontoon-bridge at Broadway Landing on the Appomattox, over which General Smith's corps moved to make the first attack on Petersburg.

PONTOON-BRIDGE WITH AN OPEN DRAW

PONTOON-BRIDGE ACROSS THE APPOMATTOX

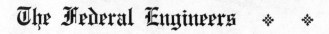

the Confederate entrenchments at Cold Harbor. But the Federals were baffled in their attempts to drive the Confederates across the Chickahominy. Colonel Michler, with his officers, was directed to assist Major Duane, chief engineer of the Army of the Potomac, in making a reconnaissance of the Confederate positions to ascertain their strength. Never were two lines of battle more closely arrayed. At places they were separated by no more than forty to one hundred yards, the men hugging the ground closely, and each army silently awaiting the determined attack of the other. The mettle of each had been felt and keenly appreciated by its opponent.

Colonel Michler and Major Duane made a careful examination of the location of the two lines, and reported to General Grant and General Meade the impracticability of storming the Confederate position, especially in front of the Second and Eighteenth corps, there being no suitable place in the rear for the massing of troops for an attack. The army was then directed to entrench on lines to be selected by the engineer officers, and until the 9th of June it lay confronting the Confederates.

On that date, Michler and Duane were ordered to select a line in rear of that occupied by the army, to be held temporarily by two divisions, which would enable the army to retire and move again by the flank, under cover. The lines were chosen by the engineers. Entrenchments were planned, and the troops began fortifying. At the same time, several of the engineer officers continued the reconnaissance to determine the best route for the contemplated movement.

On the 13th of June, by direction of the commanding general, engineer detachments proceeded in advance of the army to the James River, to reconnoiter the ground along its banks for two purposes—first, to enable the army to cross to the south side, and second, to fight a battle, if necessary, to protect the crossing. Lines covering the point of crossing were selected, entrenched, and held. Colonel Michler was

SOLDIERS BY THE UPPER PONTOON BRIDGE AT DEEP BOTTOM—JAMES RIVER, 1864

To construct a pontoon bridge the first boat launched was rowed up-stream a short distance. The anchor was let go. Its rope was then paid out sufficiently to drop the boat down into position. A second anchor was dropped a short distance down-stream, if the current proved irregular. The second boat was placed in position by the same process. Then the sills of the bridge, called "balk," could be placed across by floating the second boat alongside the first, placing the ends of the balk, usually five in number, across the gunwale, and then shoving the boat into position by pushing on the inner ends of the balk. These ends had heavy cleats so that they could be engaged over the further gunwale of each boat. The third boat was then placed in position by repeating the process. Then the "chess" layers commenced. The "chess" were the boards forming the flooring of the bridge. After the floor was laid the side rails, visible on the top of the flooring, were laid, and lashed to the balk through slits which were left between the boards for that purpose. This stiffened the whole structure and held the floor in place. Usually an up-stream anchor was necessary on every boat, and a down-stream anchor on every second or third. The floor of the bridge was usually covered with earth or straw to deaden the sound and preserve the chess. In these two photographs the engineers are just completing a bridge across the James.

THE GROUP SHIFTS—THE SENTRY RETURNS

then directed to locate a line on the south side where the Second Corps, after crossing, could entrench and protect the remainder of the army during the dangerous movement.

One hour before noon, on June 15th, General H. W. Benham, of the Engineer Corps, was ordered by General Grant to prepare a pontoon bridge across the James River for the passage of the army. In anticipation of this order, pontoons had been sent from Fort Monroe, and work was started under direction of Major Duane. General Benham was at Fort Monroe when he received the order, but arrived at the site of the bridge, just above Fort Powhatan, about five o'clock in the afternoon. The work was accomplished by four hundred and fifty men under the immediate command of Captain G. H. Mendell, of the regular service, who had for this purpose a body of regulars and volunteers under his charge.

General Benham reported to General Meade at the position selected, and was directed to proceed at once with the construction. General Meade smiled at the enthusiasm of Benham when he remarked that he would not sleep until the bridge was finished. The regulars were placed at the east end and the volunteers at the west end, and work was commenced on several parts of the bridge simultaneously—by the method known to the engineers as that of "simultaneous bays." About five and a half hours after Benham's arrival, a telegram was received from General Meade asking the progress on the bridge, and the engineer was able to reply that the last bolt was in position, that a gap had been left, according to orders, but the bay necessary to connect the span was ready, and that in fifteen minutes from the time the order was given the communication would be complete from shore to shore, a distance of twenty-two hundred feet.

The gap was closed, but the bridge was not required until six o'clock in the morning of the next day. At that time the regulars were relieved, and the bridge continued under the charge of the volunteers until it was dismantled, three days

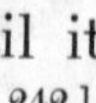

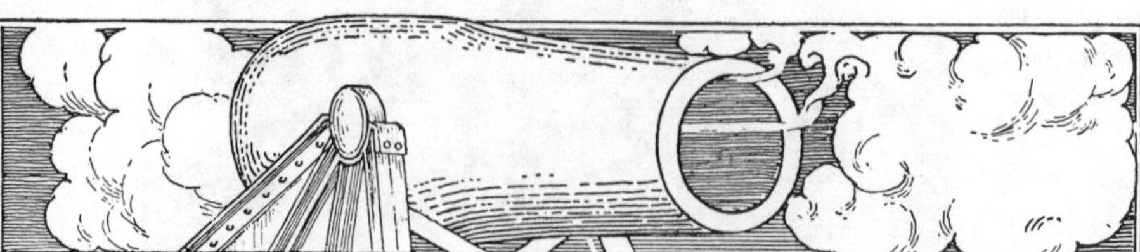

THE DUTCH GAP CANAL

NOVEMBER, '64—DIGGING

APRIL, '65—COMPLETION

After General Beauregard had repulsed the attempt of General Butler to move along the south bank of the James on Richmond, and had "bottled up" Butler at Bermuda Hundred, the Federal commander cast about for other means to accomplish his object. The opposing lines of entrenchments touched the river at Trent's Reach, a broad and shallow portion of the James completely commanded by Confederate batteries. Moreover, General Butler himself had built a line of obstructions across it after his retreat from Drewry's Bluff, much against the advice of the naval men in the river. The army seemed more afraid of the Confederate flotilla than were the men who would have to fight it on water. Butler had been fearful, however, that he would be cut off from his base of supplies at City Point, so he ordered the vessels to be sunk in the channel and made the formidable

obstructions a mile south of the Bluff, where the Confederates soon built Battery Dantzler. The river, however, was so crooked that two miles below Trent's Reach at Dutch Gap, only 174 yards separated the lower river from the upper. If the Federals could cut through this neck, they could avoid the Confederate works and move on up the river by boat as far as the works at Chaffin's Bluff and Drewry's Bluff. Captain Peter S. Michie, of the United States Engineers, later a brigadier-general, was detailed to dig a canal through at Dutch Gap. This would cut off four and a half miles of river. The excavation was forty-three yards wide at the top, twenty-seven at the water level, and thirteen and five tenths yards wide at a depth of fifteen feet below water-level. It was ninety-three feet deep at the northwest end and thirty-six feet deep at the southeast end. The total excavation was nearly 67,000 cubic yards. The greater portion of the digging was done by colored troops who showed the utmost bravery under the constant fire of the Confederate batteries on the river.

later. The repairs and the adjustments required during the continuous use of the bridge were attended to by the volunteers.

Beginning at six o'clock in the morning of June 16th, a continuous column of wagons (nearly six thousand), nearly all the artillery, cavalry, and infantry present, together with more than three thousand head of beef-cattle for the Subsistence Department continued to cross the bridge for forty hours, without a single accident to man or beast.

The officers and men in charge of the bridge were allowed very little sleep during this time, and General Benham relates that he had only about four hours' sleep in the eighty that the bridge was in operation. He said it was in anxiety, not to say in trembling, that he saw the destinies of that whole army committed to the frail structure, with steamers and other vessels drifting against it, and with so much of its planking previously worn through by careless use on the Rappahannock; while he did not dare stop that stream of men and supplies for a moment, in order to make repairs.

At length, the last animal was over by 7 P.M., on June 18th, and the guardians of the frail path commenced to breathe freely again, when, to their consternation, the Confederate artillery, about a mile away, began shelling. The pontoniers almost gave up hope of withdrawing the bridge in safety; but it was ordered up, and General Benham directed its removal in three rafts. This was successfully accomplished before three o'clock in the morning of the 19th, and the great bridge reached City Point, the Federal headquarters, about sunrise of that day, a souvenir of the most successful bridge of boats in the military history of the world.

Compared with the bridge built by the same troops over the Chickahominy two years before, this James River bridge was the greater feat. In the latter case, the water was deep for the greater portion of the distance, in some places nearly eighty-five feet, with a strong current running. In the former, the stream was comparatively shallow for most of the

SUNK BY A CONFEDERATE SHELL—BUTLER'S DREDGE-BOAT

Here is the dredge-boat that had deepened the southern approaches to the Dutch Gap canal, as it lay after being sunk by a Confederate shell on Thanksgiving Day, 1864. It was later raised and bomb-proofed to insure its finishing the work. This view is to the east, showing a Union lookout-tower on the north bank of the James River, and some monitors in the right distance. The digging of the canal was begun on August 10, 1864, and was intended to enable Union monitors and gunboats to pass up the James to Richmond. The bend of the river which it cut off was filled with obstructions placed there by General Butler himself, and was commanded by the Confederate Battery Dantzler. After September 29th, when the Confederate Fort Harrison, north of the James, was captured by the Union troops, the canal was not needed, but work was continued until some four months afterwards it was ready. After the war it was a welcome channel for vessels on the James. January 1, 1865, when the bulkhead at the northern end of the excavation was blown up with twelve thousand pounds of powder, the fallen earth and débris obstructed the entrance. It could be entered by small boats, but it was never used for the passage of armed vessels. The size of the dredge-boat can be judged by the figures of the two men beside it.

distance, and a great portion of the bridge could be built on trestles, whereas, in the James River construction, only about two hundred feet could be built of trestling.

On July 9, 1864, an order was issued directing operations against Petersburg by regular siege-works. This required a survey of the topography of the country and the positions of the lines of both armies. A map was made by the engineers which was constantly used as a reference by all the officers concerned in laying out and constructing these works. The engineers planned the regular entrenchments and approaches as far as possible, but, because of the multiplicity of duties devolving upon them, much of this work was delegated to other officers, who closely followed the plans indicated on the maps furnished.

At noon, on June 25th, a mine was begun by the troops in front of Petersburg. This was not undertaken by engineer troops, but was under the direction of Lieutenant-Colonel Henry Pleasants, Forty-eighth Pennsylvania Volunteers, and was executed by his own men. General Meade and General Grant sanctioned the project, and plans were adopted for an assault on the entire Confederate line when the mine should explode. The majority of the men employed in the work were miners from the coal regions of Pennsylvania, and the necessary expedients were familiar to them, without special instructions from the engineers. The excavation was commenced without special tools, lumber, or any of the materials usually required for such work. By late afternoon, on July 23d, the excavations were deemed complete. Eighteen thousand cubic feet of earth had been removed.

The mine was charged on the afternoon and evening of the 27th, with three hundred and twenty kegs of powder, each containing about twenty-five pounds. Altogether, there were eight magazines connected by wooden tubes which were half filled with powder. These tubes met at the inner end of the main gallery, and fuses were laid along this gallery to the exit. As

CELEBRATING AN ANNIVERSARY

ENGINEERS ON JULY 4, 1864

'hus the officers of the Fiftieth New York Engineers celebrated the victories of Gettysburg and Vicksburg in front of Petersburg July , 1864. At the head of the table sits Lieutenant-Colonel Ira Spaulding. On his right is Charles Francis Adams, later a leading Ameri-an historian. Often in front of Petersburg just a few more shovelfuls of earth meant the saving of lives. The veterans in the lower hotograph are bearded and bronzed; the muscles beneath their shabby blue tunics were developed by heavy, constant manual labor. The operations in this campaign marked a development in field-fortifications, opened virtually a new era in warfare. The siege was ot a bombardment of impregnable fortifications. It was a constant series of assaults and picket-firing on lines of entrenchments in he open. By July, 1864, the earthworks to the east had been almost finished, although much of this exacting labor had been per-ormed at night and under a galling fire. During August, the engineer corps extended the lines south and southeast of the beleaguered ity. But meanwhile the Confederates had been hard at work also. They had fewer men to hold their lines and to carry on the work, but t was accomplished with great devotion, and under able management and direction. The soldiers in the trenches lived in bomb-proofs.

GROUP OF COMPANY D, UNITED STATES ENGINEERS, IN FRONT OF PETERSBURG, AUGUST, 1864

there was not a sufficient length of fuse at hand to lay it in one piece, several pieces spliced together had to be used. An inspection of the work indicated that it was perfect.

Orders were given to fire the mine at three o'clock in the morning of July 30th. The fuse was lighted at 3.15 A.M., but the charge failed to explode. The defect was repaired, the fuse again lit, and at twenty minutes to five the mine exploded.

The shock was terrific. For nearly an hour the defenders of the adjacent works appeared paralyzed. Through a misunderstanding, the Federal assault was a failure, and many lives were sacrificed. From an engineering point of view, the enterprise was a success. Tactically, it was a failure.

From the moment the Federal troops appeared before Petersburg until the evacuation of the town, the duties of the Engineer Corps were very exacting. Every man was engaged in superintending and assisting in the construction of the technical part of the siege-works. Whenever the battalion was assembled, it was held ready for duty as infantry, and in several cases of emergency was used to strengthen weak points.

A final attempt was made by General Lee, while shut up in Petersburg and Richmond, to divert attention from himself and the Confederate capital by sending General Early up through the Shenandoah valley into Maryland and against Washington. Practically all the garrison at the Federal capital had been withdrawn from the defenses of the city to reenforce the Army of the Potomac. The troops left behind fit for duty did not suffice to man the armaments of the forts, of which the Engineer Corps and artillery had constructed a line of about thirty-seven miles in length.

Colonel Alexander, of the Corps of Engineers, was the only officer of the corps whose personal attention could be given to these defenses. Two of the officers in the office of the chief engineer were ordered to his assistance, and the officers of the corps on fortification duty on the sea-coast, north and east

WHEN IT WAS JUST A QUESTION OF TIME BEFORE PETERSBURG

It was an unexpected "war-time scene" before the cottage of Colonel Nathaniel Michler of the Engineer Corps at Brant House, near Petersburg. It recalls the prelude to Tennyson's "Princess," and the boy telling of the Christmas vacation in his deserted college halls, who "swore he long'd at college, only long'd, all else was well, for she society." How much more must the boys around Petersburg, some of whom had not seen their womenkind for three years or more, have longed for their presence and all the sweetness and daintiness and gentleness that it implied. It was only a question of time now when stoutly defended Petersburg would succumb before the vigor of the Northern assault. Now and again an officer was fortunate enough to receive a visit from his wife, or, as this picture proves, even from his little boy. The neat cottage shows with what success the Engineer Corps could turn from entrenching to the more gentle art of domestic architecture.

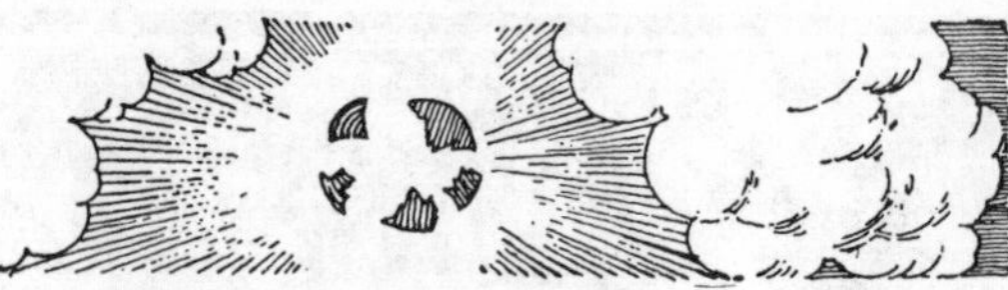

of the city, who could be sent to Washington, were detached from their duties and ordered to report at the capital at once.

But the improvised organization within the city, and the expected arrival of large reenforcements, of which Early had information, impelled him to withdraw after making a light attack, and the city was saved. The engineer officers that had been withdrawn from their work on the seaboard were immediately returned to their respective stations.

In the West, the operations of the Federal engineers shed luster on their corps. Fort Henry, Fort Donelson, and Vicksburg are names that are held in memory as demonstrating the high achievements of the scientific soldiers whose skill overcame great odds. Seventeen field- and subaltern-officers of the corps served constantly in the Western Federal armies, and though they had no regular engineer troops under them, the volunteers who received training from these officers proved their worth. Their labors at Chattanooga, Tennessee, under Captain (afterward Colonel) Merrill, rendered that important position impregnable. Knoxville, Tennessee, likewise withstood terrific onslaughts, having been fortified with great skill.

The army under Sherman had with it nine able engineers, under Captain O. M. Poe, who labored constantly in the construction of defenses for the numerous bridges along the line of railroad, fortified many strategic points, made surveys and issued maps, reconnoitered the positions of the Confederates, and managed the pontoon-bridge service.

Sherman started from Atlanta for the sea-coast, November 16, 1864. Hood had moved north into Tennessee. The Union army under Thomas had been sent to Nashville. The engineers fortified Franklin, but Schofield, with two corps of Thomas' army, was not strong enough to hold it. At Nashville the skill of the engineers, under Captain (afterward General) Morton and Captain Merrill, had enabled General Thomas to take his stand and hold on until he was ready to move against Hood.

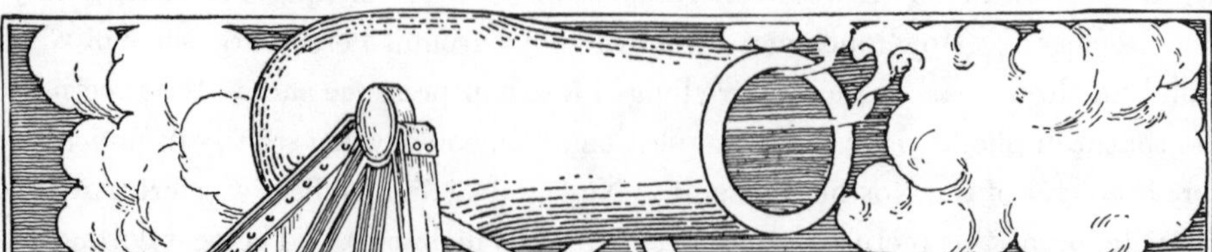

MAP-MAKING FROM PULPIT ROCK, LOOKOUT MOUNTAIN

The tripod signal in the background was erected by Captains Dorr and Donn, of the United States Coast Survey, in the triangular survey of the triple battlefield for making the official maps. In the West, the operations of the Federal engineers shed luster on their corps. Seventeen field and subaltern officers served constantly in the Western Federal armies; and though they had no regular engineer troops under them, the volunteers who received training from these officers proved their worth. The army under Sherman had with it nine able engineers under Captain O. M. Poe, under whose supervision a number of the photographs which are reproduced in this work were taken. He fortified many strategic points, made surveys and issued maps, reconnoitered the positions of the enemy, and managed the pontoon-bridge service. Captain Poe was a trained engineer officer, a graduate of West Point. He was commissioned as brigadier-general of volunteers and brevetted brigadier-general of the regular army.

A TRIPOD FOR SURVEYING THE BATTLEFIELD

THE ENGINEERS IN KENTUCKY—HEADQUARTERS AT CAMP NELSON

In the West, Forts Henry and Donelson and Vicksburg are names that are held in memory as demonstrating the high achievements of the Engineer Corps. Its labors at Chattanooga, under Colonel Merrill, rendered that important position impregnable. The work at Knoxville likewise withstood terrific onslaught. At Nashville the skill of the engineers enabled General Thomas to take his stand until he was ready to move against Hood. Throughout the Atlanta campaign Sherman showed implicit confidence in his engineers.

ALL DONE BUT THE DRAW

SPANNING THE TENNESSEE RIVER

WORK OF THE WESTERN ENGINEER CORPS

AFTER THE BATTLES AT CHATTANOOGA

THE DRAW IN PLACE

A SPAN TO BE PUT UP OR DOWN

TESTING THE FRAMING AND PULLEY-ROPES

(BELOW) READY FOR A MARCHING ARMY

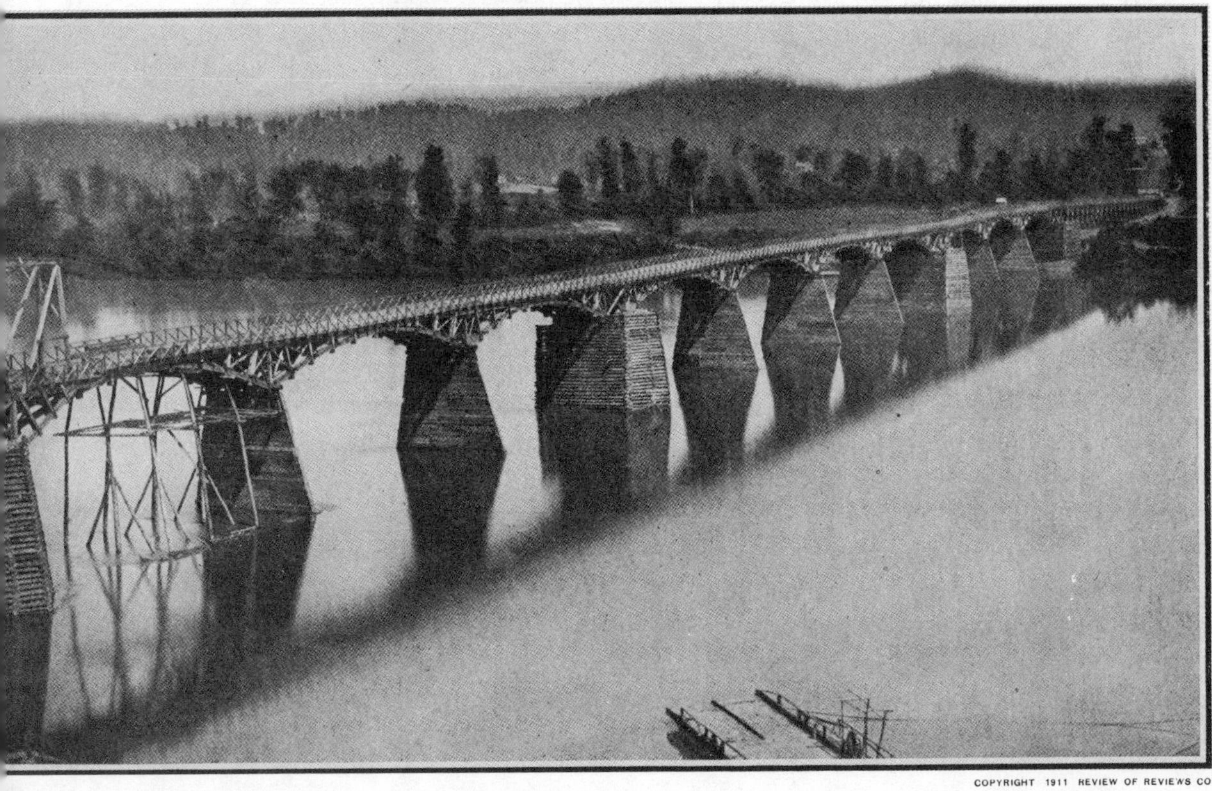

The importance of these defenses was mainly in enabling Thomas to concentrate his army at a depot well stored with munitions of war, and to hold his opponent, who was flushed with his successful march from Atlanta, in check, until the Union army was fully prepared. It is conceded by all critics that the labors of the engineer troops on these works were abundantly well spent. During the same eventful period, the fortifications constructed by them at Murfreesboro were successfully held and defended by a portion of Thomas' army.

No mention has been made of the immensely valuable services of all the engineer officers in the conduct of sieges throughout the war. No small portion of the conflict consisted in the besieging of important fortified places, and the manner in which these duties were discharged elicited high praise from all the commanding generals who had to do with such operations. Henry, Donelson, Vicksburg, Fort Fisher, the defenses of Charleston, Mobile, Savannah, and other places were all notable for the work of the besiegers, whose engineers directed and superintended the construction of the works of approach.

Justice to posterity demands that an accurate record of all the important military events of the war be preserved. No small part of that record had to be shown by maps. The chief engineer of the army directed the engraving, lithographing, photographing, and issuing of these maps, of which about twenty-four thousand five hundred sheets were sent out during the Civil War. The carefulness of the compilation often has been demonstrated. The hostile operations came to an end with the surrender of the last Confederate armed forces, but, for the construction of a basis on which accurate history might later be built, the Engineer Corps of the army continued its invaluable labors in making record of these events, which could be best depicted in map-form and in official reports. We have not even yet fully realized the immense worth of these documents of the great struggles during the Civil War.

X

THE CONFEDERATE ENGINEERS

A "COVERED WAY" IN FORT PULASKI, APRIL, 1862—THE GARRISON HERE MADE A CONTINUOUS BOMB-PROOF BY LEANING TIMBERS AGAINST THE INNER WALL OF THE FORT AND THEN COVERING THEM WITH EARTH

REMINISCENCES OF THE CONFEDERATE ENGINEER SERVICE

By T. M. R. Talcott

Colonel Commanding Engineer Troops, Army of Northern Virginia, Confederate States Army

[The text of this article is of especial value since it embraces personal reminiscences in a field where few official records or maps are available; namely, the operation of the engineer troops with the Army of Northern Virginia. The chapter is broadened by illustrations showing engineering works of the Confederate army in the West and South. —The Editors.]

THE account of the services rendered to the Southern Confederacy by its engineers must be largely, if not wholly, from memory, owing to the loss of records pertaining to this branch of the Confederate military service. The following, therefore, must be considered merely a reminiscence of the Civil War preserved in the memory of an individual participant in the events of the four years, from April, 1861, to April, 1865.

Prior to April, 1861, the State of Virginia maintained the hope that wise counsels would prevail, and urged forbearance; but mindful of the old adage, "In time of peace prepare for war," an appropriation was made for river, coast, and harbor defenses, and the services of a competent military engineer were secured to plan and superintend the work. Thus it happened that, when the Ordinance of Secession was passed by the Constitutional convention of the State of Virginia, on the 16th of April, 1861, in answer to Lincoln's call for her quota of the seventy-five thousand troops, no time was lost in organizing a State corps of engineers to prepare defenses against the then inevitable invasion of the State.

BRIGADIER-GENERAL DANVILLE LEADBETTER

MAJOR-GENERAL J. F. GILMER

CONFEDERATE ENGINEERS WHO MADE THEIR MARK

When it is realized that few of the officers in the Confederate Engineers Corps had any previous practice as military engineers, although some of them had been educated at military academies, and that no engineer troops were provided for by the Confederate Congress until 1863, the work accomplished by the Confederate engineers seems all the more marvelous. The Confederate coastwise defenses were strengthened in a way that baffled the blockading fleet, and no two armies have ever been entrenched in the field as were the armies of the South and North before Petersburg. Walter H. Stevens became major in the Confederate Corps of Engineers March 16, 1861. He was made colonel the following year, and brigadier-general August 28, 1864. He was chief engineer of the Army of Northern Virginia before Petersburg, and surrendered at Appomattox. Danville Leadbetter also became a major in the Engineer Corps March 16, 1861. He was a brigadier-general of the Provisional Army of the Confederate States February 27, 1861. J. F. Gilmer was lieutenant-colonel of the Engineer Corps in 1861. He became brigadier-general in the Confederate army in 1862, and major-general in 1863. During most of his service he was chief of the engineer bureau.

BRIGADIER-GENERAL WALTER H. STEVENS

The Confederate Engineers

The moment that the Norfolk Navy-Yard was evacuated, the erection and armament of batteries along the Elizabeth River was begun to prevent its recapture; and thus Virginia came into possession of a thoroughly equipped navy-yard, at which the *Merrimac,* some time later, was converted into the ironclad *Virginia,* and the guns needed for the speedy armament of batteries for the defense not only of the Elizabeth, James, and York rivers, but also against attacks on Norfolk and Richmond by other lines of approach, were obtained.

Subsequently, the Virginia Corps of Engineers was merged into that of the Confederate States; and the cost of completing the defenses begun by the State of Virginia was borne by the Confederate Government.

Very few of the officers in the Confederate corps had any previous practice as military engineers, although some of them had been educated at military academies. In this respect the North had a decided advantage over its opponents. No engineer troops were provided for by the Confederate Congress until 1863, when two regiments were authorized and organized, in time to take part in the campaigns of 1864. Prior to that time, such duties as pertain to engineer troops were performed by details from divisions, generally known as Pioneer Corps, under the direction of officers of the Engineer Corps attached to such divisions.

Of the two regiments of engineer troops, the First Regiment and two companies of the Second Regiment were organized for service with the Army of Northern Virginia. The other eight companies of the Second served elsewhere than in Virginia, several of them in the Trans-Mississippi Department.

During the first three years of the war when pontoon bridges were needed, they were handled by the Pioneer Corps, or other details from the ranks, under the direction of officers of the Engineer Corps. The bridge on which General Lee's army recrossed the Potomac near Williamsport after the battle of

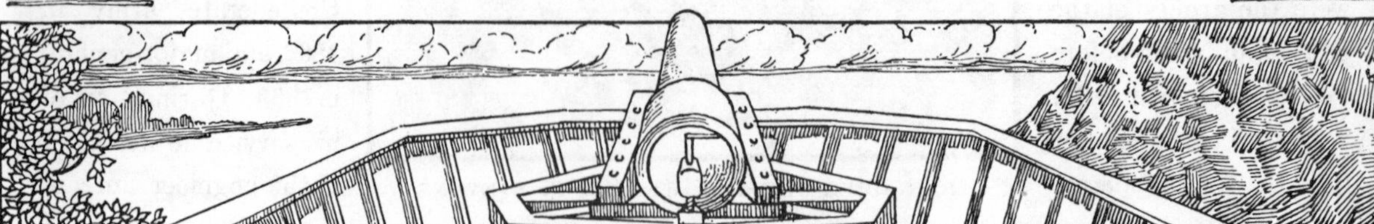

AN INGENIOUS DEVICE OF THE CONFEDERATES IN PULASKI

The Confederates had swung upwards the muzzle of this 8-inch smooth-bore sea-coast gun within Fort Pulaski, so that it could be used as a mortar for high-angle fire against the Federal batteries. General Hunter and General Gillmore's troops, supported by the gunboats, had erected these on Jones Island and Tybee Island. Fort Pulaski, commanding the entrance to the Savannah River and covering the passage of blockade runners to and from Savannah, early became an important objective of the Federal forces at Hilton Head. It was of the greatest importance that shells should be dropped into the Federal trenches, and this accounts for the position of the gun in the picture. There was no freedom of recoil for the piece, and therefore it could not be fired with the "service" charge or full charge of powder. Reduced charges, however, were sufficient, as the ranges to the opposing batteries were short. With this and other ingenious devices the little garrison kept up its resistance against heavy odds. It finally surrendered on April 11, 1862.

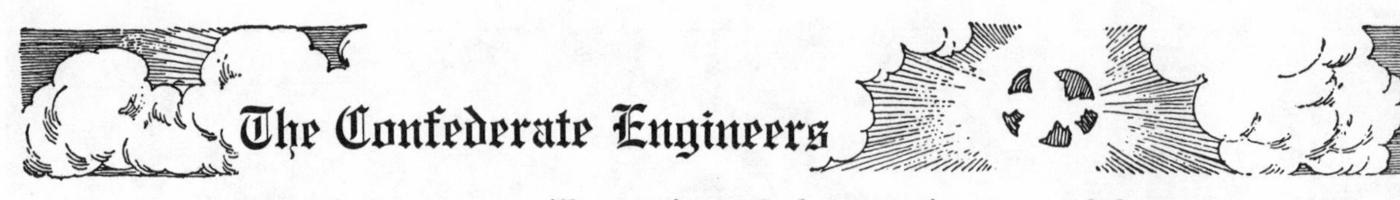

Gettysburg was an illustration of the corps' resourcefulness; for in this instance pontoon boats were lacking. The expedition with which material was collected, boats built, and the bridge constructed was most creditable.

The pontoon bridges for the engineer troops in Virginia were built at Richmond under the direction of the engineering bureau, and were in accordance with the plans and specifications prescribed by Captain (afterward General) George B. McClellan, United States Corps of Engineers, in one of the engineering papers published some years prior to the War between the States.

The pontoon bridge consisted of flat-bottomed boats, with longitudinal timbers to connect them, and planks for the flooring, all of which were lashed together with cords, so that they could be quickly assembled and as readily taken apart. The transportation of them required wagons specially constructed for the purpose. Provision had, of course, to be made to hold the boats in position against strong currents in streams to be crossed, by anchors or guy-lines to the shore.

When the campaign opened in 1864, the engineer troops attached to the Army of Northern Virginia, which was then at Orange Court House, were used first as infantry to guard the depot of supplies at Guiney's Station, and afterward to support a cavalry brigade which held the Telegraph road, on the extreme right of General Lee's position in Spotsylvania County, where it crossed the Ny, one of the four streams which form the Mattapony River. At this point earthworks were constructed, and the position was held until after the battle of Spotsylvania Court House, when it was turned by the flank movement of General Grant; and General Lee retired to the line of the North Anna River.

During General Grant's demonstration against Richmond, the engineer troops were used to strengthen the works which withstood his attacks at Cold Harbor; but anticipating the necessity at any time for a prompt movement across the

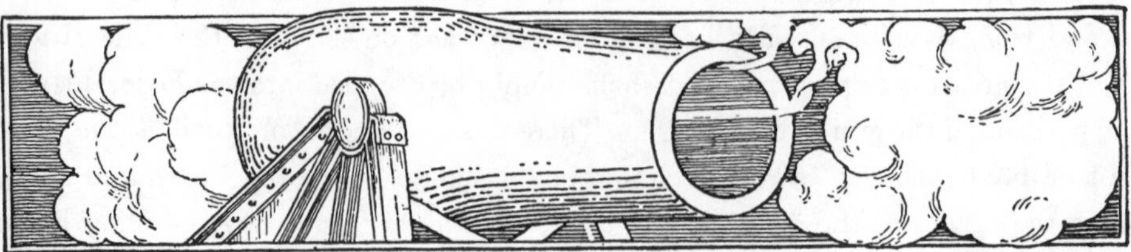

PULASKI—THE ANGLE WHERE THE FEDERALS CONCENTRATED THEIR FIRE

RIFLED CANNON VS. BRICKS

These two photographs of Fort Pulaski at Savannah, taken in April, 1862, after the bombardment by the Federal batteries, show very clearly how the Confederate Engineers learned that the old-fashioned brick wall was of no use against modern guns. The time had passed for brick and stone fortresses. Granite was found to be weaker than sand. Any yielding substance which would slow down and finally stop the great projectiles, and which could be shoveled back into position, no matter how much of it was displaced by a shell, proved far superior to any rigid substance. The ruins of Fort Pulaski taught the Confederates how to defend Fort Sumter—which was evacuated but never fell. In General Gilmore's Report on Charleston he says: "One hundred and ten thousand six hundred and forty-three pounds of metal produced a breach in Fort Pulaski which caused the surrender of that permanent and well constructed brick fortification, while one hundred and twenty-two thousand and thirty pounds of metal failed to open the bomb-proof of Fort Wagner, a sand work extemporized for the war. . . . It must not be forgotten, in this connection, that in the former case the brick wall stood nearly vertical, and all the débris formed by the shots immediately fell into the ditch, and no longer afforded any protection to the wall left standing; while in the latter the mass was so formed that a large proportion of the sand displaced fell back and again within an area attempted to be breached."

INSIDE THE BREACHED CASEMATE (SEE ABOVE)

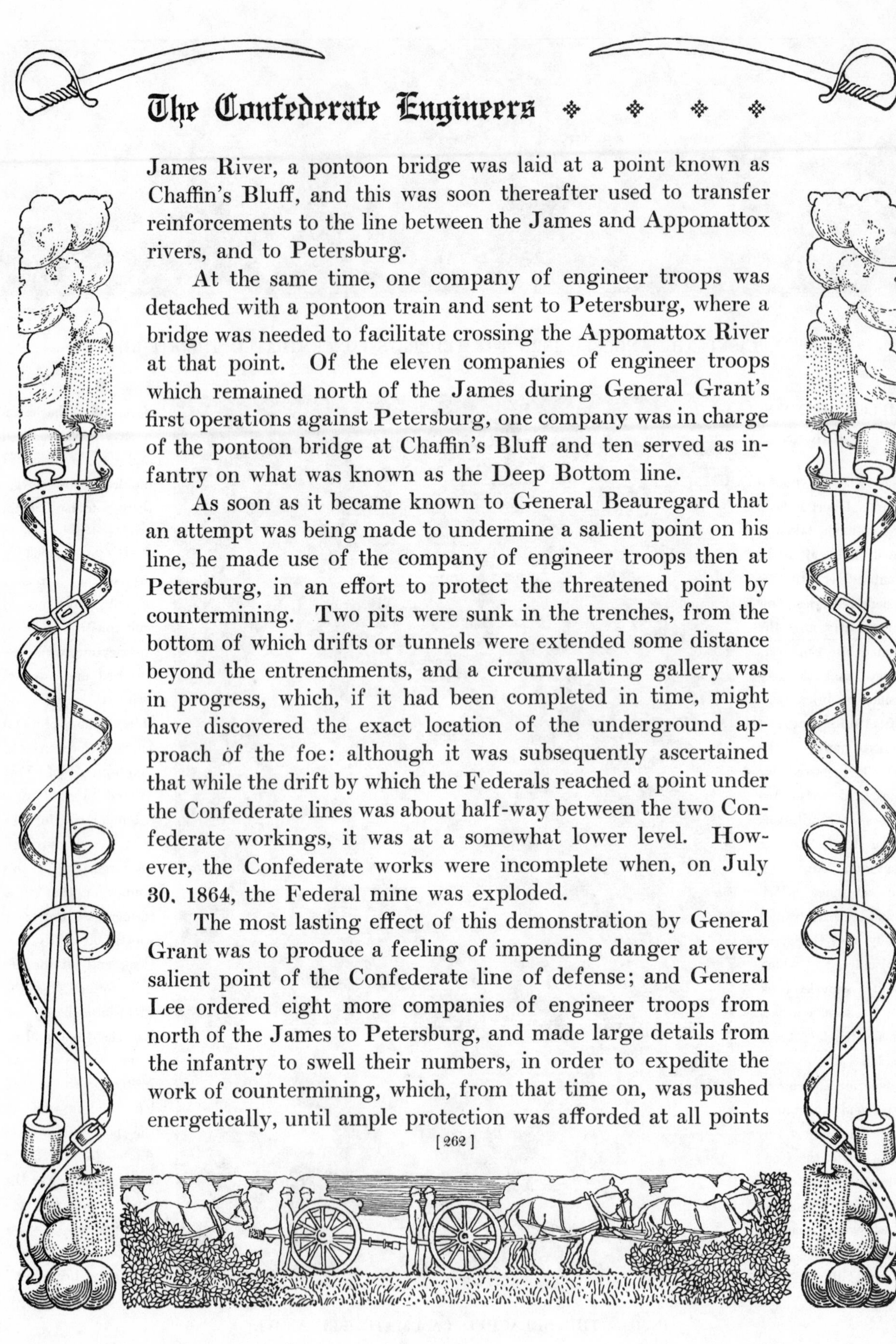

James River, a pontoon bridge was laid at a point known as Chaffin's Bluff, and this was soon thereafter used to transfer reinforcements to the line between the James and Appomattox rivers, and to Petersburg.

At the same time, one company of engineer troops was detached with a pontoon train and sent to Petersburg, where a bridge was needed to facilitate crossing the Appomattox River at that point. Of the eleven companies of engineer troops which remained north of the James during General Grant's first operations against Petersburg, one company was in charge of the pontoon bridge at Chaffin's Bluff and ten served as infantry on what was known as the Deep Bottom line.

As soon as it became known to General Beauregard that an attempt was being made to undermine a salient point on his line, he made use of the company of engineer troops then at Petersburg, in an effort to protect the threatened point by countermining. Two pits were sunk in the trenches, from the bottom of which drifts or tunnels were extended some distance beyond the entrenchments, and a circumvallating gallery was in progress, which, if it had been completed in time, might have discovered the exact location of the underground approach of the foe: although it was subsequently ascertained that while the drift by which the Federals reached a point under the Confederate lines was about half-way between the two Confederate workings, it was at a somewhat lower level. However, the Confederate works were incomplete when, on July 30, 1864, the Federal mine was exploded.

The most lasting effect of this demonstration by General Grant was to produce a feeling of impending danger at every salient point of the Confederate line of defense; and General Lee ordered eight more companies of engineer troops from north of the James to Petersburg, and made large details from the infantry to swell their numbers, in order to expedite the work of countermining, which, from that time on, was pushed energetically, until ample protection was afforded at all points

ONE OF THE GUNS THAT HAD TO BE DUG OUT—FORT McALLISTER

Digging out the guns was an every-morning duty of the garrison in Fort McAllister, defending Savannah, during the three bombardments of the Federal monitors and gunboats—January 27, February 1, and March 3, 1863. Every night the cannon in the fort became buried with dirt thrown up by the Federal shells, yet every morning they were roaring defiance again at the attacking fleet. No Federals set foot here until the little garrison of 230 men were confronted by Sherman's army of 100,000 and stormed on December 13, 1864.

FORT MORGAN, MOBILE BAY, ALABAMA

Fort Morgan, on the right of the entrance to Mobile Bay, was one of the strongest of the old brick forts. By August, 1864, it had been greatly strengthened by immense piles of sandbags, covering every portion of the exposed front toward the neck of the bay. The fort was well equipped with three tiers of heavy guns, one of the guns at least, of the best English make, imported by the Confederates.

exposed to attack by mining. These underground defenses included, besides the necessary pits, over two and one-half miles of drifts or tunnels.

In addition to the countermining at Petersburg, the engineer troops were used to strengthen the fortifications and to build a branch railroad to facilitate the delivery of supplies. During the investment of Richmond and Petersburg, two pontoon bridges were maintained across the Appomattox River, and one across the James at Chaffin's Bluff; and additional pontoon trains were provided in case they should be needed.

Anticipating the necessity for the abandonment of Richmond and Petersburg, General Lee, during the winter of 1864–65, required the engineer troops to rebuild Bevill's Bridge over the Appomattox River west of Petersburg, and to send a pontoon bridge to the Staunton River in Charlotte County.

The engineer troops also prepared a map showing the routes to the different crossings of the Appomattox River, to be used whenever the army should be withdrawn from Richmond and Petersburg. This map has since been lithographed by the United States Government.

In March, 1865, when the right of General Lee's position was seriously threatened, engineer troops strengthened the defenses at Hatcher's Run; but the main body of them served in the trenches in place of the infantry withdrawn to extend still further westward a line which was already more than thirty miles in length.

The Confederate reverse at Five Forks, which cut off a part of Lee's army from Petersburg and forced it to retire to the north side of the Appomattox River, was closely followed by the loss of a part of the entrenchments before that city, and this necessitated an interior line of defense, pending the withdrawal of the main body of General Lee's army to the north side of the Appomattox River. This new line of breastworks was thrown up hurriedly, in part by the engineer troops, but chiefly by negro laborers. This was probably the only time

SEA FACE OF FORT FISHER—MIGHTIEST FORTRESS OF THE SOUTHERN CONFEDERACY

Along the North Carolina coast, near Wilmington, guarding the port longest open to blockade-runners, lay these far-flung earthworks. Heavy timbers were heaped fifteen to twenty-five feet thick with sand, sodded with luxuriant marsh-grass. Below appears some of the destruction wrought by the fire of the Federal war-ships. Here are the emplacements next to the angle of the work on the left of the sea face, and a bomb-proof under the traverse. The first gun on the right is a 10-inch Columbiad dismounted by the assailants' fire. Only the old-style two-wheeled wooden carriage, without chassis, can be seen, at the top of the bank—ready to tumble over. The next gun is also a 10-inch Columbiad which has been knocked off its wooden barbette carriage; the third, a $6\frac{3}{8}$-inch rifle, on a two-wheeled wooden carriage. The carriage has been knocked entirely off the bank, and is lying in the pool of water. The only gun left mounted is the 10-inch Columbiad to the left. The fort finally succumbed to the terrific fire of the Federal fleet on January 15, 1865.

BEHIND THE RAMPARTS—HAVOC FROM FEDERAL SHELLS

that the Confederates required negro laborers to work under fire, and to their credit be it said that they performed their task with apparent willingness.

The engineer troops were the last to leave the city of Petersburg, for the destruction of the bridges devolved upon them. They retired from the north bank of the river early in the morning of April 3, 1865, under a scattering fire from the advance guard of the Federals.

Then followed a day's march to Goode's Bridge, and the crossing of the Appomattox River at that point, not only of the army and its wagon trains, but also of a large number of other wagons, carriages, buggies, and riders on horseback, Government and State officials, bank-officers with their specie, and many private individuals seeking safety for themselves and their belongings.

It had been planned to use the newly built Bevill's Bridge, which was the nearest to Petersburg, for the troops and trains from that point, Goode's Bridge for troops from Richmond, and a pontoon bridge at Genito for all not connected with the army; but by reason of high water, which covered the approaches, Bevill's Bridge was useless. The pontoons for Genito, which were ordered from Richmond two days before, failed to arrive, and thus everything converged at Goode's Bridge and the railroad bridge at Mattoax.

This awkward situation was relieved to some extent by hurriedly laying a rough plank flooring over the rails on the railroad bridge, which made it practicable for vehicles to cross at Mattoax.

The crossing to the south side of the Appomattox River having been effected in some confusion, but, owing to the light of the moon, without accident, both the railroad and pontoon bridges were destroyed before daylight; and the engineer troops moved on to Amelia Court House, where some rest but very inadequate rations awaited them.

Soon orders came from General Lee to push on to Flat

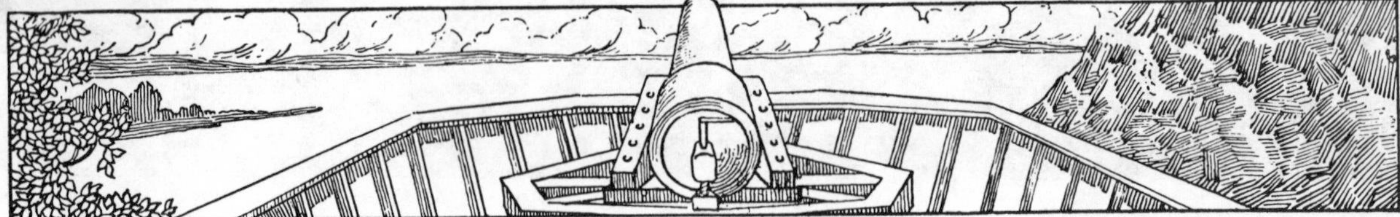

FORT FISHER

EFFECT OF THE NAVAL BOMBARDMENT OF DECEMBER, 1864

In 1864, a larger force than ever had assembled under one command in the history of the American navy was concentrated before Fort Fisher, North Carolina, under Admiral David D. Porter. Sixty vessels, of which five were ironclads, arrived in sight of the ramparts on the morning of December 20th. After a futile effort to damage the fort by the explosion of the powder-boat *Louisiana* on the night of December 23d, the fleet sailed in to begin the bombardment. The *New Ironsides*, followed by the monitors, took position as close in as their drafts would permit. The *Minnesota*, *Colorado*, and *Wabash* followed near. With a deafening roar and a sheet of flame, these frigates discharged their broadsides of twenty-five 9-inch guns, driving the garrison into their bomb-proofs. On Christmas Day, the bombardment was resumed by the larger vessels and the ironclads, while the smaller vessels covered the landing of General Butler's troops from the transports which had just arrived. The fort proved too strong to take by assault, and the troops were withdrawn. The fort did not fall until January 15, 1865. This photograph shows the effect of the terrific bombardment of the Federal fleet.

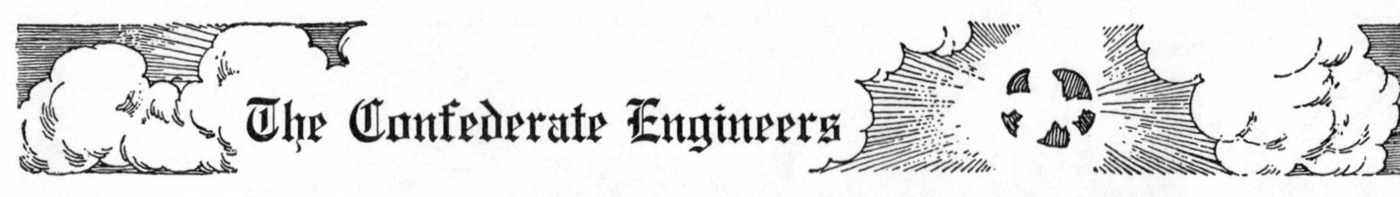

Creek, where the failure of an old country bridge and the absence of practicable fords delayed the crossing of that stream. The outlook at that point on the line of march was evidently disturbing to General Lee, for on arrival of the engineer troops late in the afternoon, for which he had waited, he impressed upon the colonel in command of them the necessity for strenuous efforts to effect as rapid a crossing of Flat Creek as possible, emphasizing his instruction by saying that a captured order from General Grant to General Ord, who was at Jetersville, indicated an attack early next morning.

Timber was felled; a new bridge was built; the last vehicle had passed over it, and the engineer troops were already in motion toward Amelia Springs, when a Federal battery unlimbered on a near-by hill and fired a few shells to expedite the movement of as tired and hungry a body of Confederate troops as could have been found that morning in General Lee's army, where fatigue and hunger were familiar conditions.

When the engineer troops, which had been rejoined by the companies detached for service north of the James River and had made a respectable showing in strength, reached Sailor's Creek, where the rear guard of the army was in line of battle, expecting an immediate attack, the general in command looked pleased and said they were just what he was looking for to reenforce a weak spot in his line. To decline such an honor was not within the range of military possibilities, but an order from General Lee, which a courier had been seeking to deliver, made it imperative to move on to the assistance of the wagon trains. A heavy ordnance train, which was stalled in an effort to surmount a steep hill over a bad road and to cross a creek through swampy ground, was causing serious delay, and a number of wagon trains were parked in the fields, waiting for their turn to move on.

While this congestion was being partially relieved, the battle of Sailor's Creek was fought, which resulted in defeat to the Confederates, who were falling back in disorder toward

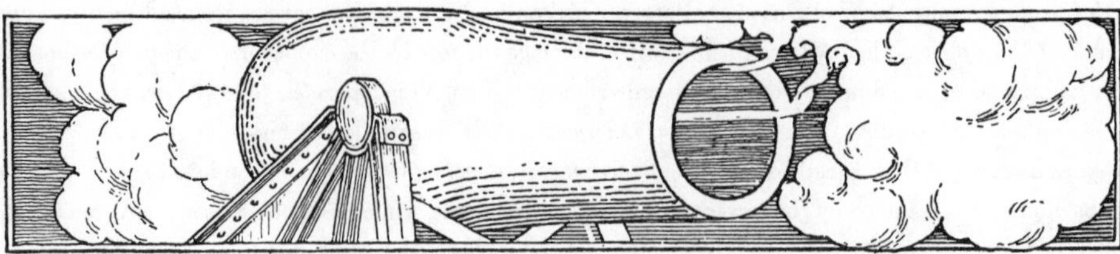

WHERE THE SAILORS ATTACKED—THE MOUND BATTERY AT FORT FISHER

In this photograph unexploded 12-inch shells can be plainly seen upon the beach, as they fell on January 13, 1865, in the terrific fire from the Federal fleet under Rear-Admiral Porter. This was the land face; the portion to the left was the angle of the work. The land assault by the sailors on January 15th, was repulsed with a loss of some three hundred killed and wounded. At the western end of the works, however, the army under General Alfred H. Terry succeeded in effecting an entrance and captured the fort that evening.

ONE OF THE HUGE TRAVERSES, AFTER THE BOMBARDMENT

A traverse in an earthwork built perpendicular to the main work in order to limit the destructive area of shells. The traverses at Fort Fisher rose twelve feet above the twenty-foot parapet, ran back thirty feet, and exceeded in size any previously known to engineers.

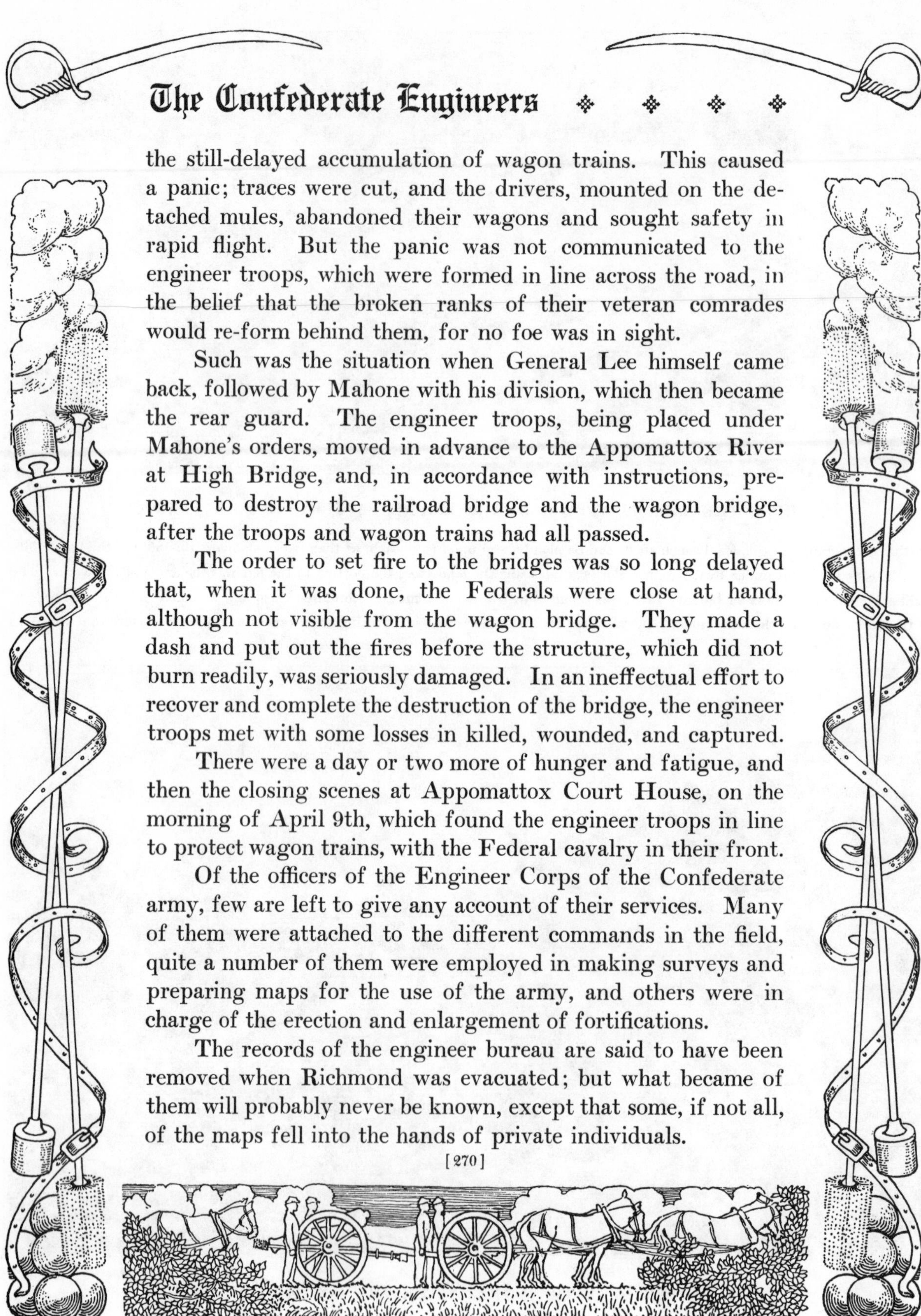

the still-delayed accumulation of wagon trains. This caused a panic; traces were cut, and the drivers, mounted on the detached mules, abandoned their wagons and sought safety in rapid flight. But the panic was not communicated to the engineer troops, which were formed in line across the road, in the belief that the broken ranks of their veteran comrades would re-form behind them, for no foe was in sight.

Such was the situation when General Lee himself came back, followed by Mahone with his division, which then became the rear guard. The engineer troops, being placed under Mahone's orders, moved in advance to the Appomattox River at High Bridge, and, in accordance with instructions, prepared to destroy the railroad bridge and the wagon bridge, after the troops and wagon trains had all passed.

The order to set fire to the bridges was so long delayed that, when it was done, the Federals were close at hand, although not visible from the wagon bridge. They made a dash and put out the fires before the structure, which did not burn readily, was seriously damaged. In an ineffectual effort to recover and complete the destruction of the bridge, the engineer troops met with some losses in killed, wounded, and captured.

There were a day or two more of hunger and fatigue, and then the closing scenes at Appomattox Court House, on the morning of April 9th, which found the engineer troops in line to protect wagon trains, with the Federal cavalry in their front.

Of the officers of the Engineer Corps of the Confederate army, few are left to give any account of their services. Many of them were attached to the different commands in the field, quite a number of them were employed in making surveys and preparing maps for the use of the army, and others were in charge of the erection and enlargement of fortifications.

The records of the engineer bureau are said to have been removed when Richmond was evacuated; but what became of them will probably never be known, except that some, if not all, of the maps fell into the hands of private individuals.

XII

THE RAILROADS AND THE ARMIES

THE LOCOMOTIVE "FRED LEACH," AFTER ESCAPING FROM THE CONFEDERATES — THE HOLES IN THE SMOKESTACK SHOW WHERE THE SHOTS STRUCK, AUGUST 1, 1863, WHILE IT WAS RUNNING ON THE ORANGE AND ALEXANDRIA RAILROAD NEAR UNION MILLS

WHAT LINCOLN CALLED THE "BEANPOLE AND CORNSTALK" BRIDGE, BUILT OVER POTOMAC CREEK

This famous "beanpole and cornstalk" bridge, so named by President Lincoln, amazed at its slim structure, was rushed up by totally inexpert labor; yet in spite of this incompetent assistance, an insufficient supply of tools, wet weather and a scarcity of food, the bridge was ready to carry trains in less than two weeks. First on this site had been the original railroad crossing—a solidly constructed affair, destroyed early in the war. After the destruction of the "beanpole and cornstalk" bridge by the Union troops when Burnside evacuated Fredericksburg, came a third of more solid construction, shown in the upper photograph on the right-hand page. The bridge below

THE THIRD BRIDGE, PHOTOGRAPHED APRIL 12, 1863—BELOW, THE FOURTH

is the fourth to be built for the Richmond, Fredericksburg and Potomac Railroad at this point. The United States Military Railroad Construction Corps by this time possessed both trained men and necessary tools. Work on this last bridge was begun Friday, May 20, 1864, at five A.M.; the first train passed over Sunday, May 22d, at four P.M. Its total length was 414 feet, and its height was eighty-two feet. It contained 204,000 feet of timber, board measure, but the actual time of construction was just forty hours. The photograph was taken by Captain A. J. Russell, chief of photographic corps, United States Military Railroads, for the Federal Government.

FEDERAL MILITARY RAILROADS

By O. E. Hunt
Captain, United States Army

WITH miles of black and yellow mud between them and the base of supplies, and a short day's ration of bacon and hardtack in their haversacks, the hearts of the weary soldiers were gladdened many times by the musical screech of a locomotive, announcing that the railroad was at last up to the front, and that in a short time they would have full rations and mail from home. The armies that operated in Virginia and in Georgia greeted, very often, the whistle of the engine with shouts of joy. They knew the construction corps was doing its duty, and here was the evidence.

In the strict sense of the term, there were but few military railroads in the United States during the Civil War, and these few existed only in portions of the theater of war in Virginia, in Tennessee, and in Georgia. Roads owned by private corporations were seized, from time to time, and operated by the Governments of both sides as military necessities dictated, but, technically, these were not military roads, although for the intents and purposes to which they were all devoted, there should be no distinction drawn. The operation of a railroad under Government military supervision, while retaining its working personnel, made of it a military road in every sense.

Great railroad development in this country began during the second quarter of the nineteenth century. The United States Government, about 1837, adopted the policy of loaning to railroad companies officers of the army who had made a scientific study of this new means of communication, and the result was a benefit to the roads and the Government.

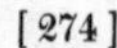

"THEY KNEW THE CONSTRUCTION CORPS WAS DOING ITS DUTY"

CAMP OF THE CORPS AT CITY POINT IN JULY, 1864

The construction corps of the United States Military Railroads had a comparatively easy time at City Point under General McCallum. There was plenty of hard work, but it was not under fire, and so expert had they become that the laying of track and repairing of bridges was figured merely as a sort of game against time. The highest excitement was the striving to make new records. It had been otherwise the year before. General Herman Haupt, then General Superintendent of all the military railroads, had applied for and received authority to arm, drill and make the military railroad organization to some extent self-protective. This was on account of the numerous depredations committed along the Orange and Alexandria Railroad. Bridges were destroyed and reconstructed (that over Bull Run for the seventh time), trains troubled by marauders, and miles of track destroyed by the armies. These men in their camp at City Point look alert and self-sufficient. The investment of Petersburg had begun, and their troubles were practically over.

Constructing companies were assisted in carrying out their ambitious projects, and the Government profited greatly by the experience gained by the officers so detailed. " In this manner army officers became the educators of an able body of civil engineers, who, to this day, have continued the inherited traditions, methods, discipline, *esprit de corps,* and the high bearing of their distinguished predecessors."

General Grant spoke very enthusiastically of the work of the railroads and wagon roads operated for him during the Virginia campaign of 1864, when his army had to be supplied by wagons over the extremely difficult roads, from the termini of railroad lines that were pushed into the Wilderness as far as possible, and from ever-shifting bases on the rivers, where the lack of dockage facilities made the work of handling freight very arduous. He particularly complimented the officers in charge of the trains on the fact that very little special protection had to be given them.

General Sherman, in his memoirs, notes that his base of supplies during the campaign of 1864 was Nashville, supplied by railroads and the Cumberland River, thence by rail to Chattanooga, a secondary base, and by a single-track railroad to his army. The stores came forward daily, but an endeavor was made to have a constant twenty days' supply on hand. These stores were habitually in the wagon trains, distributed to the corps, divisions, and regiments, and under the orders of the generals commanding brigades and divisions. Sherman calculated that, for this supply, he needed three hundred wagons for the provision train of a corps and three hundred for the forage, ammunition, clothing, and other necessary stores—a total of six hundred wagons per corps. It was recognized as impossible for the wagons to go a great distance from the terminus of the railroad and still maintain their maximum efficiency of operation, and hence the efforts made to keep his railroad construction up to the rear of his army.

The construction, operation, and repair of the railroads

GENERAL HAUPT INSPECTING THE MILITARY RAILROAD—1863

THE SCENE IS NEAR BULL RUN—GENERAL HAUPT STANDS AT THE RIGHT—THE ENGINE HAS BEEN NAMED AFTER HIM

On the embankment stands General Haupt overseeing the actual work on the railroad. This photograph gives an indication of the secret of his success—no detail was too small for him to inspect. He was a graduate of the United States Military Academy in the class of 1835. He resigned his commission soon after graduation, and entered the railroad service in the State of Pennsylvania. His especial forte was bridge-building. In 1846 he became identified with the Pennsylvania Railroad, and in 1865 he became interested in the Hoosac Tunnel project in Massachusetts, which he carried to successful completion. In April, 1862, Secretary of War Edwin M. Stanton summoned him to Washington and put him in charge of rescuing the railways and transportation service from the chaos into which they had fallen. At first employed as a civilian, he was given later the rank of colonel, and at the second battle of Bull Run was commissioned brigadier-general of volunteers. His work was magnificent, and he soon had the railroads running smoothly. On account of differences with General Pope, he retired to his home in Massachusetts in July, 1862. A few days later he received from the War Department the following telegram: "Come back immediately; cannot get along without you; not a wheel moving on any of the roads." General Haupt returned, and the wheels began to move. On September 14, 1863, D. C. McCallum succeeded Haupt.

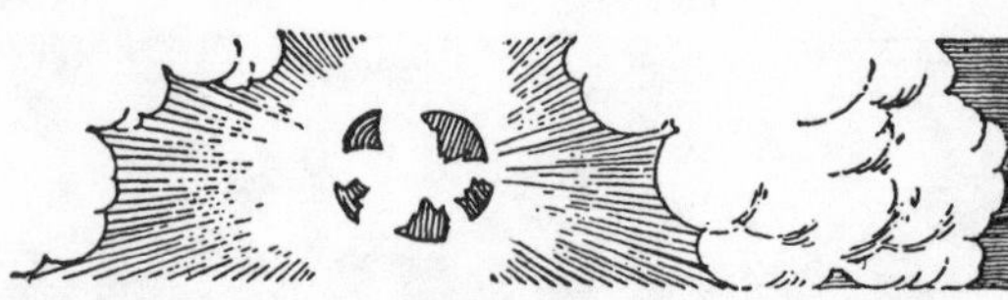

of the Federal Army of Virginia and the Army of the Potomac were, until September 9, 1863, largely in the hands of Herman Haupt, who, for a time, also held general superintendence over all the military roads of the United States.

In April, 1862, the great war secretary, Edwin M. Stanton, sent an urgent telegram to Mr. Haupt, requesting him to come to Washington. Knowing that Congress would probably exercise a certain amount of supervision over his work if he entered the Government service, and having had a discouraging experience already with legislative bodies, he hesitated to undertake the work which Secretary Stanton pressed upon him. However, having been assured by the joint committee of Congress having such matters in charge that his interests would not be sacrificed, he immediately began the task of rescuing the railway and transportation service of the Federal armies from the apparently irreparable chaos into which it had fallen. Secretary Stanton knew his ground when he confided this work to Haupt. He also knew his man, and the absolute integrity and fearless energy that he was capable of putting into any enterprise he undertook.

At first, Haupt was employed as a civilian. On April 27, 1862, however, he was appointed aide-de-camp on the staff of General McDowell, whom he had known at West Point, and with whom he was soon on the closest terms, both personally and officially. On May 28th, he was given the rank of colonel, which he held until the second battle of Bull Run, when he was commissioned a brigadier-general.

The first important work under Haupt's direction was the reconstruction of the railroad from Aquia Creek to Fredericksburg. This became, on reopening, the first strictly military road in the United States during the war. At Aquia Creek, the large wharf had been completely destroyed and the railroad track torn up for a distance of about three miles, the rails having been carried away and the ties burned. All the bridges in the vicinity had been destroyed by burning and their

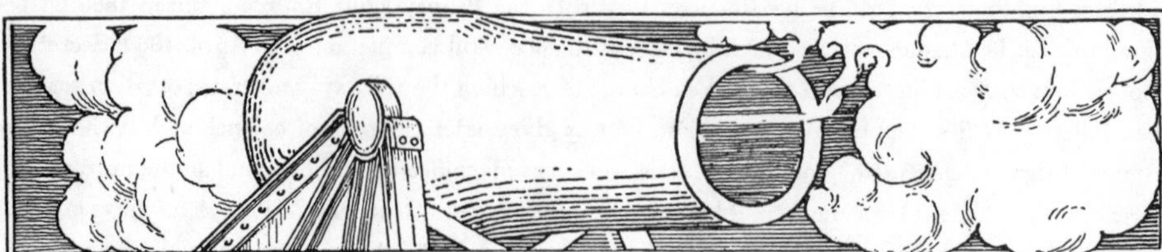

A PROBLEM SOLVED BY THE ENGINEERS.

It was a long step from Cæsar's wooden bridges to the difficulties which confronted the United States Construction Corps in the Civil War. Here is an example of its work. Time and again, during 1862–63, the bridges on the line of the Orange & Alexandria Railroad were destroyed by both sides in advance and in retreat. It remained for the army engineers to reconstruct them. It was a work requiring patience and unceasing activity, for speed was of prime importance. These structures, capable of supporting the passage of heavy railroad trains, and built in a few hours, were conspicuous triumphs which the American engineers added to the annals of war.

abutments blown up. The road-bed had been used by wagons and cavalry and was badly cut up.

The first bridge to be constructed on the line was at Accakeek Creek. This was built complete, with a span of about one hundred and fifty feet and an elevation of thirty feet, in a little more than fifteen hours on May 3 and 4, 1862. The next and most serious obstruction was the deep crossing of Potomac Creek. Here was built what is known as a deck bridge, of crib and trestle-work, four hundred feet long and eighty feet high. As before, totally inexpert labor was employed, and only a very few officers who had any knowledge of that kind of work were available. With this incompetent assistance, with an insufficient supply of tools, with occasional scarcity of food, and several days of wet weather, the work was nevertheless advanced so rapidly that in nine days the bridge was crossed by foot passengers, and in less than two weeks an engine was passed over, to the intense delight of the soldiers, by whose labor the structure had been erected. It was completed on May 13th. After President Lincoln first saw this bridge he remarked: " I have seen the most remarkable structure that human eyes ever rested upon. That man, Haupt, has built a bridge across Potomac Creek, about four hundred feet long and nearly a hundred feet high, over which loaded trains are running every hour, and, upon my word, . . . there is nothing in it but bean-poles and corn-stalks."

The railroad bridge across the Rappahannock at Fredericksburg was constructed next in about the same time as that across Potomac Creek, and was six hundred feet long and forty-three feet above the water, with a depth of water of ten feet. This structure was built under the immediate supervision of Daniel Stone.

The excitement created by General Jackson's invasion of the Shenandoah, in 1862, caused orders to be issued to McDowell to intercept him. The railroads were unserviceable, and it became Haupt's duty to make such repairs as would

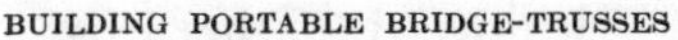

BUILDING PORTABLE BRIDGE-TRUSSES

AT WORK IN THE CARPENTER-SHOP

EXPERIMENTS WITH BOARD TRUSSES

LOADING A BRIDGE TO TEST IT

TESTING A "SHAD-BELLY" BRIDGE

TRIAL OF A "SHAD-BELLY" BRIDGE

BRIDGES WHILE YOU WAIT, BY THE CONSTRUCTION CORPS

Early in 1863, after Burnside was relieved and while the Army of the Potomac was lying at Fredericksburg under Hooker, the construction corps experimented busily with portable trusses and torpedoes. Records of the experiments were made by photographs, and these views served for the education of other Federal armies. Above are some of the very photographs that instructed the Federal armies in "bridge-building while you wait." Hooker's first plan of operations, given in confidence to General Haupt, required large preparations of railroad-bridge material. Although the plans were subsequently changed, use was found for all of this material.

enable McDowell's forces to reach the Valley, at Front Royal, in time, if possible, to get in rear of the Confederates. McDowell was then in command of the Department of the Rappahannock, and Haupt was his chief of construction and transportation.

The road to be repaired was the Manassas Gap Railroad. It was promptly put in order from Rectortown to Piedmont, but the equipment was insufficient to enable it to sustain the amount of work suddenly thrown upon it. Besides, the operation of military railroads was not understood, and the difficulties were constantly increased by military interference with the running of trains and by the neglect and, at times, absolute refusal of subordinates in the supply departments to unload and return cars. The telegraph was, at this period, so uncertain an instrument that it was considered impracticable to rely on it for the operation of trains. Consequently, a schedule was arranged. But here again there was trouble. Even the War Department consented to having this schedule broken up by unwarranted interference, and the operators were compelled to return to the uncertain telegraph for train despatching.

Colonel Haupt stated, in a report of these difficulties to the War Department on June 6th, that the road had theretofore been operated exclusively by the use of the telegraph, without the aid of any schedule or time-table for running the trains; that such a system might answer if the telegraph were always in order, operators always at their posts, and the line exclusively operated by the railroad employees; but when in operation it was frequently appropriated to military purposes. In consequence, he had, on one occasion, been compelled to go eighteen miles to get in telegraphic communication with the superintendent to learn the cause of the detention of trains, and had been compelled, after waiting for hours, to leave without an answer, the telegraph line being in use for military messages.

As a further evidence of the unreliability of the telegraph

GUARDING THE "O. & A." NEAR UNION MILLS

Jackson's raid around Pope's army on Bristoe and Manassas stations in August, 1862, taught the Federal generals that both railroad and base of supplies must be guarded. Pope's army was out of subsistence and forage, and the single-track railroad was inadequate.

DÉBRIS FROM JACKSON'S RAID ON THE ORANGE AND ALEXANDRIA RAILROAD

This scrap-heap at Alexandria was composed of the remains of cars and engines destroyed by Jackson at Bristoe and Manassas stations. The Confederate leader marched fifty miles in thirty-six hours through Thoroughfare Gap, which Pope had neglected to guard.

for railroad use, Colonel Haupt stated that, even if a wire and operators were provided for the exclusive use of the road, the line would be so liable to derangement from storms and other causes that it could be considered only as a convenience or an auxiliary. As a principal or sole means of operation it was highly unreliable, and was not a necessity.

In order, then, to get some kind of service, the use of the telegraph had again to be abandoned, and even a schedule was dispensed with. Trains received orders to proceed to Front Royal with all speed consistent with safety, returning trains to give the right of way, and all trains to send flagmen in advance. These flagmen were relieved as soon as exhausted. The trains were run in sections, and after considerable experience in this method of operation, a certain measure of success was obtained.

McDowell's orders had been to intercept Jackson; he had personally hurried through Manassas Gap with the troops in advance, and was at Front Royal when, on May 31st, an engineer officer reported to him that there was a bad break in the railroad just west of the summit of the gap, with the track torn up and rails and ties thrown down the mountainside. McDowell sent a hurried note to Haupt, who was east of the gap, and he replied by the same messenger that the general need feel no uneasiness, for, if the rails were within reach, the break could be repaired in a few hours. On June 1st, soon after daylight, the men of the construction corps reached the scene of the wreck and found it in bad shape, but set to work immediately. The broken cars were tumbled over the bank in short order. The track gang was divided into two parties, working toward each other from the ends of the break. The rails and ties were hauled up from the side of the mountain below, and by ten o'clock an engine passed over and was sent to report to General McDowell. Notwithstanding the quick work done throughout, Jackson escaped up the Valley, and the pursuit was fruitless.

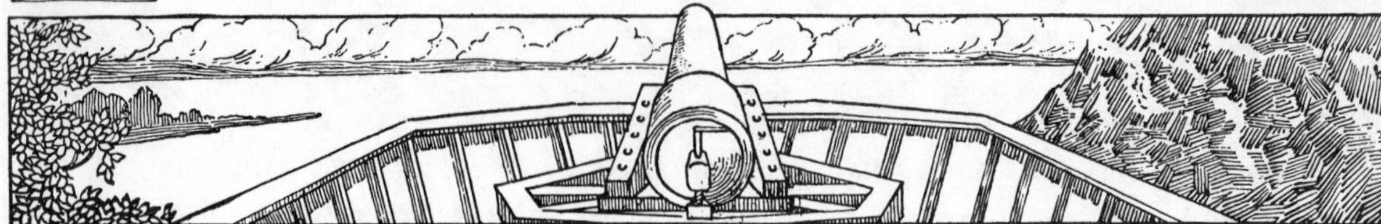

BEFORE THE FRESHET OF APRIL, '63

THE BRIDGE OVER BULL RUN THAT KEPT THE CONSTRUCTION CORPS BUSY

The United States Military Railroad Construction Corps got much of its training at this point. The bridge over Bull Run near Union Mills was one of the most frequently reconstructed of the war. This photograph, taken from upstream, shows its appearance before it was carried away by the freshet of April, 1863. On the pages following it appears in several stages of destruction and reconstruction after that event. This neighborhood was the scene of numerous guerrilla raids after the battle of Chancellorsville, May 2, 1863. It was visited with fire and sword again and again by both the Federals and Confederates, as the fortunes of war gave temporary possession of this debatable bit of ground, first to one side and then to the other.

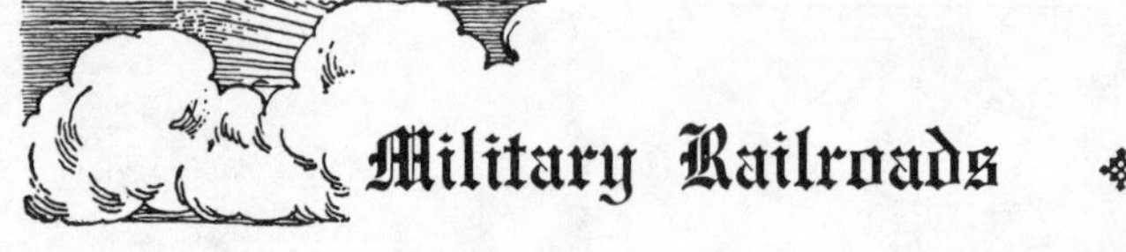

After the withdrawal of McDowell from the Valley, there was a lull in the active operations, and the construction corps was reorganized. Up to this time it had been composed of details of soldiers. It was now made up of a permanent personnel, assisted by details when necessary. Under date of June 11, 1862, a set of regulations was promulgated by Colonel Haupt for the guidance of the corps, and on June 20th, Haupt, believing that he had accomplished the purpose for which he was brought to Washington by the Secretary of War, sent in a letter of resignation, stating that the communications were then all open, the roads in good condition, the trains running according to schedule, abundant supplies of stores for a week or more in advance already transported, and no probability of any new work for the construction corps for several weeks. As characteristic of Secretary Stanton, it may be noted that this letter was never answered.

On June 26th, General Pope assumed command and persistently declined to notice Haupt or the duties he had been performing. McDowell tried to persuade him to do so, but Pope declared that all such matters should be run by the Quartermaster's Department. Consequently, Colonel Haupt went to Washington, reported the state of affairs to an assistant secretary of war, and proceeded to his home in Massachusetts. The understanding was that he was to return if needed. Soon after his arrival home he received from the War Department the following telegram, "Come back immediately; cannot get along without you; not a wheel moving on any of the roads." He reported to General Pope at Cedar Mountain, and received orders to dictate such directions as he deemed necessary to the chief of staff. Orders were thereupon issued, placing Haupt in entire charge of all transportation by railroad within the lines of operation of Pope's army. This was August 18th. On August 19th, the Secretary of War confirmed the order issued by General Pope on the previous day.

During the retreat of General Pope, the railroads under

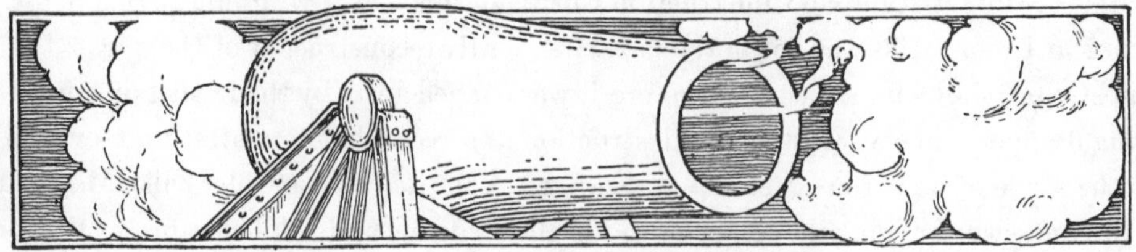

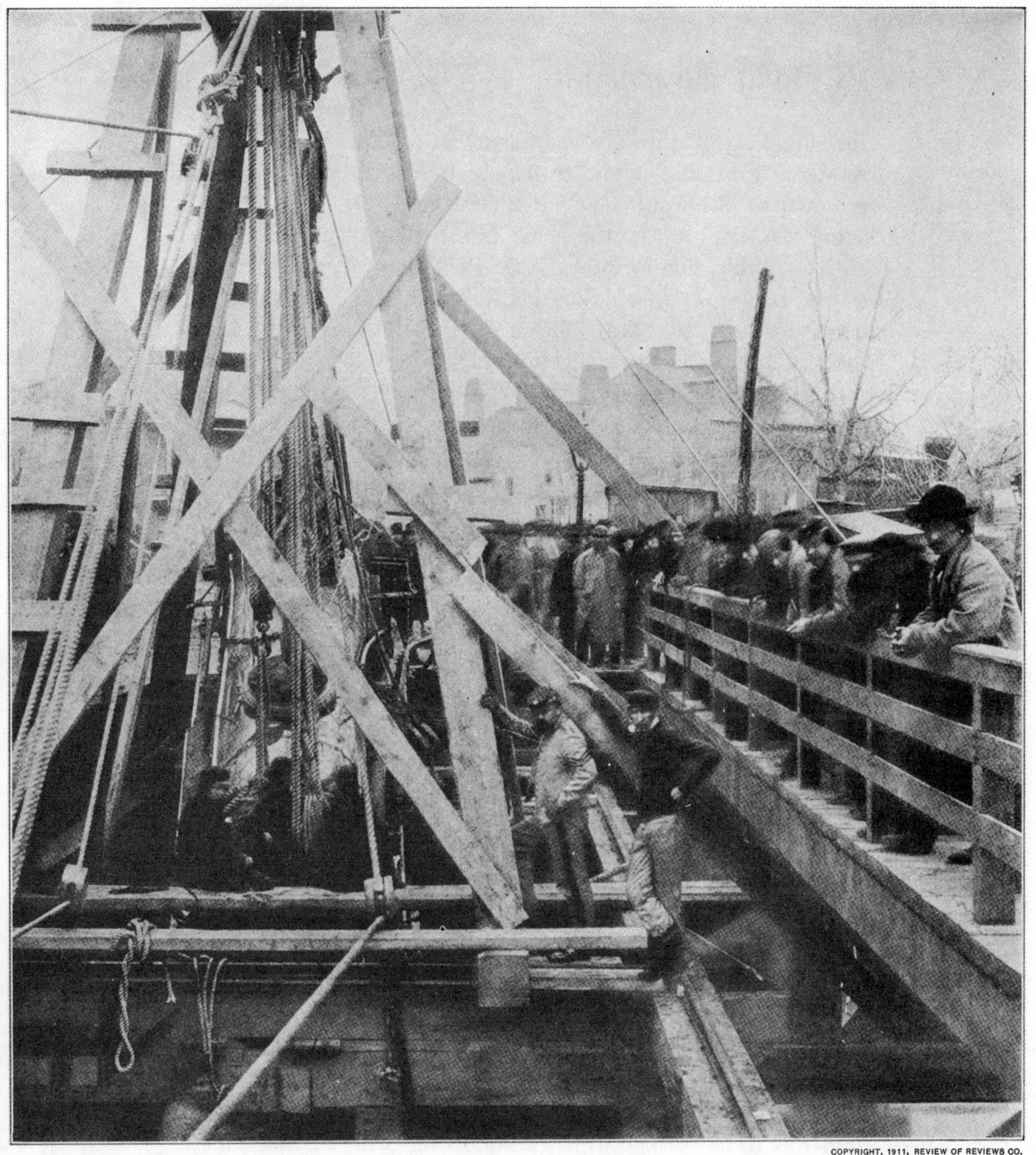

LIFTING THE 59,000-POUND ENGINE "VIBBARD" FROM THE DRAW OF LONG BRIDGE

This scene of March, 1864, suggests some of the difficulties which confronted the superintendent of military railroads during the war. Long Bridge, from the railroad-man's viewpoint, was not a very substantial structure. J. J. Moore, chief engineer and general superintendent of military railroads of Virginia, reported to Brigadier-General D. C. McCallum, under the date of July 1, 1865, that he experienced great difficulty in keeping it secure for the passage of trains. On August 22, 1864, the draw at the south end of the bridge was nearly destroyed by a tug, with a schooner in tow, running into it, and February 18, 1865, an engine broke through the south span of the bridge, the entire span being wrecked. The rescue of the "Vibbard," which weighed 59,000 pounds and cost $11,845, was apparently effectual; the same report states that it ran 5,709 miles at a total cost of $4,318.78 in the fiscal year ending June, 1865.

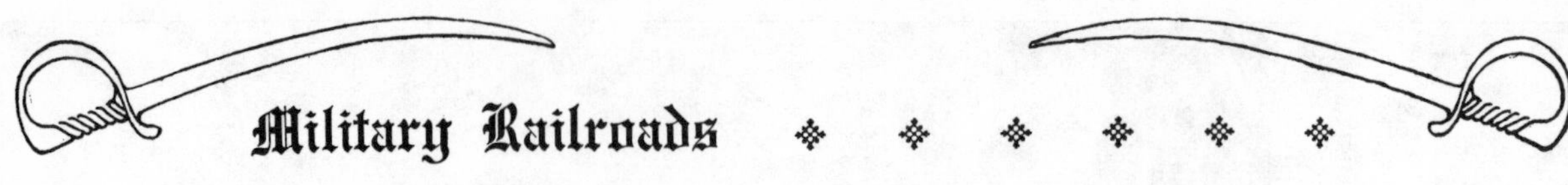

the direction of the chief of construction and transportation rendered great aid in the transportation of troops and in the removal of the wounded from the front. The supply of the army was kept up at the same time. This would have been entirely impossible in the early days of the war, yet the necessity of having one head for this service had not yet impressed itself on all the general officers of Pope's army, for we find interference with the operation of trains from officers who would not have done so if they had realized the importance of non-interference. There has been some controversy regarding the non-arrival of troops at the front during this campaign, and the point has been made that it was impossible to secure rail transportation. It appears that the railroad was a single-track one, with a limited equipment of cars and engines, and necessarily it was impossible to forward troops with the rapidity that could have been desired, but under the circumstances the operation of the trains was as successful as could have been hoped for.

In consequence of the interference by subordinates with the running of trains, a positive order was issued by General Halleck to all concerned, directing that no military officer should give any orders, except through the chief of the construction corps, that would affect the operation of the road, and that all orders must come from either General Pope or General Halleck, except in case of attack on the road, in which case the officials of the road were to consult the commander of the nearest body of troops.

By August 26th, it was evident that the railroad could be relied on for nothing more than the necessary supplies for Pope's army, except in cases where the trains should happen to be unemployed, in which case troops could be forwarded. A schedule for use in such event was provided. Transportation was to be furnished in the following order: First, subsistence for men in the field; second, forage; third, ammunition; fourth, hospital stores; fifth, infantry regiments that had seen

On September 14, 1863, General Haupt was relieved from further duty in the War Department, and turned over his duties to Colonel (later Major-General) D. C. McCallum, who was appointed Superintendent of Military Railroads. The efficient operation of the roads with the Army of the Potomac continued, and received the enthusiastic praise of General Grant. Engines for the military railroad at City Point had to be transported by water. In the lower photograph the "General Dix" is seen being landed at City Point.

MAJOR-GENERAL D. C. McCALLUM

AN OFFICER PRAISED BY GENERAL GRANT

This engine weighed 59,000 pounds and cost $9,500. It was credited with a record of 16,776 miles at the comparatively low cost of $6,136.62 during the fiscal year ending June, 1865. Behind it is the tender piled up with the wood which was used for fuel in those days. This is what necessitated the gigantic stacks of the wood-burning engines. The "General Dix" has evidently been put into perfect condition for its trips over the uneven track of the railway from City Point to the army lines at Petersburg.

LANDING THE MILITARY ENGINE "GENERAL DIX" AT CITY POINT, 1864–5

service, and staff horses; sixth, infantry regiments that had not seen service; and the following were ordinarily refused transportation, although the positive rule was laid down that nothing necessary for military service was to be refused transportation if such was available—batteries, except in cases of emergency, were to march; cavalry was to march; mules and wagon-horses were to be driven; wagons, ambulances, and other vehicles were to be hauled over the common roads.

In addition to the regular duties of construction, repair, and operation of the railroads, the construction corps did valiant service in securing information of the Confederates and also of Pope's army, which for a time was cut off from communication with the Federal capital. Their telegraph operators would go as far forward as possible, climb trees, reconnoiter the country, and send back by wire all the information they could gather. As soon as the Confederates had withdrawn from the vicinity of Manassas, the corps promptly began repairing road-beds, tracks, and bridges. Pope's army was soon resupplied and the intense feeling of apprehension allayed.

In the latter part of 1862, W. W. Wright, an assistant in the work of the corps, was placed in charge of the Cumberland Valley Railroad, which was wholly under military supervision. Later in the war, Wright was in charge of Sherman's railroads during the great Atlanta campaign in 1864. For his guidance with the Cumberland road the instructions were: First, not to allow supplies to be forwarded to the advanced terminus until they were actually required; second, only such quantities were to be forwarded as could be promptly removed; third, cars must be promptly unloaded and returned; fourth, to permit no delay of trains beyond the time of starting, but to furnish extras when necessary.

When Burnside's corps evacuated Fredericksburg upon the withdrawal of the Federal forces from the Rappahannock line before the second Bull Run campaign, all the reconstructed work at Aquia Creek and some of the bridges on the

THE CONSTRUCTION CORPS TURNS TO WHARF-BUILDING

The construction corps of the United States Military Railroads was as versatile in its attainments as the British marines according to Kipling—"Soldier and Sailor, too." This busy scene shows construction men at work on the wharves which formed the City Point terminal to Grant's military railroad, connecting it with the army in front of Petersburg. This hastily constructed road was about thirteen miles long, measured in a straight line and not counting the undulations, which, if added together, would have made it several miles in height.

TROOPS AT CITY POINT READY TO BE TAKEN TO THE FRONT BY RAIL

THE SUPPLY ROUTE WHEN THE RAILROADS WERE WRECKED

When the Army of the Cumberland under Rosecrans retreated from the field of Chickamauga, with 16,000 of its 62,000 effectives killed and wounded, it concentrated at Chattanooga. The Confederates under Bragg held the south bank of the Tennessee, and from the end of the railroad at Bridgeport there was a haul of sixty miles to Chattanooga. Twenty-six miles of railroad, including the long truss bridge across the Tennessee River and the trestle at Whiteside, a quarter of a mile long and one hundred and thirteen feet high, had been destroyed. Rosecrans' only route to supply his army was the river. It was Lieutenant-Colonel (later Brigadier-General) William G. Le Duc who saved from a freshet the first flat-bottomed boat, the *Chattanooga*, which carried 45,000 rations up to Kelley's Ferry, whence the haul was only eight miles to the Army of the Cumberland—instead of sixty. Later more boats were built, and the railroad repaired, but it was Le Duc's ingenuity in rescuing the nondescript craft, built by Captain Edwards, from the oaks along the river and an old boiler as raw material, that saved the army many pangs of hunger, if not general starvation. The sixty-mile haul over the rough mountain-roads from Bridgeport to Chattanooga was no longer whitened with the bones of the suffering draft animals who were being killed by thousands in the desperate effort to bring food to the army. In the photograph opposite the other end of the line—Bridgeport, Alabama—is shown as it appeared April 2, 1863. Prince Felix Salm-Salm, a German soldier of fortune, was the Commander of this post. He served on the staff of General Louis Blenker and later was commissioned Colonel of the Eighth New York Volunteers, a German regiment. His final rank was Brigadier-General.

ARMY BOATS ON THE TENNESSEE—1864

railroad, including the "bean-pole and corn-stalk" bridge, had been again destroyed, this time by Federal troops. General Haupt had protested against it, but without avail. On October 26th, after the memorable battle of Antietam, McClellan requested that the Aquia Creek and Fredericksburg railroad wharves and road be reconstructed. Haupt reported that the task was now much more formidable than before; that he had protested against the destruction of the wharves and the tearing up of the road, and especially against the burning of the "bean-pole and corn-stalk" bridge over Potomac Creek; that this work was a piece of vandalism on the part of Federal troops that could have been prevented, and that it was entirely unnecessary. Nothing was done immediately toward this reconstruction, but strict orders were issued to prevent further depredations of similar character.

On the replacing of McClellan by Burnside, in 1862, the rebuilding of these structures was carried to completion, and again they were in serviceable condition for the campaign which ended so disastrously to the Federals at Fredericksburg.

W. W. Wright was instructed, on December 11, 1862, to prepare for the construction of a bridge over the Rappahannock for the passage of Burnside's army. The rebuilding of the railroad bridge was again commenced, but the battle began and forced suspension of the work, and it was not finished. The battle resulted in a check to the Federal forces, and the forward movement of the Army of the Potomac was stopped. Nothing more of importance occurred in connection with military railroad operations while Burnside was in command. After he was removed, and while the army was lying near Fredericksburg under Hooker, the construction corps was experimenting with trusses and torpedoes; and the U-shaped iron for the destruction of rails was perfected.

The battle of Chancellorsville was fought; Hooker was repulsed, and the same annoyances of guerrilla raids were experienced on the Orange and Alexandria road as had been

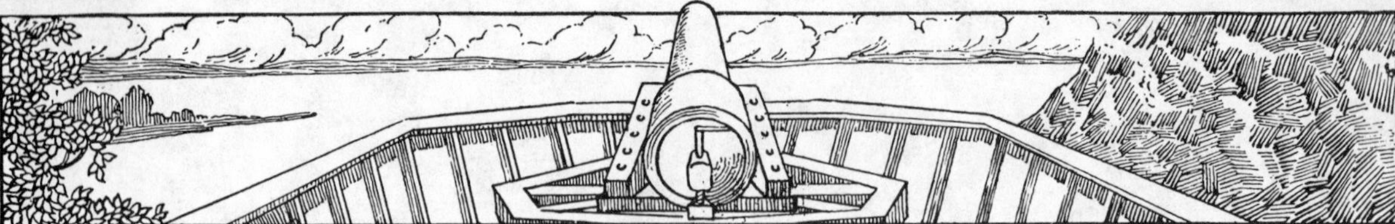

THE STRUCTURE THAT STAYED—THREE TIMES HAD THE CONFEDERATES DESTROYED THE BRIDGE AT THIS POINT—BRIDGEPORT, ALABAMA

This bridge of 1864 over the Tennessee, on the Nashville and Chattanooga Railroad at Bridgeport, Alabama, was the fourth in succession. Three previous bridges had been destroyed by the Confederates. But the United States Military Railroad Construction Corps, then under the command of Colonel D. C. McCallum, seemed like the mythical giant Antæus to rise twice as strong after each upset. So it was only for a short time that supplies were kept out of Chattanooga. So confident did Sherman become during his great Atlanta campaign of their ability to accomplish wonders, that he frequently based his plans upon the rapidity of their railroad work. They never failed him. Colonel W. W. Wright directed the transportation, and General Adna Anderson directed repairs to the road, including the reconstruction of the bridges, but this latter work was under the immediate direction of Colonel E. C. Smeed. How well it was done is evidenced by these two photographs. In the lower one the broad wagon-way below the railroad trestles can be examined.

previously felt elsewhere. On June 28, 1863, Hooker was relieved by General Meade. The crucial period of the war came at Gettysburg. The construction corps, under the personal direction of General Haupt, rendered invaluable service. Haupt had made Gettysburg his home for part of the time he was a resident of the State of Pennsylvania, and knew every road in the vicinity. He gave great assistance in divining Lee's direction of march, and by the great exertions of the corps the railroad communications were kept open, the wounded handled with celerity, and after the battle there was a sufficient supply on hand of nearly all kinds of provisions.

On September 14, 1863, General Haupt was relieved from further duty in the War Department, and turned over his work to Colonel D. C. McCallum, who was appointed superintendent of military railroads. The efficient operation of the roads with the Army of the Potomac continued, and received the enthusiastic praise from General Grant which already has been noted.

Extensions aggregating nearly twenty-two miles in length were built to the railroad from City Point, in order to supply Grant's forces in the lines before Petersburg. After the repulse of General Rosecrans at Chickamauga, in September, 1863, it was deemed necessary to send reenforcements from the Eastern armies, and the military-railroad officials were called upon to know if the movement of the number of troops designated was practicable. Colonel McCallum soon gave an affirmative answer, and the result was the transfer of Hooker, with two corps, about twenty-two thousand men, over twelve hundred miles in eleven and one-half days. For this service Colonel McCallum was appointed brevet brigadier-general.

The Knoxville-Chattanooga road was the next to be opened, and then the Nashville-Johnsonville line. In all of this work the corps introduced new methods to replace the older ones. All of this was preparatory to the advance on Atlanta, in 1864.

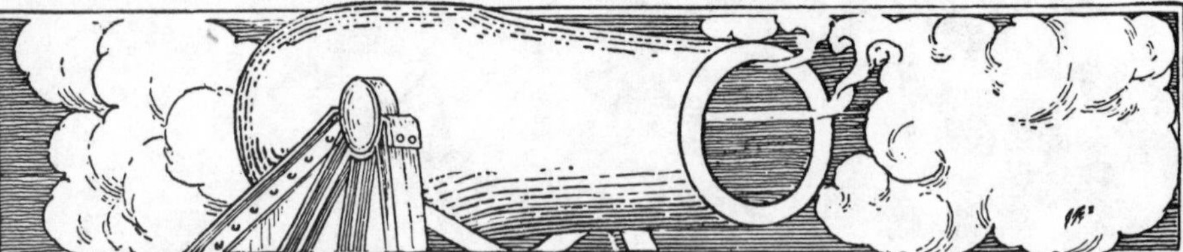

A MILL WRECKED TO BUILD A BRIDGE

CUMBERLAND RAVINE TRESTLE

This trestle across the Cumberland Ravine was rushed up from trees and other materials ready to hand. One source of supply was the mill by the mountain torrent. Few boards remain on the structure as the soldiers lounge about it. While Sherman's army advanced on Atlanta, again and again a long high bridge would be destroyed, and miles of track totally obliterated, by the retiring Confederates. But close upon their heels would come the construction corps: the bridge and track would be restored as if by magic, and the screech of an approaching locomotive would bring delight to the Federals and disappointment to the Confederates. With any materials they found ready to hand the construction corps worked at marvellous speed.

Military Railroads

In the great Atlanta campaign, the railroad work of every kind was probably the best of the war. The hard schools of Virginia and around Chattanooga had prepared the railroad corps to initiate greater exhibitions of skill and efficiency. General Sherman had such confidence in the abilities of the construction corps to keep pace with him that he frequently risked advances which depended entirely on rapid railroad work behind the corps of his army, feeling assured that the rail communications would keep up with his movements. They did, and the moral effect of a screaming locomotive constantly close in the rear of his army, notwithstanding the tremendous destructive efforts of the Confederates in their retreat, was very great on both armies. A long, high bridge would be destroyed, miles of track totally obliterated, and the Confederates would retire; the Federals would advance, cross the stream in the face of opposition, and no sooner across than, to the consternation of the Confederates and the delight of the Federals, an "iron devil" would immediately set up its heartrending (delightful) screech, announcing that, march as hard and as fast as they might, neither army could get away from the end of the railroad.

The marvelous celerity with which bridges were repaired or rebuilt, new mileage of track opened, and the operation of the road carried on, notwithstanding the numerous breaks by raiding parties, will always remain a bright page in the history of the Civil War. Colonel W. W. Wright directed the transportation and remained most of the time with Sherman; General Adna Anderson directed repairs to the road, including the reconstruction of the bridges, but this latter work was under the immediate direction of Colonel E. C. Smeed. All of these officers had had previous experience in military and civil railroading that fitted them admirably for the work. General Sherman says the operation of his railroads was brilliant; that the campaign could not have been prosecuted without the efficient service which he received; that altogether there were

MILITARY TRAIN ON THE CUMBERLAND RAVINE TRESTLE—BELOW, THE CHATTAHOOCHIE BRIDGE

Underneath this picture of the army trestle (seen from down-stream on the second page preceding) is reproduced a panoramic view of the Chattahoochie Bridge—the most marvelous feat of military engineering to date (July, 1864). It was 800 feet long, nearly 100 feet high, and contained about twice as much timber as was required for the "beanpole and cornstalk bridge," shown on page 272. It was completed in four and a half days, from the material in the tree to the finished product. This would be record time even now.

AN 800-FOOT RAILROAD BRIDGE BUILT IN FOUR AND ONE-HALF DAYS

SWIFT REPAIR WORK BY THE MILITARY RAILROAD CORPS

DISMANTLED BY A FRESHET CONSTRUCTION CORPS TO THE RESCUE

It was not only the daring Confederates with which the United States military construction corps had to contend, but the elements as well. In April, 1864, a freshet swept away this much abused structure. The standard size parts, ready prepared, were stacked in the railroad yards awaiting calls from the front. Cars were held always ready, and the parts ordered by wire were hurried away to the broken bridge as soon as a competent engineer had inspected the break and decided what was needed. The remainder of the work of the corps after this material reached the spot was a matter of minutes, or at the most of a few hours. The lower photograph shows the Bull Run bridge being repaired.

THE TRACK OVER BULL RUN CLEAR AGAIN—CONSTRUCTION CORPS AT WORK

The parts of this railroad crossing over Bull Run near Union Mills, were of the standard size found most suitable for emergencies. This was fortunate, because the bridge was destroyed seven times. A work of this character could be put up in a very few hours. Repairing the masonry abutments, of course, consumed the greatest length of time, but even these grew like magic under the efforts of the construction corps. The lower photograph shows the same bridge reënforced with trusses. These standard size trusses and other parts of bridges were carefully made by the skilled engineers of the construction corps, and tested under weights greater than any they would conceivably be called upon to bear. These parts were kept constantly on hand so that repairs could be rushed at short notice.

THE BRIDGE THAT WAS DESTROYED SEVEN TIMES

REËNFORCED WITH TRUSSES—TRANSFORMED INTO A STANDARD BRIDGE

473 miles of road from Louisville, through Nashville and Chattanooga, to Atlanta, 288 miles of which were constantly subject to raids from the foe—the portion from Nashville to Atlanta; that this single-stem road supplied one hundred thousand men and thirty-five thousand animals for one hundred and ninety-six days; and that to have delivered as much food by wagon would have been entirely impossible, since even to have hauled as much a short distance would have taken thirty-six thousand eight hundred six-mule wagons, and, when the state of the roads was considered, an attempt to supply by these means would have been an absurdity. Whereupon he reiterated that the Atlanta campaign would have been an impossibility without the railroads.

When Sherman evacuated Atlanta, preparatory to his march to the sea, he destroyed the railroad in his rear, blew up the railroad buildings in the city, sent back his surplus stores and all the railroad machinery that had been accumulated by his army, and, as far as possible, left the country barren to the Confederates. The stores and railroad stock were safely withdrawn to Nashville, and after the dispersion of Hood's army the construction corps again took the field, reconstructed the road to Chattanooga, then to Atlanta, and later extended it to Decatur, Macon, and Augusta.

At one time, just prior to the close of the war, there were 1,769 miles of military railroads under the direction of General McCallum, general manager of the military railroads of the United States. These roads required about three hundred and sixty-five engines and forty-two hundred cars. In April, 1865, over twenty-three thousand five hundred men were employed. The results of the work of the corps were recognized throughout the world as remarkable triumphs of military and engineering skill, highly creditable to the officers and men.

XIII

THE DEFENSE OF RICHMOND

THE CAPITOL AT RICHMOND UNDEFENDED, WHILE LEE AND HIS REMNANT WERE SWEPT ASIDE—APRIL, 1865

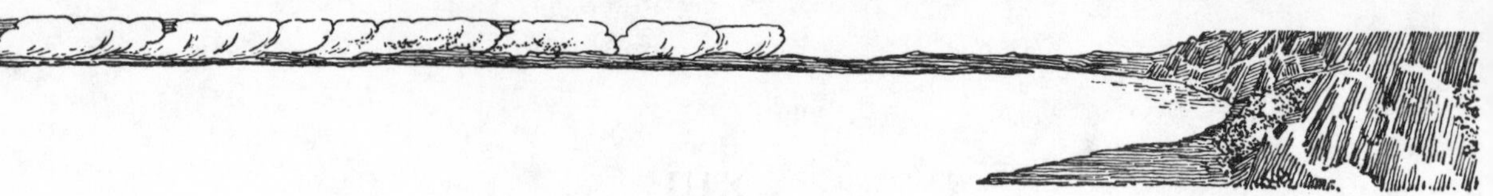

DEFENDING THE CITADEL OF THE CONFEDERACY

By O. E. Hunt
Captain, United States Army

The Editors desire to express their grateful acknowledgment to Colonel T. M. R. Talcott, C. E., C. S. A., for a critical examination of this chapter and many helpful suggestions. Colonel Talcott was major and aide-de-camp on the staff of General Robert E. Lee, and later Colonel First Regiment Engineer Troops, Army of Northern Virginia, with an intimate knowledge of the Richmond defenses and is able to corroborate the statements and descriptions contained in the following pages from his personal knowledge.

AFTER the admission of Virginia to the Confederacy, General Lee was detailed as military adviser to the President, and several armies were put in the field—those of the Potomac, the Valley, the Rappahannock, the Peninsula, and Norfolk. It was not until the spring of 1862, when Richmond was threatened by a large Federal army under McClellan, that these forces were united under Johnston's command—Lee continuing as military adviser to the President until Johnston was wounded at Seven Pines, when the command fell to the leader whose brilliant defense of the citadel of the Confederacy from that time until the close of the great struggle excited the admiration of friend, foe, and neutral, alike.

Owing to the importance of Richmond, General Lee found himself always compelled to keep the one object in view—the defense of the capital of his State and Government.

For the safety of the city it was necessary that the approaches should be rendered defensible by small bodies of

UP THE JAMES AT LAST—1865

These Federal gunboats would not be lying so far up the river—above the Dutch Gap Canal, near Fort Brady—unless the breaking of Lee's lines at Petersburg had forced the evacuation of Richmond, and of the batteries which lined the shores of the river-approach to the city. The Confederate batteries are silent now; and the dreaded Confederate fleet has been destroyed by orders of its own commander. The ironclad, *Virginia*, which never fired a shot, lies in the mud near Chaffin's Bluff opposite Fort Darling, sunk in a last desperate attempt to obstruct the approach of the Federal fleet. Now follows a scene of peace. It is wash-day, as can be seen from the lines of clothing hanging in the rigging of the gunboats and of the converted ferryboat down the river. The latter will soon return to its former peaceful use.

troops, so that the main body of the Army of Northern Virginia could be utilized in strategic operations, without danger of the fall of the capital into the hands of small raiding parties from the Federal forces.

The energies of the Richmond Government were exerted in so many directions in preparing for the struggle that the immediate preparations for the defense of the capital had to proceed very uncertainly. On June 14th, General Lee reported to Governor Letcher that the work on the redoubts which had been projected was going on so slowly that he deemed it his duty to call the governor's attention to the matter.

Lee had, during the previous month, taken the precaution to fortify the James River below the mouth of the Appomattox, by having works erected on the site of old Fort Powhatan, about twelve miles below the confluence of the two rivers, and at Jamestown Island, Hardin's Bluff, Mulberry Island, and Day's Point.

In July, 1861, the citizens of Richmond were aroused to their patriotic duty of helping in the fortification of the city, and, by formal resolution of a committee on defenses, proposed that the city bear its proportionate share of the expense, and that their officers consult with those of the general Government as to the strength and location of the works. It was decided to employ the services of such free negroes as would be available in the city, under the superintendence of competent officers. To these resolutions the Secretary of War replied on July 12th, concurring in the views expressed, and saying that the question of the division of expense should be adjusted easily, inasmuch as there was a duty on the part of the Government to provide its share toward the protection of its capital; that the militia would be armed, equipped, and drilled immediately, and that the construction of the fortifications would be pushed.

The works erected during the spring and summer of 1861 in and around Norfolk and on the James River and the Peninsula, were provided for by an appropriation by the State of

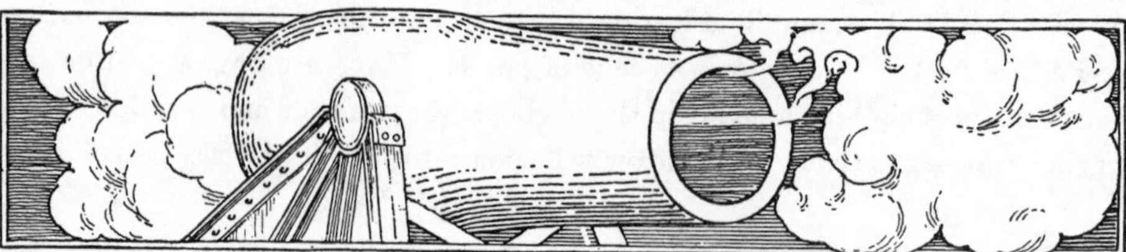

THE ARSENAL AT RICHMOND (AFTER THE FIRE)

After Richmond was selected as the Capital of the Confederate States it was deemed absolutely vital to hold the city at all costs. Aside from the impression which its fall would have made on European nations that might side with the Confederacy, its great iron-works were capable of supplying a large part of the *matériel* for the artillery of the armies and for the navy. It provided railroad supplies in considerable quantities. Its skilled artisans furnished labor essential in the technical branches of both the military and naval services during the first year or more of the war. Now, as the political center of the new Government, its importance was enhanced a hundredfold. The actual fortifications of the city were never completed. The Army of Northern Virginia, under its brilliant and daring tactician, Lee, proved the strongest defense. Field-artillery was made in Augusta, Georgia. But here, in the Tredegar Iron Works, was the only source of heavy caliber guns, of which the Confederacy stood in such woeful need.

THE TREDEGAR WORKS FOR HEAVY GUNS

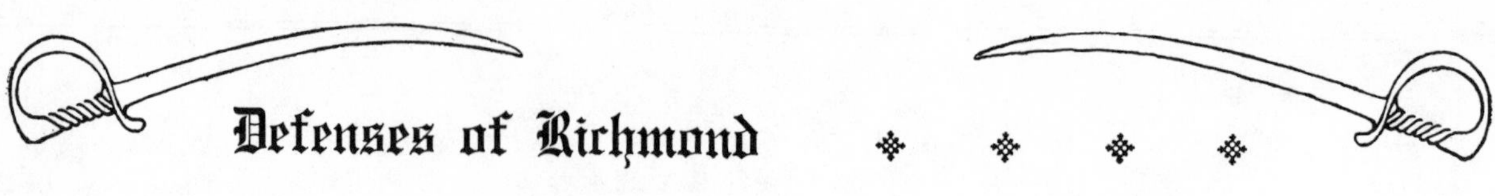

Virginia for "river, coast, and harbor defenses" made previous to the secession of the State.

On October 9th, Major Leadbetter, acting chief of the engineer bureau, reported to the Secretary of War that the pressure of work of all kinds on the city, State, and general governments had been such that but little progress had been made on the Richmond defenses. Only six guns, 32-pounders, had been mounted, while some thirty others were on hand without carriages. A few of the carriages were being built, but the work was moving slowly for the want of skilled labor to devote to that particular project. When the Norfolk Navy-Yard fell into the hands of the Confederates, there had been obtained a considerable supply of 32-pounder Dahlgrens, and army gun-carriages were being made for these at Norfolk, but this supply was limited, and the demand was so great that none could be spared for Richmond itself.

By this time, the State authorities were anxious that the whole responsibility for the fortifications should be assumed by the Confederate Government, and Major Leadbetter recommended that these wishes be observed. The greatest difficulty which he apprehended for the general Government was the lack of competent engineer officers. A number of officers of the line had been detailed as acting engineers, and with these it was hoped to carry the work to a successful conclusion.

But it was not until the end of February, 1862, that the chain of works was fairly well started. It consisted of eighteen closed or semi-closed forts, and seven outworks. The entire circuit was about twelve miles, and the designs of all the forts were good, and the proposed distances of the works from the city varied from less than a mile to more than a mile and a half from the outskirts. The complete armament would require two hundred and eighteen heavy guns.

The armament, however, was never fully furnished, for it was decided by the Virginia State authorities that the line was too near the city, and that, if closely assailed, there was

With the possible exception of Charleston at the seaside, Richmond was the best-defended city in the Confederacy. Vicksburg proved long and difficult of capture on account of the natural formation of the land, and Petersburg lay behind an army entrenched; but the series of Confederate batteries along the James River, up which the Union army and navy were trying to advance, rendered the stream impassable to the navy and the city above impregnable against the army. These guns look solitary and deserted with no one but the photographer's assistant in the picture. But each was attended by an eager crew, so long as the Confederacy held the reaches of the James. The serving of these guns marked the last great stand of the Confederacy. Union assailants will testify to how bravely and desperately they were fought. The Confederacy was calling on every man capable of bearing arms. The Federals could easily have duplicated their own armies in the field. All of these guns are mounted on old-fashioned wooden carriages. The elevating device of the gun in the upper picture differs materially from the screws for that purpose in the lower. The breech was elevated by means of handspikes, using the sides of the carriage as fulcra, and retained in the desired position by the series of checks visible on its breech. Even with these clumsy devices the guns proved too formidable for the Federal fleet.

TWO HEAVY CONFEDERATE SIEGE GUNS NORTH OF DUTCH GAP CANAL

NAVY BROADSIDE 42-POUNDER WITH REËNFORCED BREECH

danger that it might be destroyed even before the forts were taken. It was apparent that the lines should be extended further toward the Chickahominy, and also above and below the city they should be placed much further out. But the inner line of forts was so well built and otherwise judiciously located, that these works could be used as a support for the more advanced positions.

The principal objection to the armament was that the guns were all *en barbette,* thus exposing them and the men too much. But, by the end of February, only eleven guns had been mounted on the north side of the river, with twelve more ready to mount, while, on the south side, there were but two mounted and no others on hand. It was estimated that, even with the entire possible armament in sight, it would take at least three months to complete the instalment of the guns; but not one single piece more was then to be had.

So far as the heavy artillery of its defenses was concerned, Richmond was in almost a helpless condition. Every engineer who expresed himself felt that the danger, however, was not from the north, as that quarter was well protected by the field-army, but from the south by the approach of a land force, and along the James by the approach of a hostile fleet.

A certain amount of unsatisfactory progress was made on the works and armament; but to strengthen the river approaches, five batteries, mounting over forty guns, with provision for more, had been erected by the middle of March along the river at points below Drewry's Bluff.

By that time the control of the defenses had been transferred from the State of Virginia to the Confederate Government, and an officer of the Government placed in charge. The opinion that the works were too near the city was confirmed by the Government engineers, but, as much work had already been done on them, it was directed that they be completed as they had been originally planned, and that, in case of emergency, the secondary works to fill the gaps and those

THE RIVER APPROACH

To hold at bay the Federal navy, waxing strong on the rivers as it was practically supreme on the sea-coast, taxed the Confederates in 1864 especially. The James River emptying into Chesapeake Bay offered the invaders a tempting means of approach. So at every point of advantage in its sinuous course through the bottom lands of Virginia, a Confederate battery was placed to sweep a reach of the river. The big guns, cast and bored in Richmond, were mounted along the river in her defense. So skilfully was this work conducted that the Federal gunboats never reached Richmond until after Lee

UNION MONITORS HELD AT BAY DECEMBER, 1864

CONFEDERATE GUNS ALONG THE JAMES RIVER DEFENDING RICHMOND

retreated from Petersburg. The banks of the James often reëchoed to the thunder of the naval guns during the last year of the war. Battery after battery was silenced, yet Drewry's and Chaffin's Bluffs held firm, while the torpedoes and obstructions in the river made it impossible to navigate. On this page appear two of the Confederate guns that frowned above Dutch Gap. The lower one is in Battery Brooke, whence the deadly fire interfered with Butler's Canal, and is a homemade naval gun. The upper one was a Columbiad with reënforced breech. Both of them are mounted on old style wooden carriages.

to cover the city at a greater distance could be constructed by the troops assigned to the defense, aided by such other labor as could be obtained. It was decided to be an injudicious waste of labor to build the outer works before the stronger inner line was completed, even though the latter was too near the city. Very few more guns were procured, however, and it seemed of doubtful propriety to place so many heavy guns in such a contracted space.

McClellan's Peninsula campaign was bringing his army dangerously near the Confederate capital. Hurried preparation of the unfinished works placed them in as strong a condition as possible, and the outer line was started. When the Federal army began its advance from Yorktown, there were only three guns in position on Drewry's Bluff, but, owing to the fear that the Union gunboats would ascend the river past the batteries further down, several ship's guns were also mounted to cover the obstructions in the channel.

On May 15th, a fleet of Union gunboats under Commander John Rodgers ascended the James and engaged the batteries at Drewry's Bluff. The seven heavy guns now on the works proved most effective against the fleet. After an engagement of four hours the vessels withdrew, considerably damaged.

From information then in the possession of the Confederates, it was supposed that McClellan would change his base to the James in order to have the cooperation of the navy, and it was hoped that he could be successfully assailed while making the change if he crossed above the mouth of the Chickahominy. The repulse of the Union fleet at Drewry's Bluff created a greater feeling of security in Richmond, and there arose a determination that the honored capital city of the Old Dominion and of the Confederacy should not fall into the hands of foes.

The battle of Seven Pines, on May 31st, initiated by Johnston while McClellan's army was divided, stopped the progress of the Federals, but the serious wounding of Johnston caused

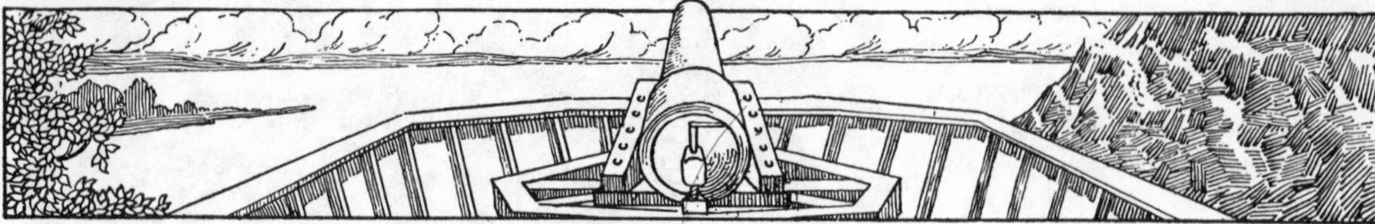

WHAT LINCOLN SAW

THE LAST OF THE UNDAUNTED CONFEDERATE FLOTILLA—"VIRGINIA," "PATRICK HENRY" AND "JAMESTOWN" SUNK

Here are some of the sights presented to the view of President Lincoln and Admiral Porter aboard the flagship *Malvern*, as they proceeded up the James on the morning of April 3, 1865, to enter the fallen city of Richmond. To the right of the top photograph rise the stacks of the Confederate ram *Virginia*. Near the middle lie the ruined wheels of the *Jamestown*. And in the bottom picture, before Fort Darling appears the wreck of the *Patrick Henry*. All these were vessels of Commodore Mitchell's command that had so long made every effort to break the bonds forged about them by a more powerful force, afloat and ashore. The previous night Lincoln, as Admiral Porter's guest on the deck of the *Malvern*, had listened to the sound of the great engagement on shore and had asked if the navy could not do something to make history at the same time. When told that the navy's part was one merely of watchfulness, the President responded, "But can't we make a noise?" Porter at once telegraphed to his fleet-captain to open upon the forts; then the air was rent with the sound of great guns up the river. Soon, rising even louder, came the sound of four great explosions one after another—the blowing up of Commodore Mitchell's vessels.

COAL SCHOONERS WRECKED TO BLOCK THE JAMES—(BELOW) DREWRY'S BLUFFS

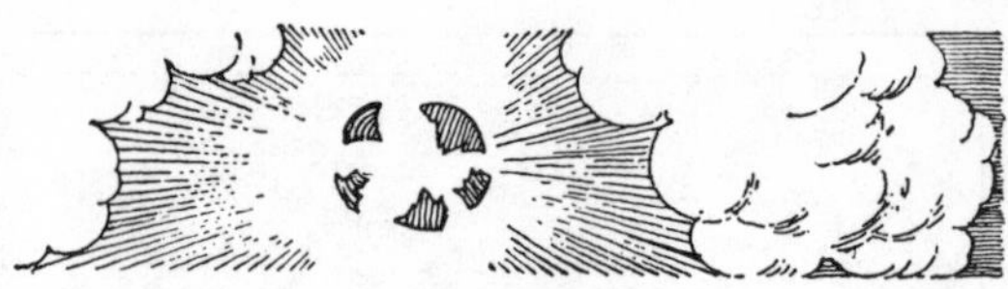

the command to devolve upon General G. W. Smith until June 2d, when President Davis assigned General Lee to the command of the Army of Northern Virginia.

Lee felt that if McClellan could not be driven out of his entrenchments, there was danger that he would move by successive positions, under cover of his heavy guns, to within shelling distance of Richmond; and to prevent this contingency, Jackson was to fall on the Federal right flank to help drive McClellan from his position. The movement was so skilfully made that the Federal commanders in the Valley and the authorities in Washington were completely deceived, and the Union army now found itself on the defensive, and the history of the Peninsula campaign records the retreat of McClellan instead of a close investment of Richmond.

During these operations, the field-works thrown up by the Confederate army constituted the principal auxiliary defenses, but as these were not in positions proper for the immediate defense of the city, they were of no particular value after the removal of the forces to other positions. As soon as the army could recover from the strain of the ordeal through which it had passed, Lee turned his attention to the fortifications immediately surrounding the capital.

On July 13th, he directed the Engineer Corps to prepare a system of defenses from Drewry's Bluff encircling the approaches to Manchester from the south, and, on the 31st, he directed that the construction of the outside lines north of the James be resumed. At the same time, more guns were ordered to be placed on the Drewry's Bluff defenses, as well as on the other works along the south side of the James. The works of Petersburg were strengthened also.

When Lee started for the Rapidan to enter on the campaign against Pope, all the troops of the Army of Northern Virginia were withdrawn from the fortifications of Richmond, and relieved from garrison duty and from the work of construction by the troops of General D. H. Hill's command.

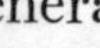

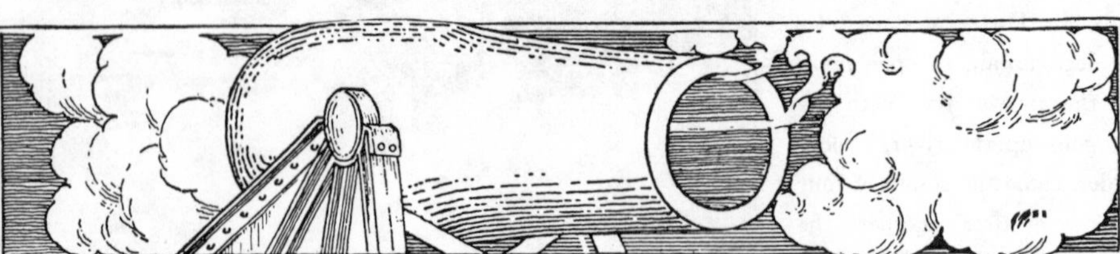

BATTERY BROOKE—GUNS THAT BOTHERED BUTLER

Halfway between the Confederate Fort Darling at Drewry's Bluff and the Dutch Gap Canal, which General Butler was busily constructing, the Confederates had dug this powerful work. Its establishment rendered the construction of the Dutch Gap Canal a futile military operation. After 140 days spent in excavating it, Butler, on New Year's Day, 1865, exploded 12,000 pounds of powder under the bulkhead; but it fell back into the opening. Under the fire from the guns of Battery Brooke the obstruction could not be removed nor could the canal be dredged sufficiently to admit of the passage of vessels. The picture looks south along the main ramparts, fronting east on the river. While the Army of the Potomac was fully occupied at Petersburg, this battery bellowed out hearty defiance to the fleet by night and day. The strong Confederate fortifications cn the James between the Appomattox and Richmond were effective in keeping General Butler bottled up in Bermuda Hundred.

BOMB-PROOF IN BATTERY BROOKE

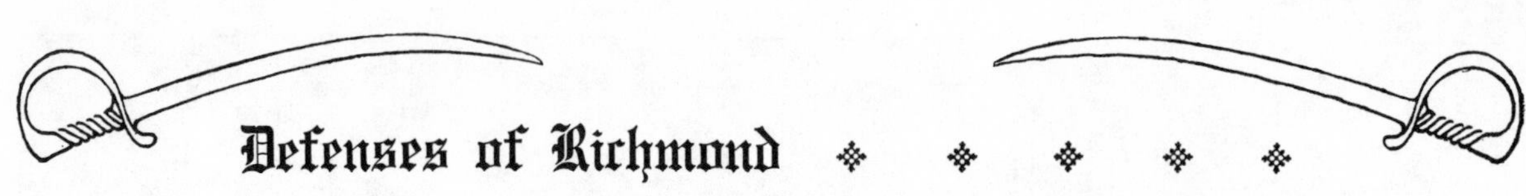

Defenses of Richmond

Previous to the movement of Lee's army, every effort had been made to advance the work of construction, so that the city could be defended easily during the absence of the main body, and by the time Lee invaded Maryland, the second line of outer works had been almost completed around the city at a distance of a mile to two miles from the first series of forts.

Outside of this continuous line were erected some small detached works, which formed the basis for a third line, built in 1864, not so complete as the second, but covering all of the principal approaches at a still greater distance from the city.

In October, 1862, during the absence of the Army of Northern Virginia from the immediate vicinity of Richmond, there were about two thousand troops assigned to the defenses, and these were engaged in keeping the works at their maximum efficiency, and in ensuring protection to the capital against small Federal raiding parties. The batteries at Chaffin's and Drewry's bluffs were held in sufficient force to prevent the ascent of the river by Union gunboats.

The works of the third line which were first built could not have much effect on a hostile army's advance, but as long as there was an opportunity of improving the strength of the general scheme of fortifications, work was continued. In some cases those of the third line at first were without proper protection on the flanks, and as it was useless to try to hold works that only jeopardized the safety of their defenders, General Hill, in July, 1863, reported that the entrenchments in that line on the west of the Brook turnpike, overlooking Brook Run, a stream flowing into the Chickahominy near Meadow Bridge, were not constructed so as to cover all the ground necessary; and that the infantry parapets were not strong enough.

At his suggestion, all the troops available were put to work at once by the chief engineer, Colonel J. F. Gilmer, all obstructions removed from the front of the works, the parapets of some of the heavier batteries made stronger, and the lines of infantry cover connecting the redoubts improved.

BIG GUNS NEAR RICHMOND

FORT DARLING JAMES RIVER

The narrow reach of the James is swept in both directions by the gun in the upper picture—a large Brooke rifle, made at the Tredegar Iron Works in the Confederate Capital. The gun below is a Columbiad with Brooke reënforcement. It is mounted within Fort Darling, and points down the James toward Chaffin's Bluff, visible beyond the bend to the left. Drewry's Bluff commanded this portion of the river so completely that it was chosen as the site of the first hastily constructed defenses of Richmond in 1862, and was subsequently so strengthened as to be almost impregnable. The guns there mounted remained the guardians closest to the Capital on the James until the withdrawal of Lee with his remnant of the Army of Northern Virginia from Petersburg rendered them useless in 1865.

THE FALL OF RICHMOND

When the news reached Richmond, April 2, 1865, that Lee's slender lines had been broken below Petersburg and that the city was forthwith to be abandoned, pandemonium ruled for a brief space of time. All that day by train and wagon, by horse and on foot, the people fled from the city. Early in the evening bands of ruffians appeared, and pillaged and caroused until the arrest of their ringleaders. The magazines were exploded, and Richmond flamed up to the sky, turning the darkness into daylight. There was little sleep

NEGRO REFUGEES WITH THEIR HOUSEHOLD GOODS ON THE CANAL

that night. Next morning an immense pall seemed to hover over the city that was a capital no more. That day the Union columns of blue marched into Richmond, and the sky was rent with their cheers as they swept into Capitol Square. Forty-eight hours after that memorable still Sunday morning when the news of the break in Lee's lines reached Richmond, the city again lay quiet, her buildings charred, her people sorrow laden. The Sunday following Lee surrendered at Appomattox. The armies in the West shortly yielded.

Defenses of Richmond

By the time of the arrival of the Confederate army at Cold Harbor, the third line of defenses had been run northeast from Chaffin's Bluff to the Charles City road, which was crossed four and one-half miles outside of the city, thence directly north to the ground overlooking the swampy lowlands of the Chickahominy, where it terminated abruptly, its flank commanding New Bridge, five miles outside of Richmond. From here, detached works held the ground upstream overlooking the river, and connected with the lines that had been started on ground overlooking the Chickahominy bottoms directly north of the city the year before. These were now completed, and the lines of detached works followed the right bank of Brook Run to its source and then bent toward the James, across the Deep Run turnpike and the plank road, four miles up the James from the outskirts of the city. The completion of this line resulted in there being three strong lines of defense.

The weary ten months which followed tested the strength of the gradually weakening defense. All realized that the fall of Petersburg meant the fall of Richmond, and that the patient toil on the miles of entrenchments around the capital finally had had the effect of causing the blow to fall elsewhere. Two expeditions were sent by Grant against the lines to the north of Richmond, but not in sufficient strength to test the works. The principal object was to weaken the forces defending Petersburg so as to permit a successful assault to be delivered.

The Federal army, under able leaders tested in the furnace of war, exhausted every device to break through the Petersburg lines. They tried them by assault, by mining, by flanking, and by bombardment. Lee's genius, seconded by that of his officers, and maintained by the gallant devotion of his troops, held on till the army was worn out and the stretching of the lines by constant extension to meet the Federal movements to the left, finally caused them to be so weak as to break under a Federal assault. Petersburg was abandoned, and Richmond fell.

THE CAPTURED MAP OF THE DEFENSES OF RICHMOND

This map of the defenses of Richmond was found on the body of the Confederate Brigadier-General John R. Chambliss, by Federal cavalrymen under Gregg. Chambliss had been killed in an engagement with these troopers near White Oak Branch, seven miles from Richmond, on August 16, 1864. Early that month Grant heard that reënforcements were being sent to General Early in the Shenandoah for the purpose of threatening Washington. In order to compel the recall of these troops, and to cause the weakening of the Confederate lines before Petersburg, Hancock took the Second and part of the Ninth Corps and Gregg's cavalry to the north side of the James, threatening the works of Richmond. On the morning of August 16th, Gregg advanced on the right of the Federal line toward White's Tavern, near White Oak Branch. It was here that the action, the death of Chambliss, and the capture of the map took place. Even with the plans of the Southerners thus unexpectedly in their possession, the Federals were unable to pass these defenses until Lee's little army had been forced aside.